ROADMAP™  B1+

STUDENTS' BOOK
with digital resources and mobile app

Hugh Dellar, Andrew Walkley

Contents

EXTENDED ROUTE

Contents

FAST-TRACK ROUTE

EXTENDED ROUTE

1A Eating out

> **Goal:** decide where to eat out
> **Grammar:** noun phrases 1
> **Vocabulary:** eating out

Vocabulary

1 Work in pairs and discuss the questions.

1 How often do you go out for lunch/dinner? Where do you usually go?

2 Which of the places in the photos look like your kind of place to eat? Why?

2 a Match comments 1–8 with responses a–h.

1 The **service** in there is terrible.

2 Is it very expensive?

3 It is great, but it'll be **packed**.

4 Isn't it a bit cold to sit on the **terrace**?

5 Do they only serve meat? I'm **vegetarian**.

6 How about the **fish place**? Does that **suit everyone**?

7 The café next door is quite **decent** and **good value**.

8 That new **Indian place** has a nice **set menu** at lunch.

a Yes, I know the one you mean, but I don't really **fancy** eating **spicy food**.

b No, they have those **outdoor heaters**.

c A bit, but it's **top quality** and the food's really **delicious**.

d I know. The last time I went, we **waited ages** to be served and they still **got our order wrong**.

e Actually, I'd prefer somewhere else. I'm **allergic to seafood**.

f That's OK, there's **plenty of choice**. I had a vegetable lasagne the last time I went.

g That's true. You really need to **book in advance**, but it is amazing.

h It was, but the last time I went they'd **put up the prices** and the food wasn't so great.

b Work in pairs. Take turns saying and responding to one of the comments (1–8) in Exercise 2a. Then try to continue each conversation.

> **A:** *The service in there is terrible.*
> **B:** *I know. The last time I went, we waited ages to be served and they still got our order wrong.*
> **A:** *Really? What did you have?*

3 Work in groups and discuss the questions.

1 Have you ever experienced **bad service**?

2 Do you go anywhere that is often **packed**?

3 Do you know a restaurant with a **terrace**? Is it nice?

4 Do you know anyone who's **vegetarian**?

5 Do you like **spicy food**?

6 Are you **allergic to** anything?

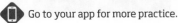 Go to your app for more practice.

Listening

4 ◁)) 1.1 **Listen to a group of people who are deciding where to have lunch. Answer the questions.**

1 How many people are going?

2 Do they all know each other?

3 What three places do they talk about?

4 Where do they decide to go?

5 Listen again. Explain why ...

1 they had to wait for Nina.

2 Tom told Jess about Carmen.

3 they didn't choose the pizza place.

4 they didn't choose the French café.

5 they chose the Lebanese restaurant.

Grammar

6 a **1.2 Listen to the sentences from the conversation. Complete them with two or three words that define the nouns in bold. Contractions count as two words.**

- **a** Carmen's the **friend** _____ telling you about.
- **b** I mentioned you might have a **room** _____ .
- **c** Let's find **somewhere** _____ first and then we can talk about it.
- **d** How about that lovely little **pizza place** _____ ?
- **e** I have a **friend** _____ to bananas.
- **f** What about that French **café** _____ which does the set lunch menu?
- **g** Anyway, the last **time** _____ , it was completely closed.
- **h** Nina and I went to a Lebanese **place** _____ , which was nice.

b Read the grammar box. Then match sentences a–h in Exercise 6a with 1–3 in the box.

Noun phrases 1

You can clarify and define the thing, person or place you are talking about by adding information after the noun. You can do this in various ways:

1 a prepositional phrase
the place **near here**   a café **with a terrace**

2 an infinitive with *to*
a place **to have lunch**   someone **to talk to**

3 a relative clause
the one **where we went for my birthday**
a restaurant **that does a set menu**

Relative clauses can always start with a relative pronoun (*that, who, where*, etc.). However, if the relative pronoun is the object of the relative clause, you can leave it out.

This is my friend (who/that) I was telling you about.
(= I was telling you about my friend.)

7 a **1.3 Listen and notice how the underlined words are stressed.**

1 There's a <u>place</u> next <u>door</u> which does <u>sandwiches</u>.
2 It's a <u>great</u> place to <u>eat</u> and <u>watch</u> the <u>world</u> go by.
3 It's the <u>best</u> place I've <u>eaten</u> in.
4 <u>Jane's</u> the <u>friend</u> with the <u>dog</u> I was telling you about.

b Listen again and repeat the sentences.

8 Add one word in each space if it is needed.

1 That's the restaurant _____ I was talking about.
2 Brad is the friend _____ owns the restaurant _____ Tenth Street.
3 There's a great place _____ I went to last week _____ the city centre.
4 There's a nice old place _____ the main square _____ you can eat outside.
5 It's a really nice place _____ have lunch.
6 We could go to the restaurant _____ we had the office party.

9 a Complete the sentences so they are true for you. Try to use all three different ways of defining the noun from the grammar box.

1 There's a nice _____ restaurant _____ .
There's a nice Italian restaurant in San Bernardo Square which does fantastic pizzas.

2 _____ is the best place _____ .
3 _____ is the friend _____ .
4 Do you know anyone _____ ?
5 What's the name of the place _____ ?

b Work in pairs. Say your sentences. Your partner should try to respond.

A: *There's a nice French restaurant at the end of my street.*
B: *Oh, OK. How often do you go there?*
A: *Maybe once or twice a month.*

📱 Go to page 136 or your app for more information and practice.

Speaking

PREPARE

10 Work in groups. You're going to decide where to eat lunch/dinner. First, work on your own and:

1 think of at least two places you could suggest. Write down how you would define them and why you think they are good.
2 think of one or two places that you wouldn't go to if they were suggested and why.
3 think about the language you could use from this lesson.

SPEAK

11 Work in groups. Discuss and decide where to eat lunch/dinner. If you don't know each other, introduce yourselves first. Use the Useful phrases to help you.

Useful phrases

What does everyone fancy?
How/What about (a pizza)?
Let's go to (that Turkish restaurant).
Sounds good.
I'd prefer somewhere else, if no one else minds.

Develop your writing
page 86

1B

A place to live

Vocabulary

1 **Discuss the questions.**

1 How often do people usually move house in your country?

2 Is it common for people you know to improve their flats/houses?

3 What reasons do people give for moving or improving their flat/house?

2 **Work in pairs. Check you understand the words in bold. Then match sentence halves 1–9 with a–i.**

1 It's an old apartment and was **freezing** in the winter,

2 We **could do with** a bit more space to put things in,

3 The kitchen was **tiny**,

4 It's quite **rough** round here,

5 Being in the country **surrounded by** fields was great,

6 Our kids had **moved out**, and we're not as fit as we were,

7 I needed a bigger place, but didn't want to **move away** from the area,

8 My **landlord** wants to **put up the rent**,

9 It's not in very **good condition**

a but now the kids need somewhere a bit more **lively**.

b so I'd like to move to a slightly safer **neighbourhood**.

c so we're covering the balcony to give us more **storage**.

d so we **knocked down** one wall and made it much bigger.

e but it's cheap to buy and I can **repair** most things myself.

f so we **put in central heating**.

g so I made **the basement** bigger.

h so we bought a smaller place, which is a lot easier to **keep clean and tidy**.

i so I'm going to **move in with** a friend and **share the cost**.

3 a **Work in pairs. Put the words and phrases in bold in Exercise 2 into the correct groups.**

1 Connected to or describing apartments/houses

2 Describing areas

3 Connected to moving or home improvement

b **Choose five words or phrases in bold from Exercise 2 and make sentences about where you live.**

We have a basement, which we use for storage.

Go to page 156 or your app for more vocabulary and practice.

Reading

4 a **Look at the photos of Notting Hill in London and discuss the questions.**

1 Do you know what the area is famous for?

2 What do you think it was like in the 1940s?

b **Read the article about Notting Hill and check your answers.**

5 **Read the article again and answer the questions.**

1 Who were the houses first built for?

2 Why weren't some houses sold and what happened to them?

3 Why were some houses knocked down?

4 Who moved into the area in the 1960s?

5 How have the house prices changed since the 1960s?

6 **Work in groups. What might be good and bad about the changes in Notting Hill since the 1990s? Are there any areas like this where you live?**

THE CHANGING FACE OF

©WESTMINSTER CITY COUNCIL

NOTTING HILL

London's Notting Hill is famous for Portobello Road market and its annual carnival – the biggest street party in Europe. Today it is a rich area, but, like many neighbourhoods in big cities, its character has changed over time. Originally, it was built in the mid-nineteenth century as a new development for professionals and upper-class people, but it was right next to one of the roughest parts of the city, where there were very poor houses, criminals and even pig farms. Because of this, many of the lovely new houses built on Portland Road, on the edge of the neighbourhood, could not be sold and were rented cheaply to poorer people.

For example, in the 1940s, the Andrews family lived at 157 Portland Road. The six members of the family lived in just two rooms on one floor. They shared the house with four other families. Many houses were even more crowded. One three-floor building housed 48 people – with no bathroom or heating. Because landlords did not have nearly enough money for repairs, the houses ended up in a terrible condition. Eventually, some were knocked down and replaced by lots of government-built flats.

In the 1960s, new people started to move into Portland Road, many of them professional people with young families. These families had often lived in tiny places in nearby Chelsea, and bigger places there were far too expensive. By buying houses in bad condition on Portland Road and then doing the repairs themselves, they could get much more space. As the houses were improved, more middle-class people moved there and in the 1990s, the neighbourhood became popular with people who worked in the finance industry. Portland Road became far more expensive to live in, and houses that had sold for around £10,000 in the 1960s were now worth over £1 million. One house on the street sold last year for over £10 million.

Grammar

7 Read the grammar box and choose the correct alternatives.

Modifying comparisons

You can add words before a comparative adjective or *too* to show how big the difference is between things.

To show a [1]*big/small* difference, use *far, much, a lot.*
*We made it **much** bigger.*
*It's **a lot** easier to keep clean and tidy.*
*Houses in Portland Road became **far** more expensive.*
*Bigger places in Chelsea were **far** too expensive.*

To show a [2]*big/small* difference, use *a bit, slightly.*
***a bit** more space*
***a slightly** safer neighbourhood*

When you use *not ... enough* and *not as ... as,* you can use *quite* to show a [3]*big/small* difference and *nearly* to show a [4]*big/small* difference.
*We're **not quite as** fit **as** we were.*
*It's **not nearly** cheap **enough.***
*Landlords didn't have **nearly enough** money for repairs.*

When you add *even*, it shows the comparison is [5]*surprising/small.*
*Many houses were **even** more crowded.*

8 Complete the sentences with the words in brackets and a comparative structure.

1 It's a bit too expensive. I'd like somewhere ___slightly cheaper___ . (slightly / cheap)

2 When we got married, we got an apartment which was _____ from my job. (a lot / far away)

3 You hear about crime there sometimes, but it is not _____ as it was before. (nearly / rough)

4 They've really improved the area. It's _____ than it was. (much / green)

5 I lived in a tiny flat when I was a student. It was _____ than this one. (even / small)

6 Our heating bills are far too expensive. We need to put in some _____ windows. (much / good)

7 It's a nice flat, but it doesn't have _____ for all my clothes! (nearly / storage)

8 It's a great area, but you'd need to earn _____ than I do to buy somewhere there. (a lot / money).

📱 Go to page 136 or your app for more information and practice.

9 Work in pairs. Turn to page 166. Look at and compare the photos. Also compare them to where you live.

The flat in this photo looks quite like mine, but I think my flat is a bit bigger and older.

Speaking

PREPARE

10 a 🔊 1.4 You're going to talk about where you live. First, listen to two people talking about where they live. Which question are they answering?

1 How many places have you lived in? Why did you move? How did the different places compare?

2 How happy are you with the place you live now? Say at least one thing that would improve it.

3 What's the area you live in like? Has it changed while you have lived there?

b Now work on your own and think about how to answer the questions in Exercise 10a.

SPEAK

11 a Work in pairs. Ask and answer the questions in Exercise 10a. Use the Useful phrases to help you.

Useful phrases

I've moved around quite a lot.
I like my new place the best.
I'm fairly happy with where I live now.
It's not changed much, but it's not quite as nice as before.
It's changed hugely. It's far more crowded now.

b What are the main similarities and differences between your experiences?

Develop your reading
page 88

1c A late night

> **Goal:** describe a night out
>
> **Grammar:** non-defining relative clauses
>
> **Vocabulary:** going out, staying in

Vocabulary

1 **Work in groups and discuss the questions.**

1 How often do you stay up late?

2 Have you had any late nights recently? What did you do?

2 **Complete the sentences with the pairs of words in the box.**

> got/bed   stayed in/tidied up   missed/fortune
> ~~stayed up/episodes~~   play/home   threw/celebrate
> queue/worth   went out/went on

1 I ___stayed up___ really late watching a new drama series called *Broken Vows*. I watched six ___episodes___ in a row!

2 I _____ for dinner with a client and then we _____ to a late-night bar in the old town.

3 It was packed so we had to _____ to get in, but it was _____ it.

4 I _____ talking to some friends online and didn't get to _____ till three.

5 The _____ finished at eleven, but we got stuck in traffic, so we didn't get _____ till after one.

6 Some friends _____ a surprise party for me to _____ my 21st birthday. It was brilliant!

7 I _____ the last metro home and had to get a taxi. It cost a _____ !

8 My flat was in a bit of a mess so I just _____ and _____ .

3 **Work in pairs. Can you think of:**

1 three other things you can **stay up really late** doing?

2 two other things you can **go out for**?

3 two other places where you might have to **queue to get in**?

4 three other situations where you might **get talking** to someone you don't know?

5 three other reasons why you might not **get home** till after one?

6 three other ways you could **celebrate** your birthday?

 Go to page 156 or your app for more vocabulary and practice.

Reading

4 a **Read the responses to a post about late nights in different countries. Order them from 1–3 (where 1 = the best).**

b **Work in pairs and explain your answers.**

Me and my friends always celebrate 1st March, **when** spring really begins. My big sister, **who I'm really close to**, lives near this lovely park, so last time we all met there and stayed up late just playing guitars and singing songs and dancing together while the neighbours' dogs barked and different friends came and went. It was lovely, but I didn't get home until two fifteen, **which is why I was late into school the next day!** Daria

I don't go out much these days, to be honest, but I did go and see a Chinese Opera performance the other night, **which** was great. I went with my partner and a whole group of his friends, **most of whom** are huge opera fans. I wasn't expecting to enjoy it, but it was actually very powerful – and quite violent, too. We then went on a behind-the-scenes tour of the theatre, **where** we were introduced to the performers. Alex

I met some old friends last night and we went to Akropolis, **which** was brilliant. We used to go there when we were students and being there again really reminded me of the old days – although the food's even better now than it used to be. Anyway, we finished around eleven, **when I'd usually go home**, but then my friend Michaela, **whose** husband's a DJ, suggested going on somewhere. So in the end, we went dancing, **which meant** I didn't get home till after four! I was exhausted the whole next day, but it's my own fault, I suppose. Milan

5 **Read the text again. Who ...**

1 met some new people?

2 doesn't normally stay out past midnight?

3 generally stays in and doesn't go out?

4 had the cheapest night out?

5 remembered happy times from the past?

6 does something special every year?

Grammar

6 Read the grammar box. Then look at the non-defining relative clauses underlined in the text in Exercise 4a. Complete 1–7 with the correct relative pronouns/phrases in bold.

Non-defining relative clauses

Use non-defining relative clauses to add extra information to sentences. The sentences would still make sense without these clauses. You can use most relative pronouns (*which, whose,* etc.) in non-defining clauses, but you can't use *that*. The pronouns cannot be left out.

In written English, you can tell when a clause is non-defining because it comes after a comma and usually ends with a comma or a full stop.

*We went to an amazing place in the old town, **which** did wonderful local food.*

*I went to the cinema with Leyla, **who** I work with, and we saw a really great film.*

Use the following relative pronouns/phrases to add extra information about:

1 places _____
2 how we felt _____
3 reasons and results _____ / _____
4 dates and times _____
5 possession or connection _____
6 larger part of a group of people _____
7 people _____

7 a 🔊 1.5 **Listen and notice the short pause after the comma.**

1 We got in free because of Yoko, whose brother works there.
2 We ate at Incanto, where I took you for your birthday.
3 I didn't get to bed until six, when the sun was rising.
4 She used to work with me, which is why I know her.

b Listen again and repeat.

8 a Complete the sentences with the correct relative pronoun or phrase.

1 I went out for dinner with Jill, _____ I've known since we were at school together.
2 I lost my wallet and had to ask a stranger for money for the metro, _____ was embarrassing!
3 For our anniversary, I took my wife to The Reno, _____ we used to go when we first met.
4 I got talking to this girl called Ellen, _____ party it was, and then I missed the last bus home.
5 I missed the bus, _____ I had to walk home.
6 In the end, we stayed there until about four in the morning, _____ they asked us to leave.
7 There were about thirty people at the party, _____ I'd never met before.
8 I paid for him to get in and he never paid me back, _____ we're not talking!

b Work in pairs. Think of a different relative clause you could add to each sentence in Exercise 8a.

I went out for dinner with Jill, which was lovely.

📱 Go to page 136 or your app for more information and practice.

Speaking

PREPARE

9 a 🔊 1.6 **You're going to describe a night out. First, listen to someone describing their night out. What were the main things that happened?**

b Work in pairs and compare your ideas.

c Work on your own and make notes about a night out that you've had. Think about ...
- where you went, who with and what it was like.
- any problems you had.
- what time you got home and how you felt the next day.
- how you can use non-defining relative clauses to add extra information.

SPEAK

10 a Work in groups. Tell your group about your night out. Ask each other questions to find out more. Use your notes and the Useful phrases to help you.

Useful phrases
Who did you go with?
How often do you go there, then?
What time did you get home?
What was it like?
Was it very expensive?

b Report back to the class. Who had the most interesting night?

Develop your listening
page 90

1D English in action

> **Goal:** express preferences and give reasons

1 a Make a list of five things that are important to you when you are choosing a place for a holiday.

It's important that the food there is good.

b Work in groups. Compare your lists and discuss good places to go for the things on your lists.

New York is one of the best places for restaurants.

2 🔊 **1.10** Listen to three friends, Lisa, Jo and Domi, trying to decide where to go on holiday. Which of the places in the photos would Domi rather visit? Why?

3 Listen again and complete the sentences with three words. Contractions count as two words.

1 To be honest, Jo, it looks like the kind of place _____ !

2 Here you'd be stuck in one place by the sea, _____ 'd be able to escape the crowds.

3 Personally, I just like _____ doing nothing for a week.

4 No. I _____ up in the mountains somewhere.

5 _____ to just stay at home.

4 Read the Useful phrases box and check your answers.

Useful phrases

Expressing preferences

I'd rather be up in the mountains.
I'd prefer (not) to stay at home.
If it was just up to me, I'd go for this place.
(But) I think this place looks much more relaxing.
It looks like the kind of place I'd hate/love.
It's (not) my kind of place.
I don't have any strong feelings either way.

Giving reasons

It would be more fun/less stressful.
You'd be able to escape the crowds.
You'd be stuck in one place.
You could probably go diving there.
I like the idea of doing nothing for a week.
Here you'd be stuck in one place, whereas there you'd be able to escape.
I've heard some good/bad things about it.

5 Complete the sentences with the words in brackets.

1 _____ (rather) go on holiday in the summer. _____ escaping the cold. (the idea)

2 _____ (prefer not) go to the beach. _____ too hot. (be)

3 _____ (not my kind) of place. _____ a bit boring. (looks)

4 _____ (feelings) either way. _____ good things about both places. (heard)

5 _____ (looks like) I'd love. _____ skiing and swimming in the same day! (could)

6 Work in pairs. Ask and answer the questions. Give reasons for your answers.

Would you rather/prefer to ...

1 go on holiday with friends or with family?

2 go somewhere really hot or somewhere really cold?

3 have six one-week holidays or one six-week holiday?

4 cook for yourself when you're on holiday or eat out?

5 go somewhere you've never been before or visit a place you already know?

7 a Work in groups. Turn to page 166. Look at the photos. Which sort of holiday would you rather go on? Explain your answer.

Turn to page 166.

b Who would be the best person from your group for you to go on holiday with? Why?

Go online for the Roadmap video.

Check and reflect

1 Complete the sentences with the best word. The first letter is given.

1 When the weather's nice, you can eat outside on the t_____ there.

2 The last time I went, the s _____ was terrible. The waiters were so rude.

3 It's a v_____ place, so it doesn't s_____ everyone. It's no good if you want meat!

4 The food there is top q_____, but you have to book in a_____ if you want a table.

5 It was very good v_____ for money before, but they recently put up their p_____ .

6 It's a good p_____ to go for lunch. They do a very good set m_____ there.

2 Cross out one word in each sentence which is incorrect or not necessary.

1 There's a really good pizza place is on my road.

2 I went to a place which it does really good fish dishes.

3 There aren't any places for to have dinner near here.

4 The café that I went to for lunch was good.

5 When I book a holiday, I always look for a hotel that near a beach.

6 On my last holiday, I had a room with on a balcony.

3 a Match verbs 1–6 with endings a–f.

1	move in	a	the kitchen with three other people
2	move away	b	my rent
3	knock down	c	from the area
4	share	d	with my wife's family
5	put in	e	new central heating
6	put up	f	half the street

b Work in pairs. Why might people do the actions in Exercise 3a? Which do you have experience of?

4 a Complete the sentences with one word. Sometimes more than one answer is possible.

1 Now we have three kids, we have a _____ less space than we did before.

2 Seville's not _____ as big as Valencia, but it is a fairly similar size.

3 It's _____ nearly as big as my last place, but it's much, much cheaper.

4 They're more or less the same size. Well, maybe this one is a _____ bigger.

5 It's a lot _____ expensive than the other place, but I prefer this neighbourhood.

6 Tokyo isn't cheap, but London is _____ more expensive. It's crazy here!

7 My flat's _____ too small. I don't have _____ enough space. It's terrible.

8 I guess it'd be nice to live in a _____ greener area, but I'm basically fine where I am.

b Think of two places you know, e.g. apartments, houses, areas, towns, cities or countries. Make comparisons between them. Work in groups and compare your ideas.

5 Complete the sentences with the words in the box.

a taxi	episodes	get home	stayed up
tidy up	worth		

1 I don't like taking the metro. I usually just get _____ instead.

2 My flat's in a mess, so I'm just going to stay in and _____ tonight.

3 It's my favourite series. I stayed in last night and watched five _____ in a row!

4 I _____ until 3 a.m. studying English.

5 I went out for dinner with some friends and didn't _____ until 1 a.m.

6 I spent a fortune over the weekend, but it was _____ it. I had so much fun!

6 a Complete the sentences with the correct non-defining relative clause. Add commas if necessary.

> none of whom I'd met before
> which meant I had to get a taxi
> when I'm usually getting up
> where my family has a summer house
> who lives in Geneva
> whose father runs the place

1 We spent two weeks in Formentera _____ .

2 I missed the last metro home _____ .

3 Jim brought all his work friends _____ to my party.

4 My sister _____ is visiting me in the UK at the moment.

5 At 6 a.m. _____ I finally got home and went to bed.

6 My friend Sergio _____ got us all in for free.

b Write three sentences that are true for you. Use three of the non-defining relative clauses in the box in Exercise 6a. Work in groups and compare your sentences.

Reflect

How confident do you feel about the statements below? Write 1–5 (1 = not very confident, 5 = very confident).

• I can describe different places to eat
• I can discuss homes and areas
• I can talk about nights out
• I can explain where I want to go on holiday – and why.

Want more practice?
Go to your Workbook or app.

2A > Getting better

> **Goal:** talk about your free time
> **Grammar:** present simple and present continuous
> **Vocabulary:** learning new skills

Vocabulary

1 **Look at the photos and answer the questions.**
1 Which of the activities are you very good/OK at?
2 Which have you tried to do, but aren't good at?
3 Which have you never tried?

2 **Complete the sentences with the pairs of words in the box.**

downloaded/exchange   interested/skilled
expert/progress   technique/way
challenge/improve   try out/go over
keen/train   useless/go

1 I'm very _____ on running. I want to do a 10K race this year, so I _____ every day before work.
2 I play golf every Sunday. I'm slowly developing my _____ , but I still have a long _____ to go.
3 I'm learning Italian at the moment. I've _____ a few apps and I do a language _____ with an Italian girl.
4 Painting has always _____ me – maybe because my mum's a highly _____ artist.
5 I started baking last year. I'm no _____ but I've made a lot of _____ .
6 It's been a bit of a _____ at times, but I can feel I'm starting to _____ , so that's good.
7 I'm _____ at it, but it's nice to have a _____ .
8 I like to _____ new skills, but it's also important to _____ what I've already learnt to do.

3 **Work in pairs and discuss the topics.**
• something I'm **keen on** and has always **interested** me
• a time I **made a lot of progress**
• something that was **a bit of a challenge** for me
• something I'm **useless** at, but enjoy doing anyway

 Go to page 157 or your app for more vocabulary and practice.

Reading

4 **Read the article. What is its main purpose?**
1 to explain why so few people get really good at things
2 to explain why so many people love *MasterChef*

5 **Read the article again. Why are the things in the box mentioned?**

2005   more than 100   bread-making machines
over 50   every weekend   over 200

THE LONG ROAD TO SUCCESS

It's official: a TV programme in which people compete against each other in the hope of becoming famous for their cooking is now the most successful cookery programme ever. Since it was first shown on British TV in 2005, *MasterChef* has spread around the world, becoming huge in Asia, Australia, Latin America and the Middle East. Over 50 different countries now make their own versions of *MasterChef*, and the programme is watched in over 200 countries. More than 100 winners are working in the food industry and many have become best-selling writers, too.

Of course, the programme has created a lot of interest in cooking. In fact, you can be sure that somewhere in the world, someone is practising a special dish and dreaming of winning the programme right now. The success of *MasterChef* is part of a growing trend. We lead busy and stressful lives, and many of us want to get back to basics and enjoy the simple things of life. More and more people are having a go at cooking, gardening and craft activities like making things with paper. However, while many people spend every weekend trying out another new recipe or improving their baking techniques, others are giving up. After finding that it is not so easy to copy what they have seen on TV, people stop believing they can ever make real progress and as a result cupboards are filling up with cookery books, bread-making machines and other expensive equipment.

What very few of us want to accept is that no one becomes highly skilled overnight – and if you want to get good at something, you need to give it time!

6 **Work in pairs and discuss the questions.**
1 Are the trends described in the article also happening in your country?
2 Do you agree with the main point at the end?

Grammar

7 Read the sentences from the article. Underline the present simple and present continuous forms. Then match the sentences with explanations a–f in the grammar box.

1 Over 50 different countries now make their own versions of *MasterChef*.

2 Somewhere in the world, someone is practising a special dish right now.

3 More and more people are having a go at cooking.

4 Many of us want to get back to basics.

5 More than 100 winners are working in the food industry.

6 Many people spend every weekend trying out another new recipe.

Present simple and present continuous

Use the present simple:

a to describe habits and routines.
*I usually **go** round the park a few times before work.*

b for things we see as facts.
*She **belongs** to the gym round the corner.*

c with state verbs.
*I **understand** what you **mean**, but I **don't agree**.*

Use the present continuous:

d to talk about current trends.
*Lots of young people **are leaving** social media.*

e for actions in progress at the moment of speaking.
*I**'m trying out** a new recipe for lunch.*

f for actions that are happening 'around now', but not necessarily at the moment of speaking.
*I**'m doing** a course in cooking skills at the moment.*

8 a 🔊 **2.1 Listen and notice what happens to the underlined auxiliary verbs in normal-speed speech.**

1 I <u>am</u> training for a marathon at the moment.

2 She <u>is</u> learning how to surf at the moment.

3 He <u>is</u> slowly getting better at it.

4 We <u>are</u> not making enough progress.

5 They <u>are</u> improving all the time.

b Listen again and repeat.

9 Complete the article with the correct form of the verbs in the box.

> become   belong   collect   get   have   join   know
> learn   look for   sound   spend   want

I guess it ¹_____ a bit strange, but believe it or not, I ²_____ hair. Not just any hair, though – it must be the hair of someone famous. I ³_____ to an online club, so I'm in touch with other collectors all over the world. We already ⁴_____ over 1,000 members and more and more people ⁵_____ all the time. Collecting hair ⁶_____ popular all over the world. I ⁷_____ most of my spare money on bits of hair – and I ⁸_____ better at asking people for hair as well. At the moment, I ⁹_____ a piece of Donald Trump's hair! I ¹⁰_____ it won't be cheap! Oh, and I ¹¹_____ how to design websites because I ¹²_____ a space online where I can show my collection.

10 a Look at the topics in the box and think about current trends in your country. Answer the questions about each trend.

> fashion   food and drink   free time activities   work
> social media   technology

1 Why do you think it's happening?

2 What does it involve?

3 Does anyone you know follow this trend?

b Work in pairs and compare your ideas. Try to use the present simple and the present continuous.

📱 Go to page 138 or your app for more information and practice.

Speaking

> **PREPARE**

11 🔊 **2.2 You're going to talk about your free time. First, listen to two people talking about things they're learning. Answer the questions.**

1 What new skills do they mention?

2 How are things going?

12 Make notes about something you're getting better at/learning to do at the moment. Think about ...

- how often you do it.
- how/when you started doing it.
- anything special you're doing to help you improve.

> **SPEAK**

13 a Work with different students in the class. Take turns telling each other about something you do in your free time. Ask and answer questions.

b Work in pairs and discuss what you learnt about other students in the class. Who is learning the most interesting things?

Develop your listening page 91

First days

> **Goal:** give a talk about where you work/study
> **Grammar:** present habits
> **Vocabulary:** starting work

Reading

1 **Look at the photos and discuss the questions.**

1 What's happening? How do you think the people feel?
2 Have you ever experienced a first day at work/school? What happened?
3 Did you feel welcome? Why/Why not?

2 a **Read the posts from an online discussion about first days at work. Who had the best day?**

What should you expect on your first day at work?

We asked our readers. Their answer? Expect the unexpected!

I knew the company had flexible working hours, but they forgot to tell me that on the first day they expected me in the office at a particular time. Anyway, I got there at ten and quickly realised I was late. I'd missed most of the welcome meeting. I also found out that I had to share a desk and there were people playing games near me, so it was hard to work. Finally, after lunch, there was what I thought was a practice drill, but was actually a real fire, so we all just went home. Very strange! **Gabriel**

My first day was just welcome meetings and information about the building. As engineers, there are always lots of health and safety rules. We were also shown around the site and given our ID cards. There's a lot of security there, as you can imagine. My main memory, though, is just how friendly everyone was. They're a great team and made me feel very comfortable. I've been here ever since! **Mona**

I was expecting some kind of welcome, but when I arrived, they just showed me to my desk and left me to get on. I didn't really know what to do, so I actually spent most of the day on the internet. Oh, and I got very hungry because I had no idea what time the lunchbreak was and was too afraid to ask! As soon as I left the office, I went straight to the nearest restaurant. Anyway, it got better after that, but it was never a friendly place to work in. **Alenka**

b **Read the posts again. Which person:**

1 didn't get any kind of welcome?
2 got something to help them get in and out of the building?
3 finished early?
4 is still working in the same place?
5 found it hard to think in their workplace?
6 didn't do anything useful?

3 **Work in pairs and discuss the questions.**

1 Do you feel induction (welcome) meetings are a good idea when people join a new place of work/study?
2 What sort of things do people need to know?

Vocabulary

4 **Match sentence halves 1–6 with a–f.**

1 We expect you to wear **formal clothes**
2 If you're a **union member**, you can contact
3 Everyone has to do a **first aid course**
4 I need to explain the **health and safety rules**
5 If you have to **take time off**,
6 We have **flexible working hours**

a before I can show you around the **building** site.
b but they're fixed if you work **night shifts**.
c your **union representative** for help.
d you don't get paid. We have a **strict policy** about that.
e but **casual dress** is OK on Fridays.
f and we do a practice **fire drill** once a week.

5 **Do you think the rules and suggestions in Exercise 4 are good or bad? Work in pairs and compare your answers.**

 Go to page 157 or your app for more vocabulary and practice.

Listening

6 **2.5 Listen to an induction for adult students on their first day at a language school. Number the topics in the order that you hear them.**

a school values

b smoking policy

c break times

d the social programme

e what to do if there's a fire

f toilets

g lateness policy

h how long the breaks are

7 Listen again and complete the sentences with up to four words.

1 There isn't an exact time for the break, but it _____ be around 10.30.

2 Unfortunately, they are _____ doing roadworks round here.

3 … Please tell Jenny at the reception desk. _____ , people tend to go out to one of the cafés along this road.

4 These are _____ cleaned so we don't tend to have any problems with them.

5 Activities are open to everyone and they _____ filling up quickly.

6 They may organise class trips _____ .

7 And finally, _____ , we have a free barbecue on the first Friday of every month.

8 We usually have a practice drill every two months but we _____ tell staff.

Grammar

8 a Match the words and phrases from the gaps in Exercise 7 with meanings 1–5.

1 always _____

2 usually or generally _*tends to*_ , _____ , _____

3 don't usually _____

4 often _*regularly*_ , _____

5 sometimes _____

b **Read the grammar box and choose the correct alternatives.**

Present habits

Use the present simple to talk about habits.
*I usually **work** from 8 till 6.*
*We **have** weekly meetings on Fridays.*
Adverbs of frequency like *regularly* are placed
1 *before/after* the main verb.
Frequency expressions like *from time to time* go at
the beginning **2** *or/but not* at the end of a clause.
Use *(don't) tend to* + **3** *infinitive/ -ing* to talk about
things that you usually do or that are generally true.
Use *has/have a habit of* + *-ing* or the present
continuous with *always/constantly* to talk about a
regular action that you find **4** *annoying/positive*.

9 a **2.6 Listen to the sentences. What happens to the letters in bold?**

1 We don'**t** ten**d** to lock the office.

2 We ten**d** to go for a coffee at 11.

3 We usually have a staff meeting the las**t** Monday of the month.

4 Things have a habit of goin**g** missing.

5 The printer's always breakin**g** down.

b **Listen again and repeat.**

10 Rewrite the sentences using the words in brackets so that they mean the same.

1 People normally wear casual clothes in the office. (As a rule)

2 People don't usually take all their days of holiday. (tend)

3 On the whole, students call the teachers by their first names. (tend)

4 Rather annoyingly, people often leave their dirty cups on the table. (habit)

5 People sometimes forget their ID card, which can cause a lot of problems. (from time to time)

6 The system has a habit of crashing. (constantly)

11 a Write five sentences about the habits of people/ machines/places you know. Use the structures in the grammar box.

As a rule, the lifts tend to break down once a year.

b **Work in pairs and compare your ideas.**

Go to page 138 or your app for more information and practice.

Speaking

PREPARE

12 a You're going to give an induction talk to new staff/ students at your place of work/study. First, work in pairs and discuss the topics you will include, e.g. the dress policy, health and safety rules.

b **Work on your own and prepare your talk. Use the language from this lesson and the Useful phrases.**

Useful phrases

The first thing I need to tell you about is (health and safety rules).

OK. Moving on, I'd like to say a bit about (night shifts).

If you have any problems with (your working hours), talk to (your manager).

As a rule, we tend to/tend not to (work late).

Right. I think that's all. Any questions?

SPEAK

13 Work in groups. Take turns giving your talks. At the end of each talk, ask the speaker questions.

Develop your writing
page 92

2c > Changing world

Reading

1 a Look at the photos and discuss the questions.

   1 Do you think children play differently now compared to in the past?

   2 Do you think children get enough exercise?

   3 Do you think children use technology too much?

  b Read the article. Does it mention any of your ideas?

2 Which of points 1–6 are made in the article?

   1 75 percent of British kids don't do any physical activity.

   2 In the past, there weren't so many cars on the roads.

   3 Mobile phones give kids more opportunities.

   4 Learning to deal with problems is an important part of growing up.

   5 Parents in Spain worry about how much their children have to read.

   6 Some things never change.

3 Work in groups. Do you think the general trends described in the article are also true in your country? Why? Give examples.

Grammar

4 Read and complete the grammar box by crossing out the forms that are not possible. Use the examples in bold in the article to help you.

used to, would and past simple

Used to, would and the past simple can all be used to talk about things that happened in the past but don't happen anymore.

- To talk about repeated past actions or events, use:
  1 *used to* + infinitive/*would* + infinitive/the past simple.

- To talk about past states such as being, having or liking, use:
  2 *used to* + infinitive/*would* + infinitive/the past simple.

- To talk about single events in the past, use:
  3 *used to* + infinitive/*would* + infinitive/the past simple.

Make negatives of *used to* with *didn't use to* or *never used to*.

My parents didn't use to know where I was half the time – and never used to ask for any details.

Make questions with *Did you (ever) use to?*

Did you use to go out on your own when you were a kid?

Give kids an outside chance

A global study of children's fitness has suggested that kids are not doing enough exercise. For example, in China, Chile and Qatar less than 20 percent of kids get involved in physical activity. Another study found that 75 percent of British children spend less time outside than people in prison.

One reason for this is that from Beijing to London, there's less green space in our cities – and far more traffic. While kids in the past **would play** games in the streets, that is almost impossible these days, even if parents let their kids go outside. But that's the second problem – worried parents want to control their kids more, and technology is allowing this to happen. Parents don't just constantly text and call now; they also have apps that allow them to see where their kids are!

Such things simply **didn't exist** when I **was** young. In fact, my parents **didn't use to know** where I was half the time – and **never used to ask** for any details. We**'d** sometimes **go** to friends' houses but often we**'d run around** the neighbourhood and explore: parks, woods and empty buildings. I remember once we even **went** into an old factory. Sure, we**'d** sometimes **get** into trouble when we were out, but I'd say that was good for our development.

What's more, parents these days don't seem happy with their kids indoors, either: kids play too many games and don't read enough. Or rather they play the wrong games and read the wrong things. A study in Spain actually **found** that kids are reading more these days. However, they're not reading as much for pleasure as we did.

It seems, then, that kids are simply worse than they **used to be** – which is perhaps the one thing that never changes. This was Socrates almost 2,500 years ago: 'Children now love luxury. They have bad manners, don't respect people in authority, and chat instead of exercising.'

5 a **2.7 Listen. Notice that when the sounds /t/ or /d/ occur before a consonant sound, they may not be pronounced.**

1 I use**d** to walk to school on my own.
2 We'**d** go to the library every weekend.
3 When I was young, we'd ea**t** fish every Friday.
4 I'd always spen**d** the holidays with my gran**d**parents.

b Listen again and repeat.

6 Read the text and cross out the alternatives that are not possible.

My life ¹*used to be/would be* much more complicated before I ²*got/used to get* my first mobile phone. In those days, I ³*always arranged/would always arrange* exactly where and when to meet my friends and we ⁴*tried/used to try* our best to get there on time.
Sometimes we ⁵*used to wait/would wait* hours for people to turn up. I remember once I ⁶*rang/would ring* a friend's mum to tell her I was going to be late, and my friend then ⁷*called/used to call* home to see if there had been any messages! People did things like that then. I also ⁸*knew/would know* loads of phone numbers by heart. Now I can hardly remember my own! It's funny, though, because even though I now carry my phone everywhere, I actually think I ⁹*called/would call* my friends more back then. I guess it's because we ¹⁰*never used to have/wouldn't have* emails, texts or messaging apps.

7 Work in pairs. Choose a piece of technology that has changed your life and explain how.

Go to page 138 or your app for more information and practice.

Vocabulary

8 Complete the sentences with the words in the box.

arrangements authority complicated control
entertain experience feel free force let
manners trouble watch over

1 You can't _____ kids all the time to check what they're doing. You have to let go!
2 It's important that children learn good _____ like saying 'Please' and 'Thank you'.
3 You shouldn't _____ your kids play in the street. It's too dangerous.
4 Children should always respect people in _____ , like teachers and police officers.
5 Getting into _____ is just part of growing up.
6 It's important to _____ the technology that kids use and give them time limits.
7 Children should _____ to say whatever they want.
8 Parents should _____ their kids to eat everything.
9 Children only learn to become independent if they _____ difficulties in life.
10 A lot of parents make too many _____ for their kids, like after-school and weekend activities.
11 It's good for children to be bored so they learn to _____ themselves.
12 Life is more _____ for kids than it was in the past. There are so many things they are expected to do.

9 Choose six sentences from Exercise 8 that you agree with. Why do you agree? Then work in pairs and compare your ideas.

I think parents should definitely control technology. I think kids should only get smartphones when they are 16 and parents should give them a limit of one hour a night on the internet.

 Go to your app for more practice.

Speaking

PREPARE

10 a **2.8 You're going to discuss how life was different when you were younger. First, listen to two people doing the same. Answer the questions.**

1 Which two topics in the box do they talk about?
2 Did they have the same experience?

technology parents entertainment holidays
fashion home life school and studying sport

b Choose four topics from the box. Think about what you and other children did when you were younger and if those habits and experiences have changed for young people today.

SPEAK

11 a Work in groups and compare your ideas. Did you have any of the same habits or experiences when you were younger? How do they compare with life for young people today? Use *used to, would* and the Useful phrases.

Useful phrases
Did you ever use to do it in the past?
Did you use to do much sport?
How often did you use to go?
I think it's better/worse for kids now because (they have a lot of freedom).
Which do you think is better?

b Work in groups. Is life better for children now or when you were younger? Explain your answers.

Develop
your
reading
page 94

2D English in action

> **Goal:** end conversations politely

1 Look at the pictures. What do you think is happening?

2 🔊 2.9 Listen to three conversations. Why does each person need to end the conversation?

3 a Listen again and complete the sentences with three words. Contractions count as two words.

1 Listen, I'm really sorry, but I'm actually _____ .
2 I'll call you. It'd be great _____ .
3 Sorry to interrupt you, but _____ seen my friend Jordan and I really need to talk to her about something before she goes.
4 It's been great _____ .
5 Anyway, if I don't see you, enjoy _____ your evening.
6 Oh no! I've _____ ! I've got a class at 7.30.
7 I know! Sorry _____ like this.
8 Well, give me a call when you hear. Thanks for the coffee. _____ !

b Read the Useful phrases box and check your answers.

Useful phrases

To bring a conversation to an end, you can:

a Show you want to say something
Anyway, …
Listen …
Sorry to interrupt, but …

b Say you have to go
I've got to go.
I need to get going.

c Explain why
My train/bus is about to leave.
I'm (actually) in a rush.
I've just seen my friend and I need to talk to her before she goes.
I'm meeting a friend at six.
I have an early start tomorrow.
I've got a class at 7.30.

d Say something positive
It was great to catch up.
It was great meeting you.
It'd be great to catch up.
It's been great to meet you.
Enjoy the rest of your evening.
Fingers crossed.

e Add an apology
Sorry to rush off like this.
I'm afraid I can't stop.

4 a Put the words in brackets in the correct order to complete the sentences.

1 I think _____ . (going / I'd / get / better)
2 Anyway, listen, _____ . (useful / been / a / really / meeting / it's)
3 I'm really sorry I _____ . (more / and / stay / talk / can't)
4 Sorry to _____ ? (time / you / what's / but / the / interrupt)
5 I have something on _____ . (work / can't / late / and / I / be / at)
6 Sorry, but I've just had _____ (someone / a / from / call) and I _____ . (out / it / sort / to / need)

b 🔊 2.10 Listen and check your answers.

c Listen again and repeat.

5 Match the sentences in Exercise 4a with functions a–e in the Useful phrases box. Sentence 2 has two functions.

6 a You're going to start and end conversations with two students in your class. First, think about:
- how you could start each conversation.
- what you will talk about.
- how you could end each conversation.

b Work in pairs and have your first conversation. Use the Useful phrases to help you. Try to make the conversation last as long as possible.

c Change partners. Repeat but end the conversation in a different way.

Go online for the Roadmap video.

Check and reflect

1 a Complete the sentences with the best word. The first letter is given.

1 I know I make mistakes when I'm speaking, but I like to h_____ a go.

2 I'm not very k_____ on grammar, but I like speaking and listening.

3 I've d_____ a few apps, which I study from most days.

4 Every day after class I go home and go o_____ what we've done in class.

5 I'm making good p_____ with my English. I'm much better than I was last year.

6 I do an online language e_____ with an English woman once a week.

b Which sentences in Exercise 1a are true for you? Work in pairs. Say three more things that you do to improve your English. Who do you think has the better study skills?

2 Complete the sentences with the correct form of the verbs in the box.

agree	bake	get	learn	start	train

1 I _____ how to dance tango. I have classes twice a week.

2 I really love football. I'm in a team and we _____ three times a week after work.

3 More and more people _____ their own businesses.

4 It's not a popular opinion, but I _____ with you.

5 I'm very keen on cooking. I _____ all my own bread – and I _____ better all the time!

3 a Match verbs 1–6 with pairs of endings a–f.

1 explain   a night shifts/late

2 work   b a suit/formal clothes

3 wear   c a union member/a manager

4 be   d the health and safety rules/a policy

5 do   e time off/a holiday

6 take   f a first aid course/a fire drill

b Choose three verbs and endings from Exercise 3a that are connected with your life. Work in groups. Explain your choices.

4 Complete the text with the correct habit structure words.

On the ¹_____ , I'd say I'm fairly fit. I don't ²_____ to have much energy in the evenings, so as a ³_____ , I get up early and do things before I go to work. I ⁴_____ running four or five times a week and I go cycling from time to ⁵_____ as well. The only problem is, I have quite an old bicycle and it has a ⁶_____ of breaking down! I don't ⁷_____ exercise on Sundays, though, because everyone needs a day of rest! Oh, I ⁸_____ to eat quite healthily too: no junk food, not much red meat, that kind of thing.

5 a Rewrite the sentences using the words in brackets so that they mean the same. In two cases, this is not possible.

1 I spent hours and hours listening to music when I was a teenager. (used to)

2 When I was eight or nine, we went to Mexico for a month. (used to)

3 When I was a kid, I always cycled to school. (would)

4 I really loved the movie *Star Wars* when I was a kid. (would)

5 I never ate vegetables when I was younger, but now I'm a vegetarian! (used to)

6 I used to have really long hair. I only used to cut it once or twice a year. (would)

b Think of five things that were true for you in the past, but aren't true anymore. Work in groups and compare your ideas. Try to use *used to* and *would* instead of the past simple.

6 a Match sentence halves 1–6 with a–f.

1 I never got into

2 I experienced

3 My parents used to force

4 My parents used to control

5 My parents made sure I learnt

6 My parents used to let

a good manners.

b any trouble when I was younger.

c me sleep as much as I wanted.

d some real difficulties when I was a kid.

e me to study every day.

f how much I used the internet.

b Which sentences in Exercise 6a are true for you? Work in pairs and explain your answers.

Reflect

How confident do you feel about the statements below? Write 1–5 (1 = not very confident, 5 = very confident).

- I can describe trends and talk about new skills I'm learning.
- I can give a short talk about where I work/study.
- I can describe differences between customs now and in the past.
- I can end conversations politely.

Want more practice?

Go to your Workbook or app.

3A Places to see

> **Goal:** recommend places to go on holiday
> **Grammar:** present perfect simple questions and answers
> **Vocabulary:** tourist places

Vocabulary and listening

1 Work in pairs and discuss the questions.
  1 What kind of places do you like going to on holiday?
  2 What kind of things do you most like doing?

2 a Read the extract from a travel brochure about Thailand and match the words in bold with photos A–E.

  b Work in pairs and discuss the questions.
  1 Which places would you most like to visit?
  2 Which things would you most like to do?

3 a Complete the collocations with an underlined word from the brochure.
  1 _____ to the top of the dam/the cliff/the tower
  2 a guided .../a coach .../a walking _____
  3 the temple/the old town/the painting has been _____
  4 _____ remains/cities/temples
  5 have a great _____ of the valley/the whole city/ the surrounding landscape
  6 a _____ path/hill/cliff

  b Work in pairs. Use words in bold from the brochure and collocations from Exercise 3a to talk about places you know.
  There's a medieval old town in Tallinn, the capital of Estonia. It's amazing!

  Go to your app for more practice.

4 🔊 **3.1** Listen to a conversation between two people who are travelling in Thailand. Match the things and activities in the box with places 1–3.
  1 Chiang Mai
  2 Sukhothai
  3 the countryside near Chiang Mai

  > an amazing landscape a zip wire across a waterfall
  > the night market ancient temples and remains
  > an elephant reserve medieval walls the old town
  > rafting down a river

5 Listen again. What were they discussing in these sentences?
  1 I'm thinking of going there later for something to eat.
  2 I guess I might go and have a look around later on.
  3 It's supposed to be amazing.
  4 It was really cool.
  5 It's more of an environmental thing.

THE LAND OF SMILES

Home to incredible beaches, friendly people, amazing scenery and delicious food, Thailand has everything you could wish for. Here are five of our favourite places to visit:

1 Phra Nang
You can get to this beautiful sandy beach through a **cave**, and once there, you can swim, sunbathe, or even climb the steep **cliffs** if you really want to.

2 Ao Thalane is a **nature reserve** on the west coast, where you can see a huge range of wildlife, including crab-eating birds. You can also kayak on the river, surrounded by stunning mountains and beautiful forests.

3 Chiang Mai
Sometimes called the Rose of the North, Chiang Mai has something for everyone: you can visit the recently restored **Wat Phra Singh temple**; you can enjoy the wonderful view from the mountains around the city; or you can take a Thai cookery course at one of the many local schools.

4 Bangkok
The best way to see Thailand's capital city is to take a guided tour with a local. Learn more about the medieval **Mahakan fort**, take a boat up the river or go shopping in the lively street markets. It's up to you.

5 Ayutthaya city
Visit the ancient **remains** of Ayutthaya city, which was built in the twelfth century.

Grammar

6 Read and complete the grammar box with the phrases in the box. Use the examples in the grammar box to help you.

> *be going to*   past simple   present simple
> *be thinking of + -ing*   *would like/love to*
> present perfect simple

Present perfect simple questions and answers

Use the present perfect simple to talk about your experiences. When you answer present perfect questions like *Have you (ever) been to ...?*, you can use a range of structures.

1 _____ : to talk about experiences from the past to now
Yeah, I've been to Thailand three times now.

2 _____ : to give details of a past experience
Yeah, I did some rafting down the river near there.

3 _____ : to give your current opinions based on experience
Yes, it's wonderful there.

be supposed to: to show opinions based on what you have read or heard
No, but it's supposed to be amazing.

4 _____ : to show your hopes for the future
No, but I'd love to go sometime during my trip.

5 _____ : to show a possible plan
No, but I'm thinking of going there later.

6 _____ : to show a firm plan about the future
Yes, I'm going to this elephant reserve tomorrow.

You can also respond by asking questions of your own:
Yeah, I have. What did you think of it?
No. Have you?
No. What's it like?

7 Work in pairs. Read the conversations and cross out the alternatives that are not possible. Explain why.

1 A: Have you ever been to Australia?
   B: Yeah, *it's/it's supposed to be* an amazing country.

2 A: Have you ever been on a zip wire?
   B: No – and *I didn't want to/I've never wanted to*. I'm scared of heights!

3 A: Have you been to Bangkok?
   B: No. *What's it like?/Have you?*

4 A: Have you been to the fort in the old town?
   B: Yes, *we took/we've taken* our kids there yesterday.

5 A: Have you been to Chiang Mai?
   B: *I didn't hear of it./I've never heard of it.* Where is it?

6 A: Have you visited the museum?
   B: No. *I'm thinking of going tomorrow./It's supposed to be a bit boring.*

7 A: Have you tried any of the local food yet?
   B: No, not yet, but *I'd like to/I'm going to*. I've heard it's delicious.

8 a **3.2** Listen to the questions from Exercise 7 said slowly and then more quickly. Notice the weak forms in the faster versions.

b Listen again and repeat.

9 a Write five *Have you (ever) ...?* questions about travel experiences. Use the ideas in the box.

> countries   places to visit   holiday activities   food

b Work in groups. Ask and answer the questions. Use the most appropriate structures from the grammar box. Try to continue each conversation.

📱 Go to page 140 or your app for more information and practice.

Speaking

PREPARE

10 a You're going to recommend holiday destinations to three groups of people:
- students on a one-month backpacking tour
- a young family on a two-week summer holiday
- a couple in search of interesting/unusual places to see

🔊 **3.3** First, listen to two people discussing a holiday destination and answer the questions.

1 What places do they recommend?
2 Who for?
3 Have they both been to the places they talk about?

b Think of three holiday destinations in your country for each group of people in Exercise 10a.

SPEAK

11 a Work in pairs. Take turns asking and answering questions about the destinations you chose. Decide which places are best. Use the Useful phrases to help you.

A: Have you ever visited Toledo?
B: No, never. What's it like?
A: Oh, it's very beautiful and romantic. Perfect for couples.

Useful phrases
It's perfect for (couples/families/students).
It's (not) very easy to get to.
It's great value for money.
There's lots to do there.
I've heard it's amazing.

b Report back to the class. Which are the most popular destinations?

Develop your reading
page 96

3B ⟩ Big issues

> **Goal:** discuss an article
>
> **Grammar:** present perfect simple and continuous
>
> **Vocabulary:** science and research

Vocabulary and reading

1 **Work in groups and discuss the questions.**
   1 Do you know anyone involved in science or technology? What do they do?
   2 What do you think are the most important problems relating to science and technology at the moment?

2 **Match sentence starters 1–7 with pairs of possible endings a–g.**
   1 The **global birth rate**
   2 These days we are at **risk**
   3 Recently, there's been a lot of **research**
   4 Scientists don't know what **causes**
   5 Our country has **invested** billions
   6 We still can't **predict**
   7 We should **invest** more in **exploring**

   a in developing **solar power**/in finding a **cure** for Alzheimer's.
   b **cancer cells** to grow/climate **change**.
   c future **earthquakes**/exactly how we will **be affected** by climate change.
   d into **identifying genes**/into new **sources** of energy.
   e has been **falling steadily**/has **increased dramatically**.
   f the bottom of the oceans/space.
   g of **running out of** oil and gas/of getting more cancer.

3 a **Work in pairs and think of one more way you can finish 1–7 in Exercise 2.**
   The global birth rate is very high.

   b **Which sentences in Exercise 2 do you think are true?**

 Go to page 158 or your app for more vocabulary and practice.

4 a **Read the article. Does it mention any of the issues you discussed in Exercise 1?**

   b **Read the article again. Are the sentences true (T) or false (F)?**
   1 The global birth rate is 50 percent lower than in the 1960s.
   2 Scientists are developing ways to grow food without fields and land.
   3 Scientists have shown that all cancer is caused only by smoking.
   4 Treatment of cancer has improved a lot over the last 50 years.
   5 More than a quarter of China's electricity comes from solar power.
   6 Scientists have discovered how to use water as a fuel.

Ask the experts about some of the biggest problems of our time

Can we feed everyone?

Although the global birth rate has fallen a lot since the 1960s (it's half what it was), the global population has been growing steadily over the last 50 years. By 2050, there may be over nine billion of us! As there are already problems with hunger in some parts of the world, we may be at risk of a global food crisis if the population continues to increase. However, scientists are already working on a number of solutions, including indoor farms in cities and meat grown in laboratories.

Can we find a cure for cancer?

Ever since US President Nixon began a 'war on cancer' in the 1970s, huge amounts of money have been invested in research to try to understand the cause of the disease and find a cure. While we know smoking dramatically increases the risk of getting cancer, scientists haven't actually discovered one single cause of all cancers. The latest idea is that cancers develop by chance, which may make finding a complete cure impossible. However, some hope that using genes to attack cancer cells will work. And scientists have been making good progress in helping people live with the disease – around 60 percent of people now survive over five years compared to less than 30 percent 50 years ago.

Can we produce more energy?

We've known for ages that we are running out of oil and gas, so we need to find other sources of energy. The use of solar power has grown dramatically, and it now provides almost 40 percent of Germany's electricity and 30 percent of China's. Scientists have also been exploring other ways to use the sun's energy, particularly for transport. One idea is to use sunlight to divide water (H_2O) into oxygen and hydrogen. The hydrogen would then be used as a clean fuel for engines.

5 **Work in pairs and discuss the questions.**
   1 Did you find any of the facts surprising or worrying?
   2 Which of the challenges seems easiest to solve? Why?

Grammar

6 Work in pairs. Read the article again and find three examples of the present perfect continuous and five examples of the present perfect simple.

7 Read the grammar box and choose the correct alternatives.

Present perfect simple and continuous

Use the present perfect to talk about actions or events that started before now and have a present connection or result.

Use the present perfect [1] *simple/continuous* to focus on the completed action. It often explains how much or how many (including none).
The birth rate has fallen since the 1960s. (how much)

Use the present perfect [2] *simple/continuous* to focus on an action that lasts for a period of time and/or that is unfinished now. It often explains how long.
Scientists have also been exploring other ways to use the sun's energy. (action unfinished)

Don't use the present perfect [3] *simple/continuous* with passive verbs or state verbs.
A lot of money has been invested in cancer research.

8 a 3.4 Listen and notice the weak forms of *have* and *been*.

1 How long have you been doing that?
2 I've been busy studying for my exams.
3 She's always been good with numbers.
4 They've been looking for ages, but they still haven't found anything.

b Listen again and repeat.

9 Complete each pair of sentences with a verb from the box. In one sentence use the present perfect simple, in the other use the present perfect continuous.

> do   explore   hurt   think   try

1 a They _____ lots of different ways of predicting earthquakes, but none have worked.
  b They _____ to find a cure for cancer for ages, but it still kills millions every year.
2 a The spacecraft _____ the edge of our solar system for the last ten years.
  b So far, we _____ only _____ a tiny part of the ocean floor.
3 a I _____ often _____ that there's very little difference between humans and animals.
  b I _____ about this question for 30 years, and now have an answer to it!
4 a Recently we _____ research into the effects of climate change on the local wildlife.
  b I'm sorry. I _____ all I can to help you.
5 a He _____ his knee, so he's not playing today.
  b I'm not sure what I've done to my back, but it _____ quite badly for the last few days.

10 a Complete the sentences with a present perfect form. Try to use at least three examples of the present perfect continuous.

1 It's a bit surprising, but I've never ...
2 I _____ for ages.
3 I'm proud of the fact that ...
4 I'd love to do some research on _____ because ...
5 I've decided to _____ because ...
6 I've been thinking of _____ because ...
7 How long ... ?
8 Have ... ?

b Work in pairs. Compare your ideas for 1–6. Then ask and answer 7 and 8.

Go to page 140 or your app for more information and practice.

Speaking

PREPARE

11 3.5 You're going to read and summarise a short article. First, listen to two people doing the same. Which of the stories from the article in Exercise 4 are they discussing?

12 Work in pairs. Student A: Turn to page 174. Student B: Turn to page 167.

SPEAK

13 a Take turns asking and answering questions about the articles. Use the questions in the Communication bank. Try to keep the conversation going by commenting or asking further questions. Use the Useful phrases to help you.

> **Useful phrases**
> That's awful/amazing!
> I had no idea.
> Do you think that's really possible?
> Can't they do anything about it?
> That's not something I worry about.

b Discuss which scientific area from the articles you think should get extra investment for more research and why.

Develop your writing
page 98

3c Living abroad

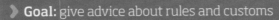

> **Goal:** give advice about rules and customs
>
> **Grammar:** obligation and permission
>
> **Vocabulary:** rules and customs

Listening

1 **Work in pairs and discuss the questions.**

1 Would you like to spend a long time in another country? Why?/Why not?

2 What advice and information would you want to get before you go?

2 🔊 **3.6 Listen to a podcast for students planning to study in London. In what order are topics a–d mentioned?**

a using public transport

b what to do if you need a doctor

c different ways of greeting people

d what to do when you first arrive

3 **Listen again. Are the sentences true (T) or false (F)?**

1 Everyone entering the UK to study has to register with the police.

2 If you have a short-term study visa, you can stay in the country for almost a year.

3 If you get very ill, you should call 911.

4 It's not possible to see a doctor unless you make an appointment first.

5 You don't need a ticket to use public transport in London.

6 People often kiss each other on the cheek – even in business meetings.

Grammar

4 🔊 **3.7 Listen and choose the correct alternatives.**

1 You *are required to/must* register with the police.

2 If you have a short-term study visa, then *you don't have to /you're not required to* register.

3 If your visa says *you can /you're allowed to* enter the country for up to 11 months, then this doesn't apply to you.

4 I'm afraid *we're not allowed to/we can't* give advice on visa issues.

5 You *don't have to/needn't* pay by cash or buy a ticket if you're taking tubes or buses in London.

6 You *ought to /should* wear headphones if you're playing music or watching videos on your phone.

7 When you're at a pedestrian crossing, *you're not supposed to/you shouldn't really* cross until you see the green man.

5 **Read the grammar box and cross out the alternatives that are not possible.**

Obligation and permission

Use *needn't, must, have to, should* and *can* to show obligation or permission. They are followed by an [1]*infinitive/infinitive with to.*

You can also use other structures:

be required to means you [2]*have to/can/should* do something (absolute obligation)

be not required to means you [3]*mustn't/don't have to/needn't* do it if you don't want to (no obligation)

be supposed to means you [4]*must/should/ought to* do something (weak obligation)

be not supposed to means you [5]*mustn't/shouldn't/ought not to* do something (weak obligation)

ought to means you [6]*have to/must/should/can* do something (weak obligation)

be allowed to means you [7]*must/can/need to* do something (permission)

be not allowed to means you [8]*ought not to/can't/needn't* do something (no permission)

6 a 🔊 **3.8 Listen and notice the weak forms of *you're* and *to.***

1 You're required to register.

2 You're allowed to have two passports.

3 You're supposed to carry ID.

4 You're not supposed to talk in here.

b **Listen again and repeat.**

7 Rewrite the sentences using the correct form of the words in brackets so that they mean the same.

1 If you already have a driving licence, you don't have to take lessons here before taking a test. (require)
2 You should really carry your ID card with you at all times, but lots of people don't. (suppose)
3 If you're in the UK already, you don't have to worry about it. (need)
4 You can join the army when you are 16 if your parents agree. (allow)
5 If you want a visa, you have to go to the capital for an interview. (require)
6 You can't cross the road until you see the green light. (allow)

8 a Write down at least one thing for categories 1–5.

1 something you're required to do at work or college that you don't like
2 something you're supposed to do at work or home that you sometimes don't do
3 a rule you have broken
4 a rule you would like to introduce
5 things schools should/shouldn't do so their children become good citizens

b Work in pairs. Take turns reading out and explaining what you wrote.

 Go to page 140 or your app for more information and practice.

Vocabulary

9 a Complete the sentences with the words in the box.

access	charge	fine	let	personal	privacy
respect	return	split	swear		

1 You have to register with a local doctor to _____ healthcare.
2 You shouldn't really _____ in public – even if talking to friends.
3 People's _____ space is important. Don't get too close or touch when talking.
4 You ought to _____ everyone off the train or bus before you get on.
5 There's no _____ for using any ATM run by any bank.
6 If people offer to buy you a drink, it's polite to offer to buy them a drink in _____ later.
7 If you drop rubbish in the street, you may have to pay a _____ of up to £1,000.
8 It's normal to _____ the bill evenly when paying in a group, whatever you choose to eat.
9 November 1st is a public holiday when people are supposed to show _____ to their dead relatives.
10 People don't tend to ask about your personal life in order to respect your _____ .

b Underline the collocations in sentences 1–10 that include the words in the box.
access healthcare

c Work in pairs. Do you know any countries where the sentences in Exercise 9a are true?

 Go to page 158 or your app for more vocabulary and practice.

Speaking

PREPARE

10 🔊 3.9 You're going to give advice about rules and customs. First, listen to someone doing the same. Which two topics are mentioned? What is the advice?

- in someone's home
- health
- transport and driving
- greetings
- things that are illegal
- going out
- things that are impolite
- visas

11 Prepare some advice for a visitor about living in the country you're in now. Do the following:

1 choose four topics from the list in Exercise 10.
2 think of at least two rules and customs you would tell the visitor about each topic.
3 think of five questions you would ask about other rules and customs if you were a visitor.

SPEAK

12 a Work in pairs. Take turns giving advice and asking questions. Use the Useful phrases to help you.

> **Useful phrases**
> Is there anything I should know about (greetings)?
> Are you allowed to (talk) here?
> Are you required to (register with a doctor)? What happens if you don't do that?
> Is it polite to (shake hands)? Do people get angry if you don't?
> What should I do if I want to (stay in the country longer)?

b What was the most useful advice you heard?

Develop your listening
page 100

> **Goal:** ask for and give explanations

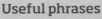

Useful phrases

Asking for an explanation
I haven't heard of that before.
What does that mean?
I don't know what that is, I'm afraid.
You got tickets for what?
What is it exactly?

Showing you don't know a word
I've forgotten the word for it.
I'm not sure what you'd call it in English.
I'm not sure how to explain it.

Explaining something in a different way
It's a kind of (soup).
It's a bit like (lemon), but (sweeter).
It's a thing for (cutting wood).
It's for (making couscous).
It stands for (the National Union of Students).
It's the place where you go if (you've had an accident).

Checking understanding
Do you know what I mean?
Does that make sense?

Showing understanding
Yeah. I know what you mean.
OK. Thanks. I've got it now.

1 🔊 3.14 **Listen to four conversations and match them with photos A–D.**

2 a 🔊 3.15 **Listen and complete the sentences with three words. Contractions count as two words.**

   1 a I've _____ for it. I used to know it.
      b Does _____ ?
   2 a You got _____ ?
      b Do you know _____ ?
   3 a Oh, it's _____ traditional Russian soup.
      b OK. Thanks. _____ it now.
   4 a I'm not sure what _____ it in English, actually.
      b Yeah. I know _____ .

  b **Listen again and repeat.**

3 **Match one sentence from Exercise 2a with each of functions a–e. Then read the Useful phrases box and check your answers.**
   a Asking for an explanation
   b Showing you don't know a word
   c Explaining something in a different way
   d Checking understanding
   e Showing understanding

4 a **Write down some things in your own language that someone from another country may not know.**
   • an acronym (e.g. NATO)
   • three different kinds of food/drink
   • two objects
   • a game
   • a special day in your country
   • an unusual animal/plant/flower

  b **Work in groups. Give explanations for your list of things and check understanding. Use the Useful phrases to help you.**

Go online for the Roadmap video.

Check and reflect

1 a Complete the sentences with the words in the box.

remains	reserve	temple	tour	tower	town

1 They have a big nature _____ there with elephants and lions and everything.
2 There's an old _____ that you can climb up. You get a great view from the top.
3 You can go on a guided _____ round the old castle there.
4 The city is famous for its ancient _____ .
5 They're restoring the old _____ , so you can't see all the buildings, but it's still nice to walk round.
6 There's an ancient Buddhist _____ in the forest that you can visit.

b Work in groups. Have you visited anywhere like the places described in Exercise 1a? When? What were they like? If not, would you like to? Why?/Why not?

2 a Complete the answers to the *Have you ever been to ...?* questions with the correct form of the verbs in brackets.

1 Yes, I have. I _____ there four or five times, actually. (go)
2 Yes, I have. I _____ it there. It _____ so beautiful! (love / be)
3 No, never, but it _____ great. (suppose)
4 No, never, but I _____ go one day. (love)
5 No, never, but I _____ there next summer, actually. (think / go)
6 No, but I _____ there next month, actually. (go)

b Think of five places you like visiting in your town/city/country. Work in pairs. Take turns asking and answering *Have you ever been to ...?* questions about the places.

3 a Complete the sentences with the best word. The first letter is given.

1 The global birth r_____ has been falling steadily over recent years.
2 I heard they've started doing more r_____ into the causes of grey hair.
3 Several cities are at risk of r_____ out of drinking water sometime soon.
4 They can now p_____ who you'll vote for by looking at your online habits.
5 They're promising to i_____ more in technology for schools.
6 They're going to spend more on helping scientists to e_____ space.

b Work in groups. Which sentences in Exercise 3a describe good news and which describe bad news? Explain your answers. What's the best/worst news?

4 Rewrite the sentences using the present perfect continuous. In some cases, this is not possible.

1 I haven't worked here very long.
2 How long have you lived here?
3 The birth rate has risen dramatically over recent years.
4 I've been there six or seven times.
5 I've done a bit of research into it recently.
6 They've looked for a cure for ages, but they still haven't found one.
7 A lot of money has been invested in this project.
8 I've always been interested in science.

5 a Complete the sentences with one word. Negative forms count as one word.

1 I don't _____ to work weekends, but sometimes I do.
2 We're not _____ to do a first aid course, but I just thought it might be useful.
3 We're not _____ to use social media during work hours.
4 We _____ really make personal phone calls at work, but people sometimes do.
5 We _____ wear smart clothes if we don't want to, but it's generally best to.
6 We _____ start work any time between 8 and 11, but if we start later, we _____ to finish later.

b Work in groups. Which sentences in Exercise 5a are true for you or people you know? Why or in what circumstances might 1–6 happen?

6 a Match verbs 1–6 with endings a–f.

1	drop	a	the bill
2	split	b	in public
3	respect	c	respect to elderly people
4	let	d	rubbish in the street
5	swear	e	people's privacy
6	show	f	people off the bus first

b Work in pairs. Which of the actions in Exercise 6a are common in your country? Are there any actions that you think don't happen enough? Explain your ideas.

Reflect

How confident do you feel about the statements below? Write 1–5 (1 = not very confident, 5 = very confident).

* I can describe my travel experiences.
* I can summarise and comment on short articles.
* I can talk about rules and customs.
* I can ask about and explain unknown words.

Want more practice?
Go to your Workbook or app.

4A A big mistake

> **Goal:** talk about accidents and mistakes
> **Grammar:** past simple and past continuous
> **Vocabulary:** accidents and mistakes

Reading

1 **Look at the photos. What accidents and/or mistakes might happen in these situations?**

2 a **Read the thread from a discussion forum and answer the questions.**
   1 What job did each person have when they made their mistake?
   2 What did they do wrong – and why?

b **Which was the easiest/worst/funniest mistake in your opinion?**

I was watching an old episode of *Mad Men* yesterday, in which <u>a character was demonstrating a new machine for cutting grass and accidentally drove over a client's foot!</u> It made me think: what's the worst mistake you've made at work?

Dejan
<u>I worked for a building company for several years</u> and one time I was repairing the bathroom in a flat while the family was away. At the end of the day, I was checking the bath to see if the repair was good when I got a call from a friend. He had a spare ticket for a big game that night and I had to go straightaway if I wanted it. I was so excited, I rushed out and completely forgot about the bath. That night it completely flooded the flat and the water went through the ceiling to the flat below. There was quite a lot of damage and I ended up paying for it!

Veronica
One time I was working in a restaurant as a waitress. I was carrying a heavy tray of food and drinks to a table and for some reason I was quite nervous. As I got close to the table, I tripped over a bag on the floor. The drinks on my tray spilt all over the people at the table! It was so embarrassing. They got really wet and were very cross!

Maxim
I work for quite a big company in the IT department. One day I had to access a computer in a local office, so I sent out a message for the user of the computer to call me, but somehow I managed to send the message to every computer in the whole company – all 6,000 of them! I guess I must've checked the wrong box on the system or forgotten to uncheck one. Anyway, <u>we were getting calls to our office for days!</u>

Grammar

3 a **Read the underlined clauses in the text. Find the past simple and past continuous verbs.**

b **Work in pairs. Match descriptions a–d with the underlined verbs in the text.**
   a This is a single completed action.
   b This is an action that was in progress around the time another action happened.
   c This emphasises the repetition of an action that continued for some time.
   d This is a completed action that continued for some time.

c **Read the grammar box and check your answers.**

Past simple and past continuous

Use the past continuous to suggest that an action was in progress:
- around a time in the past.
- around the time another action happened.

Use the past simple to talk about completed actions.

You can also use both the past simple and continuous to talk about the duration of an action. The past continuous emphasises that the action was repeated over a period of time.

4 a **4.1 Listen and complete the sentences with three words. Contractions count as two words.**

1 As she _____ , she accidentally knocked the table.

2 They _____ do too many things at once.

3 He wasn't looking where _____ and he knocked into me.

b Listen again and practise saying the sentences.

5 Choose the correct alternatives. In one case, both forms are possible.

I ¹*broke/was breaking* the screen on my phone the other day! I ²*walked/was walking* along the road with a friend and we ³*chatted/were chatting* and I was laughing at the ugly cover my friend ⁴*had/was having* on his phone to protect it. I ⁵*lifted/was lifting* up my phone to show it to him and said, 'Look. I've had this for over a year and there's not a scratch on it!' Then as I ⁶*put/was putting* it back in my pocket, this guy ran past and ⁷*knocked/was knocking* my elbow. The phone ⁸*flew/was flying* out of my hand and onto the pavement where it broke, of course! What made the whole thing even worse was that my friend ⁹*found/was finding* the whole thing very funny. He ¹⁰*joked/was joking* about it for hours afterwards!

Go to page 142 or your app for more information and practice.

Vocabulary

6 Complete the sentences with the pairs of verbs in the box.

crashed/caused   mixed up/turned up
ticked/charged   measured/fit   forgot/caught
pressed/went out   knocked/spilt
slipped/went into   left/flooded   slipped/fell down

1 I accidentally _____ over a bottle of olive oil and it _____ all over the floor.

2 I _____ the tap on and I _____ the apartment.

3 I _____ into the car in front and _____ quite a lot of damage to it.

4 I _____ the wrong box and I got _____ an extra £100 for insurance I didn't need.

5 She _____ 'reply to all' by mistake and it _____ to everyone in the company.

6 They _____ the height wrong and so when they came to install it, it didn't _____ .

7 I _____ to turn off the cooker and the frying pan _____ fire.

8 He _____ and _____ the stairs.

9 I _____ the dates for the booking so when we _____ , the hotel didn't have a room.

10 The knife _____ and it _____ my leg!

7 Work in pairs and answer the questions.

1 What other things could you **spill**?

2 What might you forget to **turn off**?

3 How else might a house **flood**?

4 How could you **cause a lot of damage** to a car?

5 What else can **catch fire**? How?

6 Where else might you **slip**? Why?

8 Work in pairs and imagine you made some of the mistakes in Exercise 6. Decide how the mistakes happened and what happened next. Try to use the past simple and the past continuous.

1 *I was cooking dinner and I accidentally knocked over a bottle of olive oil and it spilt all over the floor.*

 Go to page 159 or your app for more vocabulary and practice.

Speaking

PREPARE

9 **4.2 You're going to talk about an accident or a mistake. First, listen to someone describing a big mistake and answer the questions.**

1 What was the mistake?

2 Why did it happen?

3 How did he feel about it? What was the result of the mistake?

10 Think of a time when you had an accident or made a mistake. Answer the questions. Write down a maximum of ten words or phrases.

1 When did it happen?

2 What were you doing at the time?

3 Who were you with?

4 What caused the accident/mistake?

5 What were the consequences?

SPEAK

11 Work in groups. Tell your group about your accident or mistake. Show interest and try to keep the activity going by asking questions. Use the Useful phrases to help you.

Useful phrases

How did you manage to do that?

So what happened after that? Did you (lose your job)?

And what happened in the end?

How did you feel after all that?

Develop your listening
page 101

4B Crime doesn't pay

> **Goal:** discuss crime stories
> **Grammar:** past perfect simple
> **Vocabulary:** crime in the news

Vocabulary

1 Work in groups. How many nouns and verbs connected to crime can you think of? Make a list.

2 Work in pairs. Check you understand the words in bold. Then complete the sentences with the correct form of the nouns and verbs in the box.

> **Nouns:** attack   gang   robber   theft   trial   victim   witness
> **Verbs:** arrest   attack   break into   claim   free   get away

1 Police are searching for some _____ who _____ a museum and stole jewellery **worth** ten million euros.

2 Some young men _____ an old man in the high street last week. He was quite **badly hurt** but no one stopped the _____ or called the **emergency services**. The police _____ anyone yet. It's terrible.

3 They recently _____ a **criminal** from prison and a lot of the _____ of his crimes complained that he got out of **jail** too soon.

4 I saw a YouTube video of this guy who managed to **trap** a _____ of **thieves** in his shop and **lock** them inside before they could _____ . It was great.

5 Apparently, a lot of people are **reporting** _____ to the police in order to _____ money on their insurance, but nothing has actually been stolen.

6 The leader of a **criminal** gang is on _____ at the moment and, apparently, several _____ have had **threats** made against them.

🔲 Go to your app for more practice.

Reading

3 a Read the news stories and choose the best headline for each one. There are three extra headlines you don't need.

1 **Bike-mad politician gets nasty surprise**

2 **Hang on a minute!**

3 **When animals attack**

4 **Man unable to break out after breaking in**

5 *Police hunt bear man*

6 **City transport is terrible says minister**

A Police in Alaska are currently searching for a man who was seen attacking a female bear and her cubs. Hunting such bears is illegal, but what made this attack more unusual was the fact that the man was himself dressed as a bear. A small crowd had formed at a nature reserve to watch the bears catching salmon, and they were shocked to see a man in a full bear suit run at the bear cubs. The real bears weren't hurt but the man had got away before the police arrived. The reason for the attack is unknown.

B While Belgium is famous for its love of cycling, cars remain the main method of getting to and from work, and the country has some of the worst traffic problems in Europe. However, when a government minister recently went to a meeting to discuss an increase in spending on cycle lanes, he got a bit of a shock.
He had locked his bike outside a railway station in the south of Brussels before the meeting, but when he returned half an hour later, he found that someone had stolen it. He then had to call his driver to pick him up from the station.

C Two students at a university in the north of England were walking back to their rooms on campus late one January night when they noticed something rather unusual. A man had tried to break into a building through a window, but his legs had somehow got trapped, leaving him hanging upside down with his legs and feet sticking out.
The students talked to him while also taking photographs and making videos before calling the emergency services. When the police and firefighters arrived, they also stopped to take selfies before rescuing the robber who, by that time, had been there for five hours.

b Read the stories again and answer the questions.
In which story ...

1 were there lots of witnesses?

2 was the criminal lucky that someone saw him?

3 is nothing known about the person who did the crime?

4 is the reason for the crime hard to understand?

5 did it take longer than necessary to help someone?

6 did the crime make the victim look silly?

Grammar

4 a Read the sentences. Underline the past simple, past continuous and past perfect simple forms.

1 Two students were walking back to their rooms when they noticed a man who had got trapped in a window.

2 The police stopped to take selfies before rescuing the robber who, by that time, had been there for five hours.

3 He had locked his bike outside a railway station in the south of Brussels before the meeting.

b Underline three more examples of the past perfect simple in the stories in Exercise 3.

c Read and complete the grammar box with one word in each space.

Past perfect simple

The past perfect simple is formed with ¹ _____ + the past participle.

Use the past perfect simple to make it clear that one action happened ² _____ another action in the past.

The past perfect is often used with time phrases and adverbs such as: ³ _____ *the/that time, already, until, after,* etc.

He'd already been in jail three times by the time he was 30.

We didn't do anything until we'd spoken to the police.

The past perfect is often used after 'thinking' verbs such as *realise, remember* and *notice.*

I suddenly remembered I hadn't locked the door.

5 a 🔊 4.7 Listen and notice the weak form *'d* in the positive sentences.

1 We'd reported it four times before the police finally came round.

2 He'd been to jail several times before.

3 I couldn't believe they hadn't arrested him before.

4 It was scary because nothing like that'd ever happened to me before.

b Listen again and repeat.

6 Complete the sentences with the correct form of the verbs in brackets. Use the past simple and the past perfect simple in each sentence.

1 It _____ (be) a real shock. Nothing like that _____ (happen) to me before!

2 By the time the police _____ (get) there, the gang _____ (get away).

3 It _____ (be) the third time she _____ (be) the victim of that kind of crime.

4 She _____ (stand up) to leave the café and then suddenly realised that someone _____ (take) her bag!

5 He _____ (be) in prison for six months before the trial _____ (start).

6 The emergency services _____ (not arrive) until about an hour after we _____ (ring) them.

7 Work in pairs. Think of at least two endings for the sentences. Use the past perfect simple.

1 Until I was 18, I _____ .

2 I decided to _____ after _____ .

3 When I got to home, I realised _____ .

4 _____ was arrested after _____ .

5 By the time the police arrived, _____ .

📱 Go to page 142 or your app for more information and practice.

Speaking

PREPARE

8 🔊 4.8 You're going to discuss a crime story. First, listen to two people doing the same. Which story from Exercise 3 are they discussing? How do they feel about it?

9 a Work in pairs. Student A: Turn to page 167. Student B: Turn to page 166. Read the short crime story. Write a question starting *Did you see that thing in the news about …?* to introduce your story.

b Work with another student who read the same story as you. Say what you remember about your story and how you feel about it.

SPEAK

10 Work in your original pairs. Take turns starting a conversation about your crime story using your question in Exercise 9a. Respond to each other's stories. Use the Useful phrases to help you.

Useful phrases

Seriously? How did that happen?

That's awful! What did they do about it?

That's crazy! Imagine how he/she felt!

Was anyone ever arrested for it?

So what happened in the end?

Develop
your
writing
page 102

4c It's not good enough!

> **Goal:** make a complaint
> **Grammar:** reported speech
> **Vocabulary:** complaints

Vocabulary

1 **Look at the pictures and discuss the questions.**

1 Why are the people unhappy? What are they going to complain about?

2 Have you ever complained about any of these things? When? What happened?

2 **Work in pairs. Check you understand the words in bold. Then match sentence halves 1–8 with a–h.**

1 They're still taking money from my account even though I've **paid off**

2 I paid €300 to **sort out** the **gears** and now the engine

3 When I took it out of the box, I realised it wasn't new and **the screen**

4 It was supposed to have a money-back **guarantee**, but they refused to

5 There was supposed to be fast, **free wifi**, but it

6 I was supposed to be on the cheapest **deal**, but then I found out the company

7 I was waiting all day for the **delivery**, but the guy

8 There was a **fault** with the printer, so I had to

a didn't **turn up**.

b give me **a refund**.

c **take** it **back** and **exchange** it.

d has **gone**.

e all of my **loan**.

f was **cracked**.

g was really slow and they still **charged** me for it.

h was **overcharging** me.

3 **Work in groups and answer the questions.**

1 Can you think of any reason why you might get a **loan**?

2 Can you think of any reason why a shop might not give you a **refund**?

3 Has anyone ever **overcharged** you – or **charged** you for something you didn't get?

4 Have you ever waited for someone who didn't **turn up**?

5 Why might you need to **take** something **back** and **exchange** it?

 Go to page 159 or your app for more vocabulary and practice.

Listening

4 🔊 **4.9 Listen to three conversations and answer the questions.**

1 Who are they complaining to?

2 Why are they complaining?

5 **Work in groups and discuss the questions.**

1 Do you think all the complaints are fair?

2 How far are the companies/people responsible in each case?

3 What do you think would be an appropriate solution to each problem?

Grammar

6 **4.10 Listen and complete the sentences with three words. Contractions count as two words.**

1 You said the _____ well.
2 The garage told me the engine had gone and that it _____ spending money fixing it.
3 I told you it'd had some problems with the gears and _____ go on forever.
4 I called yesterday and the person I spoke to said _____ fine for me to collect it today.
5 I explained the problem and asked if _____ sorted out.
6 The guy I spoke to told me _____ it.
7 The person I spoke to told me they'd found my luggage in Paris, I think, and he said they _____ deliver it to my home.
8 I told _____ the wrong address when I rang before.

7 **Complete the grammar box with the words in the box.**

> past continuous   *going to   would*
> past perfect simple   past simple   *might*

Reported speech

When you report what other people said, you usually move the tenses back (backshift) because what they said is now in the past.

Direct speech -> Reported speech

*The man said, 'It **isn't** worth spending more money on it.'*
*The man **told** me it **wasn't** worth spending more money on it. (*¹_____*)*

*'The car **is running** well.'*
*You **said** the car **was running** well. (*²_____*)*

*'The engine **has gone**, I'm afraid.'*
*The garage **told** me the engine **had gone**.*
*'I **fixed** it this morning.'*
*The guy I spoke to **told** me **he'd fixed** it that morning.*
*(*³_____*)*

*'It **might** not go on forever.'*
*I told you it **might** not go on forever. (*⁴_____*)*

*'It **will** be ready for you to collect today.'*
*The person I spoke to said it **would** be ready for me to collect today. (*⁵_____*)*

*'We**'re going** to deliver it to your home.'*
*He said they **were going** to deliver it to my home.*
*(*⁶_____*)*

*'**Can** you sort it out?'*
*I explained the problem and **asked if he could** sort it out.*

If you are reporting something that is still true, you usually use the same tense in the report.
'Sorry, but that's the wrong address.'
*I **told** them that**'s** the wrong address. (= It's still wrong now.)*
'I'll meet you at the cinema.'
*He said **he'll** meet us at the cinema. (= We haven't left for the cinema yet.)*

8 a **4.11 Listen to the complaints. Notice the way the speakers sound a bit angry and the way the underlined words are stressed.**

1 You <u>told</u> me it'd be <u>fine</u>.
2 You <u>said</u> you were the <u>best</u>!
3 He <u>claimed</u> he'd already <u>done</u> it.
4 I was <u>told</u> they were <u>waiting</u> for a <u>part</u>.

b **Listen again and repeat.**

9 **Read the sentences and cross out the alternatives that are not possible. If both are possible, is there any difference in meaning?**

1 Yesterday I spoke to someone at your office and they said I *have to/had to* call you or you *would/were going to* close my account.
2 I called last week and someone told me that you *had already sent/already sent* my new phone. The guy I spoke to promised it *arrived/would arrive* in a couple of days, but I still haven't received it.
3 I spoke to someone yesterday and they said that I *would only get/will only get* a refund if I *sent/send* a letter to the head office.
4 I phoned earlier and your assistant said you *talked/were talking* to someone and *couldn't/can't* come to the phone. Did he pass on my message?
5 The travel agent said the place *had/has* a balcony with a nice view and that there *was/is* a lovely pool.

10 a **Choose one of the following and prepare to tell a short story. Decide what tenses to use to report the events and what the people said.**
  • a time you complained about something
  • a memorable conversation you've had this week
  • an argument you've had with someone you know well

b **Work in groups. Tell your group what happened.**

Go to page 142 or your app for more information and practice.

Speaking

PREPARE

11 **You're going to roleplay two conversations between an angry customer and a company representative. Work in pairs. Student A: Turn to page 167. Student B: Turn to page 169.**

SPEAK

12 **Roleplay the conversations. Try to find solutions. Use the Useful phrases to help you.**

> **Useful phrases**
> What seems to be the problem?
> I'm very sorry to hear that.
> Please allow me to apologise for that.
> I'm not sure how that happened.

Develop your reading
page 104

> **Goal:** respond to news

1 Match the words in the box with photos A–H.

annoyed	excited	grateful	guilty	proud
stressed	upset	worried		

2 Work in pairs and discuss the questions.

1 Look at the people/animal in the photos. Why do you think they are feeling the way they are?
2 When was the last time you felt like that? Why?

3 🔊 4.12 Listen to three conversations and answer the questions.

1 What news is shared?
2 How is the main speaker feeling about the news? Why?
3 Do you know anyone who has been in a similar situation? What happened?

4 Listen again and tick the phrases that you hear.

Useful phrases

When someone shares good/bad news, you can respond by:

Asking a question
When did you hear about it?
So what happened?
What are you going to do?
So what happens next?

Adding a comment
Good luck with everything.
I hope you get the job.
I really hope it all goes well.
Congratulations! That's amazing!
Well done!
Seriously? What a pain!
You poor thing!
Oh no! I'm sorry to hear that.

Guessing how the person feels
I bet you're really annoyed/delighted.
I bet he's had enough by now.
You sound like you've made up your mind.

5 a Choose the correct alternatives.

1 That's amazing! I bet you're really proud *about/of* her.
2 That's awful! I hope you *will feel/feel* better soon.
3 Are you planning *to go/going* out and celebrate?
4 Oh no! I bet that *didn't/wasn't* much fun.
5 That's *a great/great* news. I bet you're really excited.
6 So what *you are/are you* going to do next, then?
7 That's brilliant. I'm really *pleased/sorry* to hear that.
8 *How come/Why* you decided to do that, then?
9 Don't worry. *I'm sure/I wish* everything will be fine.
10 So what's *happened/been happened*? Are there any new developments?

b 🔊 4.13 Listen and check your answers.

6 Work in pairs. Choose three ways of responding from Exercise 5a and invent short conversations. What was said before and after?

A: I can't come to class today. I was sick all night.
B: That's awful! I hope you feel better soon.
A: Thanks. I'm just going to stay in bed and rest today.

7 a Think of two pieces of news. Decide how you're feeling about each piece of news and what you're going to do next.

b Work in pairs and roleplay your conversations. Use the Useful phrases to help you.

Go online for the Roadmap video.

Check and reflect

1 Complete the sentences with the pairs of words in the box. Use the past simple and the past continuous in each sentence.

| cut/slip   get/turn up   sleep/hear   get/study |
| hurt/play   work/meet |

1 I _____ my back quite badly while I _____ football in the park.
2 I _____ still _____ changed when all my guests _____ .
3 I _____ vegetables when the knife _____ . It was very painful!
4 We _____ in Singapore when we first _____ .
5 We just _____ talking in a café when we _____ at the same language school.
6 I _____ when I suddenly _____ a loud noise outside my window.

2 a Match sentence halves 1–6 with a–f.

1 I spilt   a it wrong.
2 I knocked   b some stairs and hurt myself.
3 I crashed   c the dates.
4 I measured   d coffee all over my shirt.
5 I fell down   e over a glass of juice.
6 I mixed up   f into someone.

b Are any of the sentences in Exercise 2a true for you? Can you change any to make them true? Work in groups and take turns explaining what happened, when and where.

3 Complete the newspaper article with the best words. The first letter is given.

Police are ¹s_____ for a gang that last night ²b_____ into a bank in the city centre. They managed to get ³a_____ with gold and jewellery ⁴w_____ over a million pounds. The gang locked the bank staff in a small back room, although one person tried to escape and was ⁵a_____ by the thieves and ⁶b_____ hurt. There were several ⁷w_____ , one of whom called the emergency services. The police have looked at film from the bank's cameras and hope to ⁸a_____ the people responsible soon.

4 a Choose the correct alternatives.

1 He hit his head when he fell. I was worried so I *had called/ called* the emergency services.
2 I was feeling very pleased with myself. I *passed/ had passed* all my exams.
3 When I went back to look for it, it *had completely disappeared/ completely disappeared*.
4 I was just leaving when I suddenly *remembered/ had remembered* my keys.
5 I was really nervous before my first lesson because I *never drove/ had never driven* before.
6 We got there at 8.05 but *found/ had found* the train *already left/ had already left*.

b Work in pairs. Take turns adding lines to a story that begins: *I was feeling great because I'd ....* Start each extra line with *Before that* and use the past perfect simple.

5 a Put sentences a–i in the correct order. Sentences 1 and 2 are given.

a I ordered a tablet a couple of months ago. *1*
b I wanted a refund, but the shop refused to give me one.
c They sorted out the fault in the shop, but they charged me for it.
d When it finally turned up, I noticed that the screen was cracked.
e After I'd ordered it, I waited ages for the delivery. *2*
f They let me exchange it, though.
g I then found there was a fault with the new tablet.
h I had to take that back to the shop as well.
i I've now finally paid off the loan I took out to pay for the tablet!

b Choose two things from Exercise 5a that have happened to you. Work in pairs. Say as much as you can about what happened. Can you think of any other examples of bad customer service?

6 a You met an old friend last week. She said 1–7. Report what she said. Start *She said ....* Sometimes more than one answer is possible.

1 'I don't know what Nick's doing.'
2 'I'm working too hard at the moment.'
3 'My brother got married recently.'
4 'I haven't seen Kim for a long time.'
5 'I'm starting a new job next month.'
6 'I might go to Morocco this summer.'
7 'You can stay at my place if you want to.'

b Think of the last time you saw an old friend. Write down five things they said. Work in groups and compare your sentences. Use reported speech.

Reflect

How confident do you feel about the statements below? Write 1–5 (1 = not very confident, 5 = very confident).

- I can talk about accidents and mistakes.
- I can retell familiar crime stories in the news.
- I can make a complaint.
- I can report and respond to personal news.

Want more practice?
Go to your Workbook or app.

5A A bright future

> **Goal:** interview someone about future plans
> **Grammar:** future forms
> **Vocabulary:** running a company

Vocabulary

1 a Write down the name of ...
1 a company you like and buy from a lot.
2 a company you don't like and don't buy anything from.
3 a company you think would be great to work for.

b Work in pairs and compare your answers.

2 Read the article and complete definitions 1–12 with the words in bold.

Tallulah Lovett and Blake Grey from Ironbridge talk about their long road to success.

We **set up** the business about ten years ago now. To begin with, it was hard because we were making a **loss**. We used up most of our savings, but after a while we started **breaking even**, which meant we could pay ourselves basic **wages** every week. After another four or five years, we finally started making a healthy **profit**. With this money, we then decided to **expand** into other **markets** and so we started to **export** to Canada and the United States. Last year, we managed to **take over** one of our biggest **competitors**, so we're now one of the biggest players in our **field**. The future looks bright, and over the coming months we're **launching** a range of new products.

1 If one company sells the same products or services as another, it's a direct _____ .
2 If a company is _____ , it's neither losing nor making money.
3 If you _____ a company, you start it.
4 If a company manages to _____ another company, they buy part or all of it, and take control.
5 If a company is _____ a new product or service, they're starting to sell it to the public.
6 If a company is making a _____ , it's losing money.
7 If you _____ a product, you send it to another country so it can be sold there.
8 If a company is making a _____ , it's making money.
9 If a company finds new _____ , they find new places or people they can sell their products to.
10 If a company manages to _____ , it becomes bigger.
11 Your _____ is the area that you work in.
12 Your _____ are the money that's regularly paid to you for work that you do.

3 Work in groups and answer the questions.
1 Do you know any countries that **export** products?
2 What new products have been **launched** recently?
3 Do you know any companies that have been **taken over**?
4 Do you know any companies that are **expanding** at the moment?
5 Do you know anyone who's **set up** their own business? How's it going?
6 How much would you say a good/bad weekly **wage** is?

📱 Go to page 160 or your app for more vocabulary and practice.

Reading

4 Read the article about three tech companies. What five future plans are mentioned?

BRAVE NEW WORLD

Hi-tech companies have become such a part of everyday life that it's easy to forget how recently they were set up. Central to their incredible success has been a desire to expand into other markets – and their plans for the future might surprise a few of you!
One major global transport technology company is going to launch a driverless car service sometime in the next few years. It is also currently working on the world's first flying taxi service, which will help city-based customers beat terrible traffic jams. If everything goes according to plan, they'll be offering this new service from around August 2023. A major American online company, meanwhile, is going to move into the physical world and open supermarkets and specialist stores. They also want to control every part of the delivery process and own all the companies that move goods from their warehouses to your home. Finally, one of the world's biggest social networking sites is starting its own media company soon. Development has begun, with the aim of producing high-quality original films and TV series.
However, while these plans are good for the tech companies, there are worries that they will cause job losses for other businesses, such as taxi firms, delivery companies and film producers. One thing's for sure: the next few years are certainly going to be interesting!

5 Read the article again and answer the questions.

1 What does the writer claim successful tech companies have in common?

2 What problem is the flying taxi service designed to solve?

3 When is the planned launch of the flying taxi service?

4 What is the social networking site planning to make?

5 Why are some people worried about all these plans?

6 Work in groups. What do you think about the plans the three companies have?

Grammar

7 Complete the grammar box with the words in the box. Use the examples from the article to help you.

> be going to   the present continuous
> the future continuous   *might*   *will*

Future forms

There are lots of different ways of talking about the future in English.

Use **1** _____ to talk about events in the future that have already been arranged with other people.

*One of the world's biggest social networking sites **is starting** its own media company soon.*

Use **2** _____ + infinitive to talk about plans for the future that you have already made.

*One major company **is going to launch** a driverless car service sometime in the next few years.*

Use both *be going to* + infinitive and **3** _____ + infinitive to make predictions we feel sure about.

*The next few years **are** certainly **going to be** interesting.*
*There are worries that these plans **will cause** job losses.*

Use **4** _____ (or *may*) + infinitive to talk about things we think will possibly happen in the future.

*Their plans for the future **might surprise** a few of you.*

Use **5** _____ (*will be* + *-ing*) to talk about actions that will be in progress at or around a certain point in the future.

*They'**ll be offering** this new service from August 2023.*

You can often use more than one of these ways of talking about the future with little or no change of meaning.

8 a 5.1 Listen and notice the pronunciation of *'ll* and *going to*.

1 I'm going to apply for a job with them.

2 She's going to set up her own business.

3 We'll break even in a year or two.

4 I think you'll make a nice profit on that.

5 It's not going to happen. They'll never do it.

b Listen again and repeat.

9 Read the sentences and cross out the alternatives that are not possible.

1 You never know. They*'ll be taking us over/might take us over*. It's not impossible.

2 *They're going to launch/They're launching* a range of virtual reality products this year.

3 *It's not going to be/It won't be* easy. That's for sure.

4 Fewer and fewer people *are going to buy/are buying* cars in the future, so that *will/may* cause real problems for the car industry.

5 They've just announced that they*'re launching/may launch* a new phone in the autumn.

6 Their new phone goes on sale at 9 a.m. next Friday, so this time next week, tens of thousands of people *will be trying to/are trying to* buy it.

10 a Think of at least two things you plan to do this week/ this month/this year/sometime in the next few years.

b Work in pairs. Tell each other as much as you can about your plans. Try to use different ways of talking about the future.

Next week I'm going to take Friday off work and go to Venice with my wife.

Sometime in the next few years, I might do a Master's. I'm not sure yet.

Go to page 144 or your app for more information and practice.

Speaking

PREPARE

11 a 5.2 You're going to roleplay an interview between a business owner and a journalist. First, listen to a journalist interviewing a business owner and answer the questions.

1 What kind of company is it?

2 How long has the owner had it?

3 How's it doing at the moment?

4 What are the owner's plans for the future?

b Work in pairs. Student A: Turn to page 168. Student B: Turn to page 170.

SPEAK

12 a Roleplay the interview. Student A: You are the journalist. Ask your questions. Student B: You are the business owner. Use the Useful phrases to help you.

> **Useful phrases**
> I'm glad you asked me that.
> I'm really excited about it.
> I'm actually quite worried about things.
> That's a good question. I'll need to think about that.

b Swap roles.

Develop your writing
page 106

5B Living the dream

> **Goal:** talk about new projects
> **Grammar:** adverbs used with the present perfect
> **Vocabulary:** new projects

Many of us dream of changing our lives. Here we meet four people who've done just that – and find out how their new lives are going.

Klara

Two years ago, after watching *Big Dreams, Big Houses*, I decided to sell my flat in Munich, leave my job and move to Sicily to build my dream home. I bought a piece of land and applied to the local council to build on it. It took time for the plans to be approved, but eventually they were, and then the hard work really started! Fast forward 18 months and the house is finished. We've just begun to work on the garden – we've already planted ten lemon trees!

Greg

I spent years working for a finance company, making good money and living what some might see as a dream lifestyle … but I wasn't happy. Last year, I quit and started studying Surf Science and Technology at Cornwall College. I've always loved surfing and wanted to learn about it in more detail. So far, I've only completed my first year, but it's going great. I still haven't thought much about what I'll do when I graduate, I'm just taking one step at a time!

Lisa

I woke up one morning and realised that all I was doing with my life was working to buy things that made me feel better about the fact that I didn't like my job! I decided to get rid of as many possessions as possible. I found a website that helped me, and since then, I've sold my DVDs, my CDs, my books, my car and I've even sold most of my clothes! My job still isn't great, but I work less and I'm much happier.

Vana

A few years ago, I had this idea for a dating app, which is also a kind of game, and I gave up work to develop it. I've got a model of the app now and it's really cool, but selling it is hard work. I haven't made any money yet and I've already spent the loans I got. I'm struggling to live, but I don't want to give up my dream.

Reading

1 Work in pairs and answer the questions.

1 Why might someone do these things?
   - leave a well-paid job
   - move abroad
   - build their own home
   - get rid of all their possessions
2 Which is the hardest to do? Why?

2 Read the article about four people who are 'living the dream'. Which person …

1 made a change connected to a free time activity?
2 made a change because of a TV programme?
3 needed permission to do something?
4 has not left their job?
5 has invented something?
6 found help online?

3 Work in groups and discuss the questions.

1 Do you know anyone who has changed their life in a major way? How?
2 Where would your dream house be? What would it be like?
3 If you could take time off to study, what would you most like to learn about?
4 Do you think you have too many possessions, just the right amount or not enough?

Grammar

4 Put the adverbs in the box in the correct place in the sentences. Then read the article again and check your answers.

already	even	just	only	so far	still	yet

1 We've begun to work on the garden.
2 I've completed my first year.
3 I haven't thought much about what I'll do when I graduate.
4 I haven't made any money and I've spent the loans I got.
5 I've sold most of my clothes.

5 Work in pairs. Complete the grammar box with the adverbs from Exercise 4.

Adverbs used with the present perfect

Certain adverbs are often used with the present perfect simple. Note where each adverb usually goes.

1 Use *still* and *yet* in negative sentences to emphasise something is not completed but we expect it to happen.

a _____ goes before *have*.
I_____ haven't decided.

b _____ goes at the end of the sentence.
I haven't decided _____ .

2 Use _____ to show something happened very recently.
I've_____ finished my last exam.

3 Use _____ to emphasise that something is completed (often before it was expected).
You don't need to give them any money. I've_____ paid for everything.

4 Use _____ at the start (or the end) of a sentence to mean *until now*.
_____ , I've been to four different countries.

5 Use _____ to show something is surprising.
He's been everywhere. He's _____ been to Antarctica!

6 Use _____ to emphasise nothing else has been done.
I've_____ applied to the two universities I most want to study at.

6 **5.3** **Listen and repeat the sentences.**
1 So far, I've had three interviews.
2 I haven't even had time to think about it.
3 I've only looked at three different places.
4 She still hasn't decided.
5 They've just opened a new shop.

7 **Choose the correct alternatives.**
1 I've *just/so far* been offered a new job In Brussels, so I'm going to have to move!
2 I started two months ago, but I *already/still* haven't managed to paint the whole house.
3 He's lost weight, started exercising and *even/only* stopped smoking!
4 I've *already/yet* changed my mind twice about what I'll do next. I'm not going to change it again!
5 I'm not surprised they haven't offered you a pay rise *yet/just*. You've *only/already* been there a year!
6 I got a £10,000 loan two years ago. I haven't *just/even* paid 10 percent of it back *yet/still*.
7 We've seen six flats *so far/yet*, but we *still/even* haven't found anywhere we like.
8 I joined a gym last month, but *so far/already* I've *only/even* been once!

8 **Work in pairs. Tell each other about:**
• things you haven't done yet, but would like to do.
• things you still haven't done, but need to do.
• your three biggest achievements in life so far.

Go to page 144 or your app for more information and practice.

Vocabulary

9 **Match questions 1–8 with answers a–h.**
1 How's your new job going?
2 How are your studies going?
3 How's the house-building going?
4 How are the wedding plans going?
5 How are things going with your business?
6 Have you found a new place to live yet?
7 Have you decided what you're doing in the summer yet?
8 Have you met anyone recently?

a We've just received **permission** from the local council to **go ahead** and start building.

b Not really. I've been on a couple of **dates** so far but they **came to nothing**.

c No. We haven't even chosen **a holiday destination**. We keep **changing our minds**.

d I've already **quit**! I've just been **offered** a new one.

e OK. We've **sorted out** a place for the **ceremony**.

f Yes. I've already moved in. Unfortunately, I've had to **get rid of** some **possessions**, because it's so small.

g I'm **struggling**, to be honest. I've already failed two exams so I don't know if I'll **graduate**.

h Good. Our business loan has just **been approved**.

10 **Work in groups. Choose one topic each then take turns talking about it.**
• a project or task you really **struggled** with
• a plan or decision which needed to **be approved**
• a possession you decided to **get rid of**
• a time you **changed your mind** or **quit** something

Go to your app for more practice.

Speaking

PREPARE

11 **5.4** **You're going to do a roleplay about two new projects in your life. First, listen to two people talking about a new project and answer the questions.**
1 What is the new project they are talking about?
2 How's it going? Very well, OK or are they struggling?

12 **Work in pairs. Student A: Turn to page 169. Student B: Turn to page 168.**

SPEAK

13 **Roleplay the conversations and try to keep them going. Use the Useful phrases to help you.**

Useful phrases
That sounds amazing.   That's good.
What a shame!
When did you start doing all of that?
So what else do you have to do?

Develop your reading
page 108

5c A good education

> **Goal:** take part in a discussion
> **Grammar:** comment adverbs
> **Vocabulary:** education

Reading and vocabulary

1 Read the facts about education in different parts of the world. What might be good and bad about each situation?

1 Typically, Chinese education places a lot of importance on learning things by heart. At 18, students are tested in a nine-hour final exam, the *Gaokoa*, on the facts they have learnt.

2 The school day in South Korea is usually from 8 a.m. till 4 p.m. However, 75 percent of students then go to a private study school between 6 p.m. and 9 p.m.

3 In South Africa, almost 60 percent of the population have to pay for primary and secondary education.

4 On average, Russian teenagers do almost ten hours of homework a week.

5 Children in Finland don't start school until they are seven.

6 In the USA, over 1.5 million children (3 percent) are home-schooled – educated at home.

7 In Japan, the average class size in secondary school is 33 students.

8 In Iran, all children go to single-sex schools, so girls and boys are educated separately.

2 Complete the sentences with the words in the box.

attention	cover	discipline	explore
perform	pressure	raise	suit

1 Ten hours of homework a week probably puts far too much _____ on kids.
2 In larger classes, it's hard for teachers to **maintain** _____ and make sure everyone is paying attention.
3 Not starting school until seven years old means kids can play outside more and _____ the world around them.
4 Extra classes in the evenings could help students **succeed** and _____ **standards**.
5 In smaller classes, you get more individual _____ and more **feedback** from the teacher on how well you're doing.
6 With home-schooling, children can _____ more subjects than they can in normal schools.
7 Putting kids in mixed-level groups might _____ those who are finding things difficult, because they get help from the better students.
8 Single-sex schools might **encourage** some kids to _____ better in certain subjects because they are not **put off** by it being a 'girl's' subject or a 'boy's' subject.

3 Work in pairs and discuss the questions.
1 What might **encourage** people to study a language and what might **put** them **off**?
2 How much **feedback** and **individual attention** did you get at school/university?
3 What three things would most help **raise standards** in education and help students **succeed**?
4 What are the best/worst ways for teachers to **maintain discipline** in large classes?

Go to page 160 or your app for more vocabulary and practice.

Listening

4 🔊 5.5 **Listen to a radio discussion about education and UK schools and answer the questions.**
1 What is the main issue that they discuss?
2 Which speaker (Olga, Josh, Franny) is: a teacher, a parent, a student?
3 What topic do they start to discuss at the end?

5 Listen again and tick the opinions that are mentioned.
1 Kids in Russia get more homework than kids in the UK.
2 Homework is basically a waste of time, especially at primary school.
3 Schools don't do anything to encourage reading at home.
4 Not all parents read to their children.
5 Giving homework can raise standards.
6 Children should learn to cook and help in the house.
7 The time you spend at school should be enough to learn what you need.
8 It's good to study a lot just before an exam.
9 Reducing class sizes doesn't help teachers maintain discipline.

6 Work in groups and discuss your opinion of homework. How far do you agree with the different opinions in the radio discussion?

Grammar

7  **5.6 Listen to the sentences from the discussion. Add the missing adverbs that you hear. In two sentences there are two adverbs.**

1   Teachers don't set enough homework – not as much as they would back home anyway.
2   When I trained as a teacher, the research said that homework makes no difference to children's progress.
3   I find that difficult to believe.
4   Yes, but it's the same here with secondary school.
5   He's not getting enough homework.
6   I'm having to do quite a lot of homework at the moment, ... but I didn't have much before now.

8   Work in pairs. Complete the grammar box with the adverbs from Exercise 7. The first letter is given.

Comment adverbs

Many adverbs describe verbs:
*I'm studying **hard**.*
*I **usually** understand things quite **quickly**.*
You can also use adverbs to show your attitude towards a whole sentence or clause. They are usually used at the start of the sentence/clause and followed by a comma.

A_____	= this is the real fact
A_____	= this is what I heard – it may not be true
B_____	= this is the most important point
G_____	= this is usually true, but not always
Hopefully	= this is what I hope
L_____	= this is good or lucky
P_____	= this is my opinion
O_____	= this is clear and obvious
Surprisingly	= this is not what I expected
U_____	= this is sad or unlucky

9 a  **5.7 Listen and notice how we stress the comment adverbs.**

1   Obviously, it's a good idea.
2   It's a nice idea, but unfortunately, it doesn't work.
3   Actually, class size doesn't make that much difference.
4   Basically, I disagree with the whole idea.

b   Listen again and repeat.

10   Choose the best alternatives.

1   It's often said that boys are better at science than girls, but *personally/actually* there's no evidence for that.
2   *Unfortunately/Luckily*, a lot of people don't finish their university courses.
3   Without a big final exam there will be less pressure on students. *Surprisingly/Hopefully*, smaller tests over the year will also allow teachers to give more feedback.
4   *Apparently/Obviously*, you're better able to learn in the morning than in the afternoon.
5   My daughter went to a mixed school and got good grades, but *luckily/generally* girls get better exam results if they study at single-sex schools.
6   *Basically/Unfortunately*, what matters most in education is the quality of the teaching.

11 a   Complete the sentences so that they are true for you.

1   Personally, I've never really wanted to _____ .
2   Hopefully, in the next couple of years, _____ .
3   Unfortunately, I've never _____ .
4   Surprisingly, I've never _____ .
5   Generally, I think most people _____ .

b   Work in pairs and compare your sentences.

Go to page 144 or your app for more information and practice.

Speaking

PREPARE

12   You're going to take part in a discussion about education. First, read the statements on page 168 and make notes about each one.

SPEAK

13   Work in groups and have your discussion. Try to agree on two things that would make the biggest difference to students' progress. Use the Useful phrases to help you.

Useful phrases
As a parent, what do you think about this issue?
That's an interesting point.
Could we get some other views on that? [Name]?
[Name], what would you say about that?
Can I just ask what you mean by that?

Develop your listening
page 110

> **Goal:** agree and disagree

1 **Work in pairs and discuss the questions.**

1 What kind of shops do you go to most? What for?

2 Do you like shopping online? Why? What kind of products do you usually buy online?

2 a 🔊 **5.11 Listen to two people discussing a piece of news and answer the questions.**

1 What is the news?

2 Who is more concerned about the news – the woman or the man?

b **Listen again and complete the replies with up to four words.**

1 A: But when was the last time you went there?
   B: _____ . It's been a while.

2 A: We've got the internet instead.
   B: Yeah, it's _____ with that.

3 A: People don't want to go into town to shop.
   B: I'm _____ that's true.

4 B: Then they don't turn up or you're out and you have to pick it up somewhere. It's almost easier to go into town.
   A: _____ , but obviously most people don't think so.

5 B: It's sad.
   A: _____ . I feel bad for the people who were working there, but …

6 A: Most of the shops that have closed down have just failed to adapt to modern life.
   B: _____ , but it's depressing …

7 B: And it leads to crime.
   A: _____ , but they could replace the shops with cafés or an arts centre.
   B: Yeah, _____ , but part of me just wants …

8 A: You just don't like change.
   B: _____ . Anyway, …

3 **Read the Useful phrases box and check your answers.**

Useful phrases

Agreeing completely
Absolutely!
Fair point.
That's true.
Sure.
I know what you mean.

Agreeing, but not completely
Up to a point.
It's partly to do with that.
That's partly true.
I kind of agree.
I half agree.

Agreeing reluctantly
You might be right.
I suppose (so).
I guess (so).

Disagreeing politely
I'm not so sure that's true.
I'm afraid I don't see it like that.

4 a 🔊 **5.12 Listen to the phrases from Exercise 2b. Notice how we:**

- stress *partly*, *might* and *half*.
- make the phrases sound longer when we don't completely agree.

b **Listen again and repeat.**

5 a **You're going to have a discussion about how shops in town centres could be supported. First, decide which ideas will or won't work and why.**

- reduce taxes for businesses
- improve security with CCTV and police on the streets
- have free buses that go into the town centre
- have more pedestrianised streets with cafés and restaurants
- turn the shops into houses or offices
- hold regular events like music festivals

b **Work in groups. Discuss why you think shops might be closing and discuss the ideas you chose in Exercise 5a. Respond to different opinions. Use the Useful phrases to help you.**

Go online for the Roadmap video.

Check and reflect

1 Complete the sentences with the verbs in the box.

> break even   expand   launch   make
> set up   take over

1 A friend of mine _____ her own business a few years ago.
2 One of our biggest competitors is trying to _____ our company.
3 I'm hoping that we _____ a healthy profit this year.
4 We made a loss last year, but this year I think we'll probably _____ .
5 They've managed to _____ into different markets.
6 They're going to _____ an amazing new range of products over the next few months.

2 a Complete the sentences with the verbs in brackets and the verb forms in the box. Use each form only once.

> the present continuous   *will* + infinitive
> the future continuous   *may/might* + infinitive
> *be going to* + infinitive

1 I've decided that after I graduate from university, I _____ my own business. (set up)
2 Nothing's certain yet, but they're saying there _____ job losses at the factory soon. (be)
3 I _____ my boss this afternoon to see if we can sort the problem out. (meet)
4 We've been doing OK recently. I think we _____ a fairly healthy profit this year. (make)
5 I _____ in your area next week, so maybe we can meet for lunch one day. (work)

b Work in pairs. Talk about the plans of people you know. Try to use all of the verb forms in the box in Exercise 2a.

3 a Complete the sentences with the adverbs in the box.

> already   even   just   only   so far   still   yet

1 I left a message on his phone yesterday, but I haven't heard back from him _____.
2 She's travelled all over the world. She's _____ been to Antarctica!
3 A: How are the exams going?
   B: Oh, I've _____ finished them all. The last one was two weeks ago.
4 A: Are you OK?
   B: Not really. I've _____ had some bad news, actually.
5 I haven't travelled much, to be honest. In fact, I've _____ been out of the country once!
6 _____ , I've applied for over twenty jobs, but I _____ haven't had any interviews.

b Work in groups. Tell your group about two things:
• you haven't done yet, but would like to.
• you've already done and don't need to do again.
• you've just done (very recently).
• you've done several times so far, but want to do again.

4 Complete the sentences with the best word. The first letter is given.

1 They got married last month. I didn't go to the c_____ , but I went to the party afterwards.
2 We've finally received p_____ from the council to add an extra room to the house.
3 Bali is a very popular tourist d_____ , so hotel prices there are generally quite high.
4 The course is much harder than I expected. To be honest, I'm really s_____ with it.
5 I was thinking of studying Law, but I've changed my m_____ .
6 I applied for a student l_____ ages ago, but it still hasn't been approved yet.

5 Match verbs 1–6 with endings a–f.

1 put   a standards
2 perform   b too much pressure on kids
3 raise   c students from poorer backgrounds
4 explore   d better in certain subjects
5 put off   e discipline
6 maintain   f the world around you

6 a Choose the correct alternatives.

1 *Hopefully/Surprisingly*, I'll get into my first-choice university and study French.
2 *Luckily/Obviously*, I need to do well in my exams if I want to be accepted.
3 *Surprisingly/Actually*, I'm not American. I'm Canadian.
4 *Generally/Hopefully*, I quite like his films, but I found the new one a bit boring.
5 *Luckily/Apparently*, the gang have robbed six different banks in the last week.
6 *Basically/Personally*, I've never liked her music, but I know lots of people love it.

b Change three of the sentences in Exercise 6a so that they are true for you. Don't change the comment adverbs. Work in pairs and compare your sentences.

Reflect

How confident do you feel about the statements below? Write 1–5 (1 = not very confident, 5 = very confident).
• I can describe future plans and intentions in detail.
• I can explain how much of a task has been completed.
• I can take part in a discussion about education.
• I can express degrees of agreement in a discussion.

Want more practice?
Go to your Workbook or app.

6A A great show

> **Goal:** talk about films and TV
> **Grammar:** passive
> **Vocabulary:** at the cinema, on TV

Vocabulary and reading

1 **Work in pairs and discuss the questions.**

1 How often do you go to the cinema? What kind of films do you like to watch?

2 How do you usually watch TV? Live or on demand? Which TV programmes do you like?

2 a **Complete the sentences with the words in the box.**

| character dialogue dull ending episode |
| filming hilarious scene special effects useless |

1 It was such a shock! I can't believe she was **killed off**. She was my favourite _____ .

2 It's _____ . I've seen it several times now and it still **makes me** laugh.

3 I love that _____ in series two where they finally show how they first became a couple.

4 I **switched over**. I found it all a bit _____ .

5 He was so _____ it was embarrassing! I'm not surprised he was **voted off** the programme.

6 I'm not usually **a fan of** big Hollywood **blockbusters**, but the _____ were amazing.

7 The _____ was just so sad. I was **in tears**.

8 It's my favourite **series**. They're such great **characters** and the _____ is so clever and funny.

9 That short _____ where he was being interviewed was great. It was so **tense**.

10 The _____ is amazing. How did they get so close?

b **Read the sentences in Exercise 2a and find:**

1 six adjectives that can describe films/TV programmes.

2 five nouns that describe features of a film/TV programme.

3 **Work in pairs and answer the questions.**

1 What's the difference between **a scene**, **an episode** and **a series**?

2 What kind of programmes or films can be **tense**?

3 Why might a character **be killed off**?

4 In what kind of programme do people get **voted off**?

5 Can you think of three big Hollywood **blockbusters**?

📱 Go to page 161 or your app for more vocabulary and practice.

4 **Read the article. What is the main point?**

1 Writers and actors can now make more money from TV than from film.

2 Modern films use too many special effects.

3 The development of technology has led to better TV programmes.

The Golden Age of TV

Janie Jones explores how television is taking over.

In recent years, television has been completely changed by streaming services like Netflix, leading to the development of many more original drama series and what is being called a 'Golden Age'. This year, around 450 different series are being shown and even more will be produced next year, as media companies compete for audiences. But it's not just the quantity that makes this a Golden Age, it's the quality and variety that is on offer.

More and more professionals, who had previously only been attracted to film work, are now being persuaded to work in TV. Writers and actors are moving into this area, partly because they get paid more than before, but also because of the creative opportunities that are offered by the new dramas.

Previously, programmes relied on advertising, so episodes were cut up into short sections with a tense moment at the end of each section to stop people switching over. Each episode also had to be a single story, so viewers could miss one, but still pick up the story the following week, which explains all the police and medical dramas. In comparison, film used to give artists far more freedom.

Nowadays, the opposite is true. Cinema today is all about the superhero blockbusters – big on special effects, but low on dialogue and character. With streaming services, there are no ad breaks and viewers can choose when to watch episodes, and so TV writers are allowed to experiment with more varied and complex stories while actors can explore characters more fully. What's more, the quality of drama means people now expect more from reality TV programmes, documentaries and so on. The result is an amazing range of programmes, and a new problem – finding the time to watch them all!

5 Read the article again and answer the questions.

1 What two main examples does the writer give to support the idea that TV is in a golden age?

2 Why are more writers and actors moving from film to TV?

3 How has streaming changed TV?

6 Is this is a golden age for TV? Why?/Why not?

Grammar

7 a Complete the sentences with the missing subjects from the article.

1 _Television_ has been completely changed by streaming services.

2 More than _____ will be produced next year.

3 _____ , who had previously only been attracted to film work, ...

4 _____ are now being persuaded to work in TV.

5 _____ get paid more than before.

6 Many writers and actors want to work in TV because of the _____ that are offered by the new dramas.

7 In the past, _____ were cut up into short sections.

8 _____ are allowed to experiment with more complex stories.

b Work in pairs and answer the questions.

1 Which sentence(s) in Exercise 7a feature a passive form using:

a the present simple?

b the present continuous?

c the present perfect simple?

d the past simple?

e the past perfect simple?

f a modal?

2 Do the sentences focus on the person/thing that does the actions or the person/thing the actions happen to?

3 Which two sentences mention the people/thing that do the actions?

4 Which word is used to introduce the person/thing that does the action?

c Read the grammar box and check your answers.

Passive

The passive is formed by a form of *be* + past participle.

present simple
*TV writers **are allowed** to experiment more.*

present continuous
*More professionals **are** now **being persuaded** to work in TV.*

past simple
*Episodes **were cut up** into short sections.*

present perfect simple
*Television **has been** completely **changed** by streaming.*

past perfect simple
*Professionals **had** previously only **been attracted** to film work.*

modal
*More than 450 series **will be produced** next year.*

be going to
*The series **is going to be filmed** in black and white.*

You sometimes use *get* to form a passive.
*Writers and actors **get paid** more than before.*

8 a 6.1 Listen and notice how we don't stress the different forms of *be*.

1 It's been cancelled.

2 It'll be shown on Sunday night.

3 He's being paid millions.

4 The last series was filmed in Tunisia.

b Listen again and repeat.

9 Complete the sentences with the correct passive form of the verbs in brackets. In some sentences, more than one answer is possible.

1 It's about this guy who _____ by the police, but they never tell him why. (arrest)

2 Apparently, the programme _____ recently, so they won't be doing another series. (cancel)

3 I think he'll probably _____ the programme this week. (vote off)

4 It's going to _____ by Steven Spielberg. (direct)

5 I heard that he was quite angry about the film. He said he _____ in a positive way in it. (not show)

6 It caused a bit of a shock at the time because nothing like that _____ on TV before. (see)

10 a Work in pairs. Think of an example of:

1 a film that was made in your country.

2 a TV series that was filmed near where you live.

3 a blockbuster that's going to be released soon.

4 a series that has been shown on TV for a long time.

5 a TV programme that isn't shown anymore.

6 a new film that is being made at the moment.

b Work with another pair. Say your examples. The other pair tries to guess the categories from 1–6.

Go to page 146 or your app for more information and practice.

Speaking

PREPARE

11 a 6.2 You're going to talk about films and TV. First, listen to two people doing the same. Which films/TV programmes do they mention? What do they think of them?

b Think of a TV programme or film. Answer the questions. Make notes.

1 What happens in it?

2 Where was it first shown?

3 When was it made?

4 What's it like?

5 Where was it filmed?

6 What's the best scene?

SPEAK

12 a Work in pairs. Discuss your TV programmes/films.

b Report back to the class. Did anybody choose the same film/TV programme?

Develop your reading
page 111

6B A five-star review

> **Goal:** recommend services
> **Grammar:** *have/get something done*
> **Vocabulary:** services and recommendations

Reading

1 **Work in pairs and discuss the questions.**
  1 Do you ever read online reviews? If so, what for?
  2 Do you ever write reviews? If so, have you ever written a really good/bad one? Why?
  3 How much do you think you are influenced by reviews?

2 a **Read the article. Are the sentences true (T) or false (F)?**
  1 Like most people, the writer reads online reviews.
  2 The online review sites the writer mentions all use a five-star rating system.
  3 The score that most people see as OK is getting lower.
  4 The author thinks there's a possibility that reviews will become useless.

Do you rely on reviews? Apparently, 92 percent of us read online reviews and we spend a lot of time doing so. According to one survey, we spend an average of eight hours on online research before we buy a car. And reviews don't only influence what we buy; they're increasingly affecting our work lives as well. For example, one taxi driver even lost his job because his rating fell below 4.6 – out of five!

Personally, I look at reviews before I do almost anything: when choosing a film on Netflix, I look at the score on IMdB (anything above seven out of ten is OK). Not sure what to cook? I search for recipes, but only those with four or five stars. And when I got my vacuum cleaner fixed the other day, I chose the repair shop using Google maps (it scored 4.1 out of five).

However, while most of us read reviews, far fewer actually post them – and when we do, it tends only to be to say something's either great or awful. This means we have lots of high scores, plenty of low ones and very little in the middle. Also, products and services vary so much that it's hard to work out what ratings mean.

Finally, there's the problem of how far we can trust reviews – it is suggested that as many as 16 percent could be fake. Given this, it's perhaps not surprising that the score we consider 'good enough' is slowly going up. If this trend continues, everything will get five stars and we'll have to go back to relying on the recommendations of friends.

b **Work in groups and discuss the questions.**
  1 Have you heard any stories about reviews affecting people's businesses or jobs?
  2 How far do you trust reviews? Do you think you would know if one was fake? How?

Vocabulary

3 **Choose the correct verb for each group of nouns.**
  1 *deliver/do* a package/a pizza/and install a new kitchen
  2 *make/assess* the damage/your fitness/your strengths and weaknesses
  3 *deliver/replace* a flat tyre/my passport/the screen on my mobile
  4 *fix/do* a pipe/a broken light/the gears on my car
  5 *deliver/do* your nails/your hair/repairs
  6 *remove/assess* a tooth/a wall/a mark on my jacket
  7 *remove/look at* the injury/the problem/what's causing it
  8 *make/do* a photo album/a copy/a mistake

4 **Say at least one thing the people in the box can do. Use the verbs and nouns in Exercise 3.**
  A builder can deliver and install a new kitchen.

  a builder   a cleaner   a dentist   a hairdresser
  a mechanic   a personal trainer

5 **Work in pairs. How many stars out of five would you give the reviews?**
  1 He fixed it, but he didn't finish **on time** and left a lot of **mess**.
  2 We are happy – they were very **efficient** and charged a **reasonable** price, too.
  3 They won't give an exact time they'll deliver, which isn't very **convenient**.
  4 They were absolutely **useless**. Don't **trust** them.
  5 They are always very **reliable**. They do the work well and **on time**.

 Go to page 161 or your app for more vocabulary and practice.

Grammar

6 **a** **Read the sentence. Which statement (1–4) is false?**

I got my vacuum cleaner fixed the other day.

1 Someone fixed my vacuum cleaner for me.

2 I fixed it myself.

3 I asked them to fix it.

4 I paid them to fix it.

b **Read the grammar box and check your answer.**

---

have/get something done

Have/get + object + past participle is a passive structure. Use it to talk about services that you pay someone else to do for you.

Use this structure when you want to focus on both the thing that an action happens to and the person that the thing belongs to. The doer – the person that does the action – is unimportant, obvious or not known.

*I **get my nails done** here.* (present simple)

*I'm **having my hair cut** soon.* (present continuous)

*We **got a couple of pizzas delivered**.* (past simple)

*You**'ve had your hair cut**.* (present perfect simple)

*You **can get it looked at** in the garage.* (modal)

*I **had to get my car fixed** while I was in Italy.* (*have to*)

This structure is also used to focus on things that happen to us which are unexpected and often bad.

*We **had our house broken into** while we were away.*

---

7 **Complete the second sentence so that it has a similar meaning to the first sentence. Use *have/get* passives and any other words you need.**

1 a I found some old photos of my parents and want someone to make them into a nice album.

b I want to *get a nice album made* of these old photos I found of my parents.

2 a We can ask them to deliver it if you don't want to collect it yourself.

b We can _____ if you don't want to collect it yourself.

3 a I don't have my car at the moment because they're fixing the gears.

b I'm _____ on my car, so I don't have it at the moment.

4 a I had a beauty treatment for my birthday and they did my nails.

b I _____ for my birthday as part of a beauty treatment.

5 a I had to replace my passport because it was stolen while I was on holiday.

b I _____ while I was on holiday, so I had to _____ .

6 a Wipe your shoes before you get in the car. It's newly cleaned!

b We _____ just _____ so wipe your shoes before you get in!

8 **Work in pairs. Use *have/get* passives and the phrases from Exercise 3 to ask and answer questions. Use these question starters:**

- How often do you …?
- When did you last …?
- Have you ever …?

A: *How often do you get things delivered?*

B: *Quite often, actually. Maybe once or twice a week. Last night I had a pizza delivered.*

 Go to page 146 or your app for more information and practice.

Speaking

PREPARE

9 **a** 6.3 **You're going to give each other recommendations. First, listen to two conversations and answer the questions.**

1 What service does each person need?

2 Why?

3 Are any recommendations made?

b **Work in pairs. Student A: Turn to page 170. Student B: Turn to page 169.**

SPEAK

10 **a** **Take turns asking for and giving recommendations. Use the Useful phrases to help you. Try to use *have/get* passives in your conversations.**

Useful phrases

Could you recommend a garage or mechanic?

Do you know a good hairdresser?

I've been going there for ages.

I've been using him for years.

They're very reliable. They've always been good with me.

---

b **What were the best recommendations you were given?**

Develop your listening
page 113

6c ▶ Headline news

> **Goal:** discuss news stories
> **Grammar:** probability
> **Vocabulary:** in the news

Vocabulary

1 **Work in groups and discuss the questions.**

1 How closely do you follow the news?
2 Where do you get information about what's happening in the world?
3 Which of the news sections in the box do you read most often? Are there any you never read?

business   celebrity   culture   environment
opinion   politics   science and technology   sport
travel   world

2 **Read headlines 1–8 and match them with sub-headings a–h.**

1 **Record** temperatures to continue
2 PostTelecom **profits** drop
3 RedAir pilots vote to **go on strike**
4 **Breakthrough** in peace process
5 Scientists claim breakthrough in **treatment** of Alzheimer's
6 World Cup hopes **hit** by Kane **injury**
7 New **scandal** hits government
8 TV star **found guilty of** dangerous driving

a **Star player** may miss opening match
b **Sentence** to be decided today
c **Union** unhappy with airline's latest offer
d Both **sides** agree an end to fighting
e Company says it may need to **get rid of** staff
f **Opinion poll** shows 87% want president to **quit**
g Visitors advised to **keep out of** the sun between 10 a.m. and 4 p.m.
h New drug **slows** development of disease

3 **Work in groups. Discuss news stories you know about. Use the words in bold in Exercise 2.**

I read that we had record temperatures last year. It was the hottest year ever. It's scary!
I heard that the national airline's profits have dropped this year. Fewer people are flying with them.

📱 Go to page 161 or your app for more vocabulary and practice.

Listening

4 🔊 **6.7 Listen to three conversations and match them with the correct news stories from Exercise 2.**

5 **Listen again. Are the sentences true (T) or false (F)?**

1 a The injury isn't serious.
  b The national team doesn't usually perform very well.
  c They both agree that the Brazilian team are playing very well at the moment.
2 a A lot of money has been spent without producing good results.
  b They both think the Popular Party will win the election.
  c Neither of them really trust opinion polls.
3 a He's not sure what to pack.
  b The place they're visiting has been very dry for quite a long time.
  c It's going to get colder in the next few days.

6 **Work in groups. What are the most important news stories at the moment?**

Grammar

7 a 🔊 **6.8 Listen and complete the sentences.**

1 I heard there's a chance _____ .
2 I guess _____ , but I don't think so.
3 I doubt _____ now anyway.
4 We'll _____ to the first good team we play.
5 I think Brazil will _____ .
6 The Popular Party _____ outright, will they?
7 There's a good chance _____ .
8 The weather's bound _____ .
9 The temperature's _____ suddenly drop a lot.

b **Match sentences 1–9 with the degrees of probability in the box.**

sentence 1 = maybe

almost certain   almost certainly not   maybe (not)
probably   probably not

8 Read and complete the grammar box with the words and phrases in the box in Exercise 7b.

Probability

When you ask for opinions about future probability, you usually use *will*. You can also use *be going to* + infinitive.

Do you think it'll happen?

*Who do you think **is going to** win the election?*

You can express probability in different ways:

1 _____

It's bound to …
It'll …
It'll definitely …

2 _____

There's a good chance …
It'll probably …
It's (fairly) likely (to) …

3 _____

It might + (not) …
There's a chance …

4 _____

It's unlikely (to) …
There's (only) a small chance …
It probably won't …

5 _____

I doubt …
It (definitely) won't …

Sometimes you can just give short replies:

A: *Do you think it'll happen?*
B: *It's bound to.* (= almost certainly yes)
B: *I doubt it./I don't think so.* (= probably not)

9 Work in pairs. Do the underlined forms in the pairs of sentences have the same meaning or not?

1 a <u>They're bound</u> to win the election. People really like what they're offering.

 b <u>I doubt they'll</u> win. Their leader doesn't seem very popular.

2 a <u>It's fairly likely to</u> lead to more unemployment.

 b <u>There's a good chance it could</u> lead to more unemployment.

3 a <u>It's fairly unlikely</u> to make any difference.

 b <u>It probably won't</u> change anything.

4 A: Do you think they'll vote to go on strike?

 a B: <u>I doubt it</u>.

 b B: <u>Probably</u>.

5 a <u>There's only a small chance that he'll</u> quit.

 b <u>He might</u> quit, I suppose.

10 Rewrite the sentences using the words in brackets so that they mean the same.

1 It's likely to hit profits quite badly. (probably)

2 I guess they might stop the worst effects, but I'm not hopeful. (small chance)

3 I'm sure she'll be successful. (bound)

4 They're bound to hold a new election sooner or later. (definitely)

5 It's unlikely to happen anytime soon. (won't)

6 It's fairly likely that profits will drop this year. (good)

7 He might not recover in time for the World Cup. (chance)

11 Work in pairs. Choose five questions to ask your partner. Then ask and answer. Try to use as many forms from the grammar box as you can in your answers.

Do you think …

1 we'll win the next World Cup?

2 you'll ever get married?

3 you'll ever have kids?

4 you'll stay in your current job?

5 you'll continue studying after this course?

6 you'll ever speak fluent English?

7 you'll ever live abroad?

8 you'll retire early?

 Go to page 146 or your app for more information and practice.

Speaking

PREPARE

12 Work in pairs. Think of three news stories that other people will probably know something about. Then write a question for each story that could start a conversation. Use the Useful phrases to help you.

Useful phrases

Did you hear about (the fighting)?
Did you see that story about (the footballer)?
What do you think of this story about (the election)?
What do you think will happen?
Do you think (they) will (get rid of many staff)?

SPEAK

13 a Work in groups. Take turns starting a conversation about the news story using your questions. Discuss each story for as long as you can.

 b Decide which of the stories will have the biggest impact on society. Explain why.

Develop your writing
page 114

6D English in action

> **Goal:** apologise and make excuses

1 **Work in pairs. Look at the pictures and discuss the questions.**

1 Which do you think is the worst situation to be in?

2 What do you think each person would say?

3 When was the last time you had to apologise? What did you say? How did the other person react?

2 **Read the excuses and answer the questions. Have you ever used one of these excuses? Have you ever been given one of them? When? What happened?**

1 We're short of staff and we have a lot of work to finish.

2 There's been a road accident so our driver's late.

3 I'm afraid several drivers are sick at the moment.

4 It's been so crazy at work, I've hardly had time to think.

5 It's been a nightmare at work and there was a problem on the train home.

6 Something unexpected happened and I just forgot.

7 My phone was out of battery.

8 We've got a new system and I'm not very familiar with it.

3 ◁) **6.9 Listen to a man called Tomas having three conversations with different people and:**

1 tick the excuses from Exercise 2 that you hear.

2 write down what Tomas is apologising for.

4 **Listen again and complete the sentences with one word.**

1 a I'm _____ sorry.

   b There really is _____ we can do about it. I can only apologise again.

   c I guess these _____ happen.

   d Thanks for being so _____ .

2 a Well, at _____ you're here now.

   b I'll do it tomorrow, I _____ .

   c I'll do it. _____ !

3 a I'm sorry. I really can't get _____ of it.

   b Don't be _____ . I'm sure I'll be able to find someone else to go. It is _____ it is.

   c Thanks. I'll _____ it up to you.

5 **Look at the Useful phrases box. Which phrases are used more often in a professional/formal situation?**

Useful phrases

Apologising

I'm really sorry, but …   I'm terribly sorry.

I'm afraid …   I'm afraid not.

I can only apologise.

Emphasising that the excuse is real

Honestly, I really can't get out of it.

There really is nothing we can do about it.

I would if I could, but I'm afraid it's impossible.

Accepting explanations

These things happen.   It is what it is.

Don't be silly. I'm sure …   Don't worry about it.

At least you phoned/you're here now.

Promising and thanking

I'll make it a priority.   I'll make it up to you.

I'll give you the money for it.

I'll do it tomorrow, I promise.

Let me assure you that it will not happen again.

Thanks for being so understanding.

6 ◁) **6.10 Listen to some of the more formal phrases and repeat them.**

7 **Write an excuse for situations 1–5.**

1 You're late for dinner with a friend.

2 You won't be able to go to your best friend's party.

3 You haven't finished some work your boss is expecting.

4 You have technical problems during a presentation.

5 You won't be able to deliver someone's order.

8 a **Work in pairs. Choose a situation from Exercise 7 and roleplay a conversation.**

b **Swap roles and choose another situation.**

Go online for the Roadmap video.

Check and reflect

1 a Complete the sentences with the best word(s). The first two letters are given.

1 The en_____ was just so sad. Honestly, I was in tears!
2 I'm not surprised she was vo_____ off the programme. She was awful!
3 I love that programme, too. Who's your favourite ch_____?
4 I'm not really a big fan of Hollywood bl_____ .
5 It's a great film. The di_____ is just so clever and funny.
6 I have to say, I thought the sp_____ ef_____ in that film were amazing.

b Choose two of the topics in the box. Work in pairs. Take turns saying as much as you can about them.

> a film with a really sad ending
> a film with amazing special effects
> a hilarious TV programme
> a Hollywood blockbuster you love (or hate)
> a film with great dialogue
> your favourite episode of a TV series

2 a Complete the sentences with the correct form of the verbs in brackets.

1 The first series _____ currently _____ on Channel 4. (repeat)
2 The World Cup Final _____ usually _____ by over a billion people. (watch)
3 Over 600 episodes of *The Simpsons* _____ so far. (make)
4 The special effects are so good that the film should really _____ at the cinema. (watch)
5 When *Jaws* _____ first _____ in 1975, the director Steven Spielberg was only 28. (release)
6 Apparently, the next James Bond movie is going _____ in my home town! (film)

b Work in pairs and talk about:
- something that's watched by a large number of people in your country.
- something that really should be watched at the cinema.
- something that's currently being repeated on TV.
- a film that was released a long time ago that you love.

3 Complete the sentences with the verbs in the box.

> deliver   finish   make   remove   replace   trust

1 Can you just _____ a few copies of this certificate?
2 The screen on my phone is cracked. Can you _____ it for me?
3 They're not very reliable. I wouldn't _____ them if I were you.
4 I've got this strange mark on my jacket. Do you think you can _____ it?
5 Phone the pizza place. They _____ for free.
6 They didn't do a bad job, but they didn't _____ on time, which was annoying.

4 Complete the sentences with a *have/get* passive and the correct form of the words in brackets.

1 I usually _____ once a month at a beauty salon near my house. (my nails / do)
2 I _____ last week. It wasn't cheap, I can tell you! (the gears on my car / fix)
3 My tooth really hurts. I really have to _____ . (it / look at)
4 Don't go in there. We _____ at the moment. (that room / paint)
5 You _____ since I saw you last. It's nice. It suits you. (your hair / cut)
6 We should _____ . It'd make the room much bigger. (this wall / remove)

5 Match verbs 1–6 with endings a–f.

1 slow   a strike
2 keep out   b of the sun
3 get rid of   c a sentence
4 go on   d the team's hopes
5 decide   e the development of the disease
6 hit   f staff

6 a Complete the sentences with one word. Negative forms count as one word.

1 Don't worry too much about it. I mean, it _____ never happen.
2 I think it's fairly _____ that prices will go up in the next few months.
3 It probably _____ make any difference, but I've asked her anyway.
4 There's a good _____ I'll be sent abroad to work by my company.
5 I _____ it'll make any difference, but I've asked him anyway.
6 There's only a _____ chance I'll get the job, but you never know.

b Write three predictions about the future. They can be about your life, science and technology, sport, news items, etc. Work in groups and compare your ideas.

Reflect

How confident do you feel about the statements below? Write 1–5 (1 = not very confident, 5 = very confident).
- I can talk in detail about TV and films.
- I can talk about and recommend services.
- I can discuss the main points of familiar news stories.
- I can apologise and give excuses.

Want more practice?

Go to your Workbook or app.

7A Health problems

> **Goal:** discuss a health problem with a doctor
> **Grammar:** verb patterns 1
> **Vocabulary:** health problems

Vocabulary

1 Match eight of sentences 1–12 with pictures A–H.

1 You look very **pale**.
2 That's a **nasty cut**. I need to have a look at that.
3 My neck feels really **stiff**. It **aches** all the time.
4 I've **injured** it somehow. I think it might be **broken**.
5 You **have a high temperature**.
6 I think I've **strained a muscle** in my back. I **keep getting** this terrible pain here.
7 I feel really bad. I think I've **eaten something that didn't agree with me**!
8 Your arm is very badly **bruised**.
9 I just get really **out of breath** all the time.
10 I have a terrible **sore throat**. It must be that **virus** that's going around.
11 I just feel tired all the time and I have these **bags under my eyes**.
12 This rash must be some kind of **allergic reaction**.

2 Work in pairs and discuss the questions.

1 What do you think caused the problems in the pictures?
2 What's the most/least serious problem? Why?

3 Work in pairs. Choose some of the problems in Exercise 1 that you have experienced. Tell your partner what happened.

I woke up one day last week and my neck felt really stiff. I think I slept in a strange way!

 Go to page 162 or your app for more vocabulary and practice.

Listening

4 7.1 Listen to two conversations between a patient and a doctor. Answer the questions.

1 What does the patient think the problem is?
2 Does the doctor agree? Why?/Why not?
3 What advice does the doctor give?

5 Listen again. Are the sentences true (T) or false (F)?

1 a The pain in the patient's leg has been really bad for a couple of weeks.
b The patient does a lot of exercise and keeps fit.
c The patient is surprised by the doctor's advice.
2 a The patient only started feeling ill very recently.
b The doctor is happy to hear something the patient tells him.
c The patient decides to take time off work.

Grammar

6 7.2 Listen and complete the sentences from the conversations in Exercise 4.

1 I **keep** _____ this pain all down here.
2 It **started** _____ a bit strange a week or two ago.
3 I'd strongly **suggest** _____ a break from that.
4 When did it **start** _____ bad?
5 I just **need** _____ your temperature.
6 And you need to **avoid** _____ anything too physical.
7 And you might want to **consider** _____ some time off work as well, if you can.
8 I **promise** _____ .

7 Read the grammar box and add the verbs in bold from Exercise 6 to the correct group 1–3.

Verb patterns 1

When two verbs are used together, the second verb usually takes the -*ing* form or the infinitive with *to*. The choice of form depends on the first verb.

1 -*ing* form
enjoy, finish, mind, miss, practise, _____ , _____ , _____ , _____

2 infinitive with *to*
agree, arrange, decide, expect, fail, hope, offer, refuse, _____ , _____

3 Some verbs can be followed by both -*ing* and the infinitive with *to* with no difference in meaning.
begin, continue, hate, like, _____

8 Complete the sentences with the correct form of the verbs in the box. In two sentences, both forms are possible.

> be   bend   book   eat   feel   join   listen
> take   wait   write

1 If you don't mind _____, the doctor should be able to see you in about half an hour.
2 I'm off work at the moment, but I'm hoping _____ back early next month.
3 I've decided _____ a gym. I need to get fit.
4 If you don't start _____ better within the next two or three days, come back and see me.
5 I've told him again and again that he needs to stop smoking, but he refuses _____ !
6 Stand up and practise _____ your knees ten times.
7 I'll be with you in one minute – as soon as I've finished _____ this report.
8 The doctor offered _____ me an appointment with a specialist.
9 I don't like _____ time off work when I'm ill because it means more stress for everyone else.
10 They put me on a special diet. I miss _____ red meat, but otherwise, it's OK.

9 a Work in pairs. Read the sentences that both include the word *try*. Which one …
a makes a suggestion?
b suggests some kind of effort or difficulty involved?
1 Can you just try to bend your leg?
2 Try taking two tablets every six hours.

b Read the grammar box and check your answers.

> A small group of verbs can be followed by both the *-ing* form and the infinitive with *to*, but the different forms affect the meaning.
> *Can you just **try to bend** your leg?* (= I realise this may be difficult for you to do.)
> ***Try** tak**ing** two tablets every six hours.* (= This is my suggestion/recommendation.)
> *I **stopped** eat**ing** meat when I was 16.* (= I used to eat meat, but don't anymore.)
> *He **stopped to answer** his phone.* (= He was doing something, but stopped and did something else.)
> *Make sure you **remember to book** an appointment.* (= It's important to do.)
> *I **remember** meet**ing** my great-grandfather when I was five.* (= It happened and I remember it.)

10 Choose the correct alternatives.
1 a I stopped *to have/having* headaches when my last doctor changed my prescription.
   b I was very tired so I stopped to *have/having* a rest.
2 a I must remember *to go/going* to the chemist's on my way home and pick up my prescription.
   b I remember *to go/going* to bed early last night and feeling a bit strange.
3 a I really tried *to go/going* to the gym more, but it just takes too much time.
   b You should try *to eat/eating* more fruit. It'd help.

11 a Think of at least one thing that you …
1 must remember to do this week.
2 remember doing when you were really young.
3 have stopped doing in the last couple of years.
4 have tried – and failed – to do.
5 (don't) really like doing/to do.
6 would like to start to do/doing in the near future.

b Work in groups and compare your ideas.

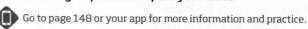 Go to page 148 or your app for more information and practice.

Speaking

PREPARE

12 Imagine you're going to visit the doctor's. Decide what's wrong with you. Use some of the health problems in Exercise 1, your own ideas or one of the roleplay cards on page 171.

SPEAK

13 a Work in pairs. Student A: You are the patient. Explain how you're feeling and what you think is wrong with you. Student B: You are the doctor. Ask questions about the patient's condition and give advice. Use the Useful phrases to help you.

> **Useful phrases**
> Come in. Sit down.
> What seems to be the problem?
> Where exactly does it hurt?
> Remember to (rest).
> Maybe you should try (doing more exercise).

b Swap roles and do another roleplay.

Develop your reading
page 116

7B Money talks

> **Goal:** discuss money issues
> **Grammar:** verb patterns 2
> **Vocabulary:** money

Listening

1 Work in pairs. How easy do you find it to talk about money? Which of the things in the box would you be comfortable talking about with friends?

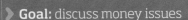

> spending on shopping   cost of living   what you earn

2 a ◗ **7.3** Listen to three conversations between two work friends, Keisha and Zara. Who do you think earns or has the most money, Keisha, Zara, Jim or Matthew?

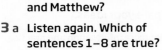

b Work in pairs. What have you learnt about Keisha, Zara, Jim and Matthew?

3 a Listen again. Which of sentences 1–8 are true?

1 Jim never buys his own coffee.
2 Jim is poor.
3 Matthew from the Spanish class seems to be wealthy.
4 Matthew is married to someone who has a lot of money.
5 Matthew is definitely in debt.
6 The women get paid £15 an hour.
7 Jim wants to buy a place to live.
8 Keisha is generous.

b Work in pairs and compare your answers.

Grammar

4 ◗ **7.4** Read the clauses from the conversations in Exercise 2a. Then listen and complete the full sentences.

a _____ he's that poor.
b _____ you bought him that coffee, too!
c _____ he does more finance stuff.
d _____ we should complain.
e _____ he's saving to buy a flat.
f _____ he earns 14 pounds an hour!
g _____ he takes milk.
h _____ he actually does for a living?
i _____ it'll make a difference?

5 Read the grammar box and match sentences a–i in Exercise 4 with categories 1–3.

Verb patterns 2

Some verbs are often followed by a clause, especially verbs connected to speech and thought, e.g. *agree, ask, bet, claim, imagine, know, forget, remember, realise, say, suppose, think, wonder, tell.*

1a You can link the verb and the clause with *that.*
*You **told** me **that** you'd pay me back today.*
*I **forgot that** I lent you that money.*
1b However, it's more common to use no linking word.
*He **said** he's earning twenty-five pounds an hour.*
*I **realised** I didn't have any money with me.*
2 You can link some of these verbs to a clause with *if* or a question word. After these linking words, use the word order of a statement, not a question.
*I **don't know if** she's coming to class today or not.*
*I **wonder how much** they pay.*
3 Questions using these verbs are sometimes called indirect questions. In indirect questions, use the word order of a statement after these verbs.
***Do you think** you'll get the job?*
***Do you know how** she made all her money?*

6 a ◗ **7.5** Listen to the sentences said quickly. Add the word *that* if you hear it.

1 I didn't know they were married.
2 Do you think we could take one?
3 I wonder what he's doing now.
4 I discovered he lives on my street!

b Work in pairs and practise saying the sentences.

7 Put the words in the correct order to make sentences.

1 you / she / lives / know / where / do?
2 how / I / wonder / earns / much / she.
3 job / found / out / I / what / is / his.
4 him / I / remember / if / I / can't / paid / back.
5 think / borrow / do / you / I / €5 / could?
6 money / I / they / have / loads / bet / of.
7 Russian / that / didn't / I / speaks / realise / Leila.
8 that / told / me / he / he / a / coffee / wants / black.

8 a Complete the sentence starters with your own ideas about famous people, recent news stories or big sporting events.

1 Did you know that … ?   3 I didn't know … .
2 Do you think … ?   4 I discovered … .

b Work in pairs. Take turns reading out your sentences and responding. Try to continue each conversation.

📱 Go to page 148 or your app for more information and practice.

Vocabulary and reading

9 a Read the article about money. Choose the correct alternatives.

b Work in pairs. Try to guess the missing numbers or place names where there is a question mark.

c Check the answers on page 171. Then discuss the questions.

1 Did you get any facts right?

2 Did anything surprise you?

3 Which facts are positive and which are negative?

4 What do you think the statistics would be for your country?

Go to page 162 or your app for more vocabulary and practice.

Money makes the world go around

Money plays a huge role in our lives, but how much do you really know about it?

1 People in **?** save the most money. On average, they keep 57 percent of their *earnings/debts* in the bank. They also have the highest average income, too: $144,000 per year!

2 **?** percent of people in the world can't get a bank *count/account*.

3 On average, women in full-time jobs in the UK *win/earn* £**?** per year less than men. That's £**?** less over their working life.

4 If you want to borrow enough money to buy a house in the UK, some banks will *lend/take* **?** times your annual salary.

5 **?** is the most expensive city to rent a place to live. On average, it costs $55.40 per square metre. A single person needs to earn around **?** per year to *owe/afford* to live in a flat on their own.

6 People from **?** borrow the most money from banks and other lenders. On average, they have *debts/wealth* of €70,000 per person.

7 According to the charity Oxfam, eight people now own **?** of all the *rate/wealth* in the entire world.

8 **?** is the most cashless society. 93 percent of all *accounts/payments* are made with a credit or debit card.

9 The government in **?** has borrowed more money than any other country in the world. It *owes/lends* almost 250 percent more than its GDP (the value of all its products and services).

10 The top *rate/payment* of income tax in Sweden is 57.2 percent for the highest earners – the highest in Europe. However, in **?** there is no tax on income at all.

Speaking

PREPARE

10 🔊 **7.6** You're going to take part in a discussion about money. First, listen to two people doing the same. Which question are they discussing? Do they agree?

1 Do you think some people earn too much money for what they do?

2 Do you agree that it is best never to borrow or lend money? Why?

3 Do you know how people avoid paying tax? Do you think it could be stopped? How?

4 How could it be made easier for young people to afford to buy their own home?

5 What would you do if you suddenly became rich?

SPEAK

11 a Read the questions in Exercise 10 again and make notes.

b Work in pairs and discuss the questions. Use your notes and the Useful phrases to help you.

> **Useful phrases**
> What do you think? Do you think it's a good idea?
> Do you know if that's true?
> Really? I'm not so sure.
> I don't agree that (he earns too much money).
> Absolutely!

c Report back to the rest of the class. Do you have the same or different views?

Develop your listening
page 118

7c ▶ Kings of the road

> **Goal:** tell a travel story
> **Grammar:** noun phrases 2
> **Vocabulary:** on the road

Reading

1 a Read the article quickly. Which cities are best for car drivers, cyclists, walkers?

b Read the article again. Why are the following mentioned?

1 a driving app	**5** an area of Fez
2 the quality of the roads	**6** footpaths
3 a 130 million euro programme	**7** road users
4 the laws of the road	**8** train carriage

2 How does your city compare with the cities in the article?

Grammar

3 a Look at the noun phrases in Exercise 1b. Divide them into two groups, depending on their form. (There is one group of five phrases and one group of three phrases.)

b Read the grammar box and choose the correct alternatives.

Noun phrases 2

You can modify or add information to nouns in different ways.
Use noun + noun.
*a **road user*** (= a user of the road)
*a **driving app*** (= an app to help you find the way)
*a **130 million euro programme*** (= a programme that cost €130 million)
In this case, the **¹***first/second* noun is the main noun.
The first noun is like an adjective so it **²***becomes/doesn't become* plural – even if it's a number.
These combinations of noun + noun are sometimes called compound nouns. Some have become fixed phrases, and sometimes they become one word.
footpath, breakdown, traffic jam, petrol station, breakdown service, cycle lanes
Use noun + *of* + noun.
*the **quality of** the roads   the **laws of** the road*
*a **programme of** 130 million euros*
In this case, the **³***first/second* noun is the main noun and both nouns can be singular or plural.
Sometimes either pattern is possible.
the quality of the roads or *the road quality*
a programme of 130 million euros or *a 130 million euro programme*
Sometimes you can combine both patterns.
the number of traffic jams

Getting to work can sometimes feel like a war in which different road users are fighting to be king of the road. Well, here are four cities where the battle has been won.

1 The best city for drivers
The driving app, Waze, found that Phoenix in the US state of Arizona came top of this list. Their decision was based on the number of traffic jams and car crashes, the quality of the roads, and support for drivers such as petrol stations, breakdown services and car parks. They also found drivers in Phoenix were very helpful.

2 The best city for subway users
Of course, if you want to avoid other road users completely, then Seoul is the place for you. Its metro system is the longest in the world and probably the most comfortable. Delays are very rare and every train carriage has free high-speed wifi, digital TVs and even heated seats in winter.

4 a 🔊 7.9 Work in pairs. Listen and write down the five sentences you hear.

b Listen again and repeat.

5 Read the sentences. Two or more noun phrases are underlined. Add *of* to the correct noun phrase.

1 There was <u>a big car crash</u> involving several vehicles and we were stuck in the middle of <u>a queue traffic</u> fifteen kilometres long.

2 We broke down in the mountains and had to wait five hours for the <u>breakdown service</u>. Luckily, we had five <u>bags shopping</u>, so we had plenty of food!

3 <u>The number accidents</u> has fallen because the police are making sure people follow the <u>traffic laws</u>.

4 In Honolulu, <u>mobile phone users</u> can get <u>a fine thirty-five dollars</u> if they walk across the road looking at their screens instead of the traffic.

5 In Singapore, there is <u>a bus stop</u> which has <u>a digital information board</u>, <u>a phone charger</u> and even <u>a selection books</u>.

6 You can reduce <u>car numbers</u> if you reduce <u>the cost public transport</u> and improve <u>passenger safety</u>.

6 Say something true about you/where you live. Use noun phrases from Exercise 5.
The police aren't very strict about traffic laws here.

📱 Go to page 148 or your app for more information and practice.

3 The best city for walkers

Some places such as Morocco's Fes el Bali were built for walking. This area of the city of Fez is thought to be the world's biggest car-free zone and nearly all trips are done on foot. Children can play in the narrow streets with the only danger coming from the donkeys used to collect the rubbish! Modern cities are also now encouraging more people to walk. Guangzhou in China has one of the highest levels of walking thanks to new footpaths that connect green spaces and tourist attractions.

4 The best city for cyclists

In Copenhagen, 63 percent of people go to work or school by bike. The city is very flat, which makes cycling easier, but it also has an average of 171 days of rain a year! The success of cycling comes from a 130 million euro programme to build cycle lanes and bridges as well as changes in the laws of the road to support cyclists.

Vocabulary

7 Complete the sentences with the pairs of words in the box.

> fine/points   pulled out/brake   driving test/park
> tyre/breakdown   gear/engine   crashed/footpath
> control/helmet   petrol station/lorry drivers

1 I failed my _____ four times because I just couldn't _____ properly.

2 I was cycling along the main road and a car suddenly _____ from a small street in front of me. I had to _____ hard to avoid hitting it.

3 When I came out of the building, a cyclist nearly _____ into me because he was cycling really fast along the _____ .

4 I got a flat _____ and had to call the _____ service to change it for me.

5 He broke down because he was driving at about 100 km per hour in second _____ and the _____ got too hot.

6 I was riding down a hill and I lost _____ of the bike and fell off. Fortunately, I was wearing a _____ so I wasn't badly hurt.

7 There was a huge queue at the _____ because there was a strike by _____ .

8 He was driving too fast so got an eighty-euro _____ and he had three _____ added to his driving licence.

8 Work in pairs. How would you describe each of the situations in Exercise 7? Use the adjectives in the box or your own ideas.

> annoying   bad luck   dangerous   an easy mistake
> embarrassing   scary   stupid

9 Who are the best/worst road users you know? Give examples.

 Go to your app for more practice.

Listening

10 a 🔊 7.10 Listen to four people talking about a travel experience. Which question does each person answer?

a Have you ever had a car crash or a bike accident?

b Have you ever had to pay a fine?

c Did you pass your driving test first time?

d What's the worst traffic jam you've ever experienced?

e Have you ever had a bike or car stolen?

b Work in pairs and answer the questions. Which speaker …

a was happy a bad thing happened?

b didn't like someone else's driving?

c made a mistake because they were nervous?

d had a series of nasty surprises?

c Listen again and check your answers.

Speaking

> **PREPARE**

11 You're going to tell a story about another travel experience. The story can be true or you can invent it. Prepare to tell your story by thinking about the answers to the questions.

- When did it happen?
- Who were you with?
- What happened in the end?
- How did you feel?

> **SPEAK**

12 a Work in groups. Take turns telling your story. Use the Useful phrases to help you.

> **Useful phrases**
> Did I ever tell you about what happened to me last year/a few years ago?
> It was early in the morning/about midnight/mid-afternoon and I was (driving to the airport).
> What happened in the end was (I missed my flight).
> When I think about it now, it was really silly.

b Choose one story to share with the rest of the class.

Develop
your
writing
page 119

7D English in action

> **Goal:** deal with problems with shops and services

1 Look at the pictures. Work in pairs and discuss the questions.
1 What might be the problem in each situation?
2 Have you had similar problems? What happened?

2 🔊 **7.11 Listen to two conversations and answer the questions.**
1 Where do the conversations take place?
2 What does the customer want to do?
3 What's the problem with that?

3 **Listen again and complete the sentences with two words.**
1 I'm sorry. We're not _____ exchange them without a receipt.
2 Is there _____ you could possibly check? I'd be really grateful if you could.
3 _____ speak to my manager.
4 Thanks. I really _____ . You've been very helpful.
5 That's a bit of a problem. _____ , I need to give her a new ticket with the same number.
6 Is there nothing you can do? I mean, _____ just go in with her and see if there's an empty seat?
7 That'd be great. You'd be _____ us out.
8 That's a relief. I can't _____ enough.

4 **Read the Useful phrases box and check your answers.**

> **Useful phrases**
>
> **Explaining rules and problems**
> We're not supposed to (exchange them without a receipt).
> I shouldn't really do that.
> Strictly speaking, I need (to give her a new ticket).
>
> **Requesting help**
> Is there (really) nothing you can do?
> Couldn't you (just go in with her)?
> Could you (maybe check with someone else)?
> Is there any way you could (possibly check)?
>
> **Persuading**
> I'd really appreciate it.
> I'd be really grateful if you could (do that).
> You'd be doing me a huge favour.
> You'd be really helping me/us out.
>
> **Offering solutions**
> Let me see what I can do.
> Let me speak to my manager.
> Let me have a look.
> I suppose I/we could (print new tickets).
>
> **Expressing thanks**
> That's great.
> I really appreciate it.
> You've been really helpful.
> I can't thank you enough.

5 a 🔊 **7.12 Listen to the sentences. Notice the extra emphasis on the underlined words.**
1 Is there really <u>nothing</u> you can do?
2 You'd be doing me a <u>huge</u> favour.
3 I'd be <u>really</u> grateful.
4 I can't thank you <u>enough</u>.

b Work in pairs and practise saying the sentences.

6 **Work in pairs. Take turns reading out the rules. Your partner should try to persuade you to change your mind using phrases from the Useful phrases box.**
1 I'm afraid we can't change the shoes without a receipt.
2 We're not allowed to let you in without a ticket.
3 We're not supposed to take $100 notes.
4 Strictly speaking, if you're checking out, we shouldn't let you stay in the room past 11 a.m.

7 a You're going to roleplay two conversations between a customer and a member of staff. Work in pairs. Student A: Turn to page 170. Student B: Turn to page 174.

b Roleplay the conversations.

Go online for the Roadmap video.

Check and reflect

1 Complete the sentences with the best word. The first letter is given.

1 When I woke up, my neck felt really s_____ . Maybe I twisted it in the night.

2 My arm was quite badly b_____ , but at least it wasn't broken.

3 I got really sick. I think I ate something that didn't a_____ with me.

4 I was playing football and I i_____ my neck somehow.

5 I had a terrible sore t_____ . I could hardly talk!

6 I had some kind of a_____ reaction to something I ate.

2 **a** Put the verbs in the box into the correct groups:

1 seven verbs usually followed by -ing

2 eight verbs usually followed by infinitive with to

3 four verbs that can be followed by both patterns without any change of meaning

agree	arrange	avoid	begin	consider	decide
enjoy	hate	hope	keep	like	mind	miss
need	offer	practise	promise	refuse	start

b Write six sentences that are true for you. Use the verbs in the box. Then work in groups and compare your sentences.

I usually avoid driving during the rush hour, if I can.

3 **a** Find the five sentences with a mistake and correct them.

1 I don't know they'll lend me the money or not.

2 Do you think I could borrow some money from you?

3 Do you know where's the nearest bank?

4 I can't believe how much you did borrow.

5 Can you ask him does he take milk in his coffee?

6 I wonder she's doing now.

b Write three sentences. Use the phrases in the box to help you. Then work in pairs and use your sentences to have conversations.

Do/Did you know …?   Do you think …?
I don't/didn't …   Could you tell me …?   I wonder …
I recently discovered …   I bet …   I realised recently …

4 Complete the sentences with the verbs in the box.

afford   earn   lend   own   pay   save

1 Fewer and fewer young people can _____ to buy their own homes.

2 People in Dubai don't _____ any tax on their earnings.

3 Some companies will _____ you money even if you're not working.

4 In many companies, men still _____ at least 10 percent more than women.

5 In the UK, the richest 1 percent now _____ over 25 percent of the country's wealth.

6 On average, in Switzerland, people _____ almost 20 percent of their earnings.

5 **a** Complete the sentences with the plural form of the noun phrases in the box.

cycle lane   cup of coffee   level of pollution
the quality of the road   road sign   train driver

1 When we stop at the garage, can you get out and get us two _____ ?

2 We got completely lost because all the _____ were in Greek and we couldn't read them.

3 Apparently, our city has one of the highest _____ in the world.

4 I probably wouldn't drive so much if there were more _____ in the city.

5 The main thing that makes driving here so difficult is _____ . It's terrible!

6 It was an awful journey. All the _____ were on strike, so we had to get a bus.

b Choose two of the noun phrases in the box that you have a story about. Work in pairs. Take turns telling your stories.

cycle lanes   the level of pollution   road signs
a bus/taxi driver   the quality of the roads
a traffic jam

6 **a** Match verbs 1–7 with endings a–g.

1	fail	**a**	control of the bike
2	crash	**b**	the breakdown service
3	wear	**c**	a helmet
4	call	**d**	my driving test three times
5	lose	**e**	points to your driving licence
6	get	**f**	a fine
7	add	**g**	into a cyclist

b When or why might you do the things in Exercise 6a? Which have you done? Which have happened to you? Make notes. Then work in pairs and discuss the questions.

Reflect

How confident do you feel about the statements below? Write 1–5 (1 = not very confident, 5 = very confident).

- I can describe basic symptoms to a doctor.
- I can exchange information about people and money.
- I can tell a story about a transport experience.
- I can deal with problems with shops and services.

Want more practice?

Go to your Workbook or app.

8A Small changes

> **Goal:** discuss environmental issues

> **Grammar:** first conditional

> **Vocabulary:** the environment

Vocabulary

1 Look at the photos. What environmental issues do they relate to? Match the photos with the words and phrases in the box.

> floods   animals dying out   plastic waste
> natural resources running out   climate change
> pollution   overpopulation   rising sea levels

2 Choose the correct alternatives.

1 We've been **experiencing** bigger **storms** and natural disasters like *plastic waste/floods.*

2 We have a big chemical industry that **causes** *pollution/storms.*

3 More of us are driving electric cars because they **produce** fewer **toxic gases**, which cause *overpopulation/pollution.*

4 We **recycle** a lot of rubbish - paper, cans and bottles - but a lot of other *toxic gases/plastic waste* just goes into the sea.

5 Lots of different kinds of plants and animals are in danger of *dying out/reproducing* unless we do something to **prevent** them from disappearing.

6 We have natural resources like oil and gas, but we should **develop** other industries in case these resources *die out/run out.*

7 We don't think enough about how we behave. We **consume** too much and *waste/recycle* too much.

8 The problem of *overpopulation/animals dying out* in big cities is getting worse, but climate change is the biggest challenge we face. We need to act fast to **solve** this problem.

3 a Work in pairs. Are the sentences in Exercise 2 true for your country? If not, change them so that they are true.

b Discuss the questions. Use as many of the verbs in bold in Exercise 2 as you can.

1 What environmental issues in your country/around the world have been in the news recently?

2 Which do you think are the most serious?

3 What do you think we can do about them?

Go to page 163 or your app for more vocabulary and practice.

Reading

4 a Read the article. What is the main point?

b Read the article again and answer the questions.

1 Why does the writer think there has been a trend towards sharing worrying statistics about the environment?

2 Why doesn't this work? Give three reasons.

3 What does the writer think is a better solution?

5 Do you agree with the article? Why?/Why not?

SHOCK treatment

Are shocking environmental statistics really a good idea?

In recent years, there has been a trend towards shocking us with worrying statistics about the environment.

Such statistics are supposed to shock us into making big changes in how we live so that we help the environment. However, psychologists have found that they may have the opposite effect. Among the most common reactions are:

Deny it: when people are told about disasters and their possible results, they often say, 'It won't happen' and refuse to recognise the problem.

Someone else will do it: People in crowds who are watching something bad happening are less likely to act as they believe someone else will help. Unfortunately, with the environment, there are seven billion of us watching!

Set goals we can't meet: We often give ourselves challenges like 'stop using plastic', but they're too big and impossible to achieve. However, we then say, 'I tried – and anyway, even if I stop using plastic, no one else will', which allows us to give up completely!

Many environmental experts now believe it's better to encourage small actions, which are both easier to achieve and also benefit us in our daily lives.

So instead of aiming to produce no waste, we could say, 'I won't create rubbish today by making my own coffee or cooking with fresh ingredients.' Or, 'Instead of getting rid of my car completely, I'll walk to work once a week and get fitter.' If we can all make these small changes, big changes will follow.

Grammar

6 a **Work in pairs. Read sentences a–d and answer the questions.**

a <u>If we can all make</u> these small changes, big changes will follow.

b <u>Unless people become</u> vegetarian, we may run out of land and water supplies by 2050.

c <u>Even if I stop</u> using plastic, no one else will.

d We have natural resources like oil and gas, but we should develop other industries <u>in case they run out</u>.

1 What structures are used in the underlined parts of the sentence?

2 What structures are used in the other part of the sentence?

b **Read and complete the grammar box with the words in the box.**

even if   may   present   should   unless   will

First conditional

Use the first conditional to talk about the possible future result of another action.

First conditional sentences have two parts: a possible future 'condition' (an action or situation) and the result of that action.

condition	result

If we all make these small changes, big changes will follow.

- In the condition clause, use a **1**_____ tense (*can* + infinitive is also sometimes possible). Start the condition clause with *if, unless, even if, in case*. *In case* means 'in order to be prepared for' something that may happen.

  2_____ means 'if not this situation'

  3_____ means that something will still be true if another thing happens.

- In the result clause, use:

  4_____ or *be going to* + infinitive to show certainty.

  5_____ or *might* + infinitive to show possibility.

  6_____ + infinitive to show you think it's a good idea.

7 a **8.1 Listen and notice the pronunciation of *will* and *won't*.**

1 If we're not careful, there won't be much countryside left in 50 years' time.

2 Industry will continue to cause pollution unless we have stricter punishments.

3 Even if we solve global warming, natural disasters will still occur.

4 We'll need to build cities in space in case we destroy the environment here.

b **Listen again and repeat.**

8 **Choose the correct alternatives.**

1 Many different kinds of animals will die out eventually *if/unless* we protect them.

2 The government are going to ban new buildings along the coast *in case/unless* sea levels rise and there are more floods.

3 I think it's too little, too late. The environment won't recover *in case/even if* we all consume less.

4 *If/Even if* you reduce your heating or air conditioning by one degree, you'll save 3 percent on your bill.

5 Climate change may continue to get worse *even if/unless* I change the way I behave, so I'm not going to!

9 **Complete the sentences with the correct form of the verbs in brackets. Use *will* or *be going to* in the result clauses.**

1 If they _____ (introduce) new environmental laws, it _____ (be) bad for the economy.

2 In future, people _____ (need to) recycle more even if they _____ (not be) happy about it.

3 Unless we _____ (clean up) the oceans, soon we _____ (not have) any fish left!

4 They _____ (start) building houses in the mountains in case global warming _____ (cause) more floods.

5 If we _____ (not change) our ways, our grandchildren _____ (not have) a future!

10 a **Make a list of four goals you would like to achieve in life and two worries you have about the future.**

I'd like to stop working when I'm 60. I'm worried about the economy. I think it might get worse.

b **Work in pairs. How can you achieve your goals? How can you overcome your worries?**

Go to page 150 or your app for more information and practice.

Speaking

PREPARE

11 a **8.2 You're going to discuss small changes that would have a positive impact on the environment. First, listen to two people doing the same. What idea do they have? Why is it a good idea?**

b **Work in pairs. Make a list of other ideas, e.g. make people pay for plastic bags. For each idea, discuss:**

- the impact it may have on the environment.
- how easy it will be to achieve.
- what benefits it will give individuals.

SPEAK

12 **Work in groups. Discuss your ideas and try to agree on the two best changes.**

Develop your listening
page 121

8B Relationships

> **Goal:** talk about different relationships

> **Grammar:** *whatever, whoever, whenever, however,* etc.

> **Vocabulary:** character

Listening

1 **Work in pairs and discuss the questions.**

1 What relationships are shown in the photos?

2 Which of the relationships in the photos do you have? How important are they?

3 Which do you think is more important, family or friends?

2 ◆ 8.7 **Listen to four conversations. What relationship(s) do they discuss? In conversation 4, they discuss three relationships.**

a sister and sister/brother

b mother and daughter/son

c stepfather and stepson/daughter

d neighbours

e boss and worker

f teacher and student

g aunt and nephew/niece

h uncle and nephew/niece

3 **Listen again. Who do the sentences describe?**

1 She's so cute! *the new niece*

2 That's generous of them.

3 She's the sensible one – good job, married, calm under pressure.

4 He's a really bright kid.

5 She's amazing, though – super talented.

6 I tried to be a bit strict.

7 He finds it so difficult to focus.

8 He doesn't seem to want to get to know me more.

9 He was a bit difficult at times to begin with.

4 **Work in pairs. How good are the relationships you heard about in Exercise 2?**

They get on very well/quite well/OK. They don't get on …

Grammar

5 a ◆ 8.8 **Listen and complete the sentences from the conversations in Exercise 2.**

1 I just can't control him. He just does _____ he wants.

2 I've tried moving him around, but _____ he sits next to, he ends up arguing with them.

3 He says 'Hi' _____ I see him.

4 He was a bit difficult at times to begin with, _____ hard I tried.

5 We always have a great time when we see each other, _____ we are.

b **Read and complete the grammar box. Choose the correct alternatives in 1–3. Complete 4–8 with answers from Exercise 5a.**

whatever, whoever, whenever, however, etc.

Whatever, whenever, wherever, however and *whoever* are conjunctions. They join two clauses together.

Use *whatever, whenever, wherever, however* and *whoever* when:

• it **1** *makes a difference/doesn't make any difference* what, when, where, etc.

• you **2** *have to/don't have to* be specific about the thing, time, place, etc.

• you **3** *know/don't know* the exact details of what, when, where, etc.

To show the thing we mean doesn't matter, use **4** _____ .

To show the way something is done doesn't matter, use **5** _____ .

To show the time doesn't matter, use **6** _____ .

To show the place doesn't matter, use **7** _____ .

To show the person doesn't matter, use **8** _____ .

6 a Listen to the sentences in Exercise 5a again. Notice the stress on the second syllable of the -*ever* words.

b Listen again and repeat.

7 a Choose the correct alternatives.
1 *Whenever/Wherever* you are in the world, you can always find people you get on with.
2 *Whoever/Whichever* you marry, the most important thing is that you love them.
3 You should try to stay together *whenever/whatever* happens.
4 *However/Whatever* much you earn, it's important to remember that money isn't that important.
5 There's no best time to get married or start a family. It's hard *however/whenever* you do it.
6 *Whatever/However* you do and *wherever/whatever* you work, make sure you don't make enemies.

b Work in pairs. Do you think the sentences in Exercise 7a offer good advice? Why/Why not?

8 a Write advice using sentence starters 1–5.
1 Whoever you are, it's important to … .
2 Wherever you go in the world, make sure you … .
3 Whenever you get the chance, try to … .
4 However hard life becomes, remember … .
5 Whatever you do, make sure you don't … .

b Work in pairs and compare your ideas. What's the best piece of advice? Why?

 Go to page 150 or your app for more information and practice.

Vocabulary

9 a Complete the sentences with the words in the box.

| active | bright | difficult | generous | patient | racist |
| strict | sweet | talented | willing | | |

1 He can be quite _____ . He just seems to oppose everything I suggest and think of problems.
2 She's a really _____ singer. I think she should try and do it professionally, but she says she's not good enough. I think she just **lacks a bit of confidence**.
3 He can be _____ , but not too much. I mean, he makes us work hard but you can have a laugh, too.
4 She's very **reliable** – always _____ to help if I need it. She can also be really funny in meetings.
5 He looks very _____ , but he can be quite **nasty** to other kids. I don't think he gets enough discipline.
6 She's really _____ . She's one of those people who gets top marks without even trying.
7 We're **politically** _____ , but for different parties! We're polite to each other, but we aren't friends.
8 He says some things and you think, 'That is actually quite _____ !' But I just think it's his generation and he's not going to change at his age.
9 What I like is how _____ she is even when we're losing. She never shouts at us. She just **stays calm** and explains how we can improve.
10 She's really _____ . She actually paid for me to come here and study English.

b Work in pairs. What kind of relationship do you think is being discussed in the sentences in Exercise 9a?

10 Work in pairs and answer the questions.
1 Apart from people, what can be **reliable**?
2 How might children be **nasty** to each other?
3 Why might someone **lack confidence** and how could you change that?
4 What might you do if you're **politically active**?
5 What can you do to **stay calm**?

 Go to page 163 or your app for more vocabulary and practice.

Speaking

PREPARE

11 a 8.9 You're going to talk about people you know. First, listen to two people doing the same and answer the questions.
1 Who is the person talking about?
2 What are they like?

b Write a list of six people who you have/had a relationship with. Use the relationships in this lesson to help you. They can be good or bad relationships. Think about the questions.
1 What's the person like?
2 How well do you get on with them?
3 What are they like? Give examples of their behaviour/character.

SPEAK

12 Work in pairs. Give your list of people to your partner and take turns interviewing each other about them. Use the questions in the Useful phrases and try to use *whatever, wherever*, etc. in your answers.

Useful phrases
Who's [name]?
Do you get on OK?
How come?
What happened?
Do you see much of each other?

Develop your reading
page 122

65

8c ▸ Big moments

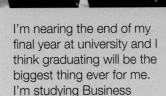

> **Goal:** describe important life events
> **Grammar:** time conjunctions
> **Vocabulary:** life events

Vocabulary

1 How many big life events can you think of, e.g. getting married? Make a list.

2 Complete the sentences with the pairs of words in the box.

> ceremony/remember   engagement/married
> separated/divorced   retire/mortgage   graduate/year
> partner/anniversary   relationship/live
> pregnant/birth

1 My son and his girlfriend have just **announced** their _____ . They're planning to get _____ in the spring.

2 Every year they **hold** a big _____ to _____ those who died in the war.

3 I really didn't enjoy being _____ , but after I **gave** _____ to my son, everything completely changed!

4 I first met my _____ five years ago now. It's actually our _____ next Friday.

5 I don't want to _____ until **I've paid off** my _____ .

6 Once I _____ from university, I'm going to **take a** _____ **off** and travel around Asia.

7 I've been in a serious _____ for quite a long time. We _____ **together** and have two cats.

8 My parents _____ when I was ten, but they only _____ last year.

3 What's the noun form of the words in the box?

engaged – engagement

> ~~engaged~~   die   divorce   graduate   married
> pregnant   retire   separated

4 Work in pairs. Think of examples of life events from Exercises 1, 2 and 3.

> *Prince Harry and Meghan Markle just got married. A big ceremony was held at Windsor Castle.*

 Go to your app for more practice.

Reading

5 Read the website article. Which is the biggest life event in your opinion?

6 Read the article again and answer the questions.

1 Who did something later than they wanted?
2 Who has had to deal with two difficult situations?
3 Who is looking forward to something?
4 Who is not looking forward to something?
5 Who got some financial help?

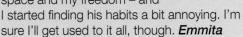

I'm nearing the end of my final year at university and I think graduating will be the biggest thing ever for me. I'm studying Business Management and doing my degree really hasn't been easy. I'd never lived away from home until I started here, so that was tough, and the course has been really hard work as well. Honestly, as soon as I finish my last exam, I'm going to go out and party for the whole weekend. It'll be great! *Max*

I got married last year and marriage has definitely been the biggest thing in my life. We'd been in a serious relationship for a long time, but we didn't live together before we were married. After the ceremony, we moved into a flat that my father bought for us, and the first few weeks were amazing. However, after that, I started missing my own space and my freedom – and I started finding his habits a bit annoying. I'm sure I'll get used to it all, though. *Emmita*

Without a doubt, the most important event in my life was the birth of my daughter. I was 41 at the time, quite old, and we'd wanted children for years, but we'd had lots of problems, so when I first held her in my arms, it was just amazing. Words can't really describe that feeling. It was just pure love. Pure unconditional love. She's 18 now and getting ready to leave home. The house will feel so empty once she's gone. *Lina*

Grammar

7 a Read the sentences and look at the underlined time conjunctions. In which sentence is the time conjunction followed by a noun and in which is it followed by a clause?

  1 I'd never lived away from home <u>until</u> I started here.

  2 <u>After</u> the ceremony, we moved into a flat.

b Read the sentences. Do they refer to the past, present or future? What do you notice about the tenses used after the time conjunctions underlined?

  1 <u>As soon as</u> I finish my last exam, I'm going to go out and party.

  2 The house will feel so empty <u>once</u> she's gone.

c Read the grammar box and check your answers.

Time conjunctions

Until, after and *before* can either be prepositions or conjunctions.

When they are prepositions, they are followed by nouns.

after the ceremony
until the anniversary

When they are conjunctions, they link two clauses and show the order in which things happen.

I'd never lived away from home until I started here.
We didn't live together before we were married.

As soon as, when and *once* only function as conjunctions. They can only be followed by a clause.

When I first held her in my arms, it was just amazing.

When you talk about future events and actions, use a present simple or perfect form in the clause that follows the time conjunction.

As soon as I finish my last exam …
… once she's gone.

The present perfect emphasises the action will happen before the other action/event.

8 a 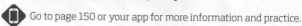 **8.10** Listen and notice how the underlined words link together.

  1 <u>Once I've</u> graduated, I'm going to go travelling for a year.

  2 <u>As soon as I</u> heard the news, I started crying.

  3 I couldn't understand a word <u>when I</u> first moved here.

  4 I'll be busy <u>until I've</u> finished my exams.

  5 I've still got lots of things I'd like to do <u>before I</u> retire.

  6 <u>After I've</u> decided, I'll let you know.

b Listen again and repeat.

9 Complete the sentences with the correct verb or noun form of the words in brackets.

  1 Once I _____ , I'll have a lot more freedom. (move)

  2 As soon as I _____ there, I felt at home. (arrive)

  3 I'm planning to go travelling after my _____ . (graduate)

  4 Things _____ better until I've found a job. (not get)

  5 We're doing up the whole house before my son _____ (born).

  6 I might move abroad after _____ . (retire)

10 a Complete the sentences so that they are true for you.

My life will change quite a lot after I finish my master's degree next year.

  1 My life will change quite a lot after _____ .

  2 Once I've _____ , I'm going to _____ .

  3 As soon as I _____ , I _____ .

  4 It might surprise you to learn that I'd never _____ until I _____ .

  5 I first _____ when I _____ .

b Work in pairs and compare your ideas.

Go to page 150 or your app for more information and practice.

Speaking

PREPARE

11 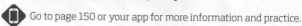 **8.11** You're going to describe big events in your life. First, listen to Ben talking about a big event in his life. Are the sentences true (T) or false (F)?

  1 He moved to Brazil when he graduated from university.

  2 He went to Brazil to do some unpaid work.

  3 He's been married twice.

  4 He's been there nearly 13 years.

12 Think of three big events in your life. They can be things that have already happened to you or things that you know are going to happen in the future. Think about:

  • when the events happened/are going to happen.

  • why they're so important.

  • what difference they made/will make to your life.

SPEAK

13 a Work in groups. Take turns telling the group as much as you can about your events. Use the Useful phrases and the language in this lesson to help you.

Useful phrases

It completely changed my life.
It was something I'd always wanted to do.
It was an amazing day.
I never really planned it. It just happened.
It was the best/worst/most interesting thing that's ever happened to me.

b Were any of your events similar?

Develop your writing
page 124

> **Goal:** make phone calls

1 Work in pairs and discuss the questions.

1 Have you ever made a phone call in English? Who to? Why? How did you find it?

2 In general, how much do you speak on the phone? Do you prefer texting to speaking?

3 Do you leave spoken phone messages? If so, who to? If not, why not?

2 🔊 **8.12 Listen to the first line of nine phone calls. Who/what kind of place is being called?**

1 a bank

3 a 🔊 **8.13 Listen to the continuation of the phone calls in Exercise 2. What is the reason for each call?**

1 needs a new PIN for a debit card

b Work in pairs and compare your answers.

4 Listen again. Tick the phrases in the Useful phrases box you hear.

Useful phrases

Accepting a call
Hello, [company name].
Thank you for calling [company name]. You're through to [name/department name].
If you know the extension number you require, please dial now.
[Name] speaking.
How can I help you?/What can I help you with today?
What can we do for you?

Giving reasons for calling
I'd like to (know/order/get) …
I'm ringing about (our heating).
I was ringing to (see if it was still available).
I have a problem with … and I wondered if you could …
I'm interested in (classes …). I wanted to know if …

Redirecting the call
Let me put you through to [department name]/my colleague.
Please hold the line (while I put you through).

5 Match reasons for calling a–i with people or places 1–9 in Exercise 2.

a I'd like to book a table for lunch, if possible.

b I was just ringing to wish you happy birthday.

c I ordered a bed the other day and I'm phoning to find out what time it might be delivered.

d I'm ringing about my rent, which is due this week.

e I have a friend who is staying with you tonight and I'd like to get in touch with him.

f I have a problem with one of my radiators and I wondered if you could come and look at it today.

g I'm interested in the master's degree courses you offer and was phoning to speak to someone from the Law Department.

h I'm supposed to be starting a course on Monday, but my flight was cancelled so I'm ringing to say I'll be late.

i I'm interested in getting a loan and I just wanted to know what you have on offer.

6 a Work in pairs. Think of one more reason to call the people and places in Exercise 2.

b Write three short phone calls like those in Exercise 3a. Use your ideas from Exercise 6a. Try to use as much language from the Useful phrases box as possible.

c Work with another pair. Roleplay your phone calls. Take turns making the call and receiving the call.

Go online for the Roadmap video.

Check and reflect

1 Complete the sentences with the best word(s). The first letters are given.

  1 Several different kinds of animals in my country are in danger of d _____ o_____ .

  2 By the time I retire, we won't have any more natural re_____ like oil or gas.

  3 In most big cities, air po_____ is reaching dangerous levels.

  4 We're all going to experience more natural di_____ in the future.

  5 We need new laws that force people to re_____ paper, bottles and cans.

  6 Everyone can see how cl_____ ch_____ is affecting our country.

2 Match sentence halves 1–6 with a–f.

  1 They're going to die out unless

  2 They're going to die out if

  3 We should be ready in case

  4 Unless we fight for cleaner air,

  5 Even if we start consuming less,

  6 If we start consuming less,

  a all the oil and gas run out.

  b we are still going to face serious challenges.

  c we might be able to stop climate change.

  d action is taken soon.

  e it's going to be impossible to live in some cities.

  f something isn't done soon.

3 a Complete the sentences with the words in the box. Use each word once only.

> however   whatever   whenever   wherever
> whoever

  1 _____ I go and visit her, she always cooks for me.

  2 He never really thinks about other people. He always just does _____ he wants to do.

  3 She always told me I could be _____ I wanted to be.

  4 He always finds something to complain about _____ we go.

  5 She's always kind to me, _____ badly I've behaved.

b Do you know anyone like the people in Exercise 3a? Work in pairs. Take turns comparing your ideas.

4 a Match the adjectives in the box with descriptions 1–6.

> very bright   very generous   quite nasty
> very patient   quite strict   very talented

  1 She always stays calm and never gets angry with us.

  2 He's a great singer and a very good musician.

  3 She's good at maintaining discipline in the classroom.

  4 I asked if I could borrow £20, and he just gave it to me.

  5 She gets top marks in every single subject.

  6 He says some awful things to the other children.

b Which adjectives in the box describe you? Which describe other people in your family? Work in groups and compare your ideas. Give examples.

5 a Complete the sentences with the noun form of the words in the box.

> engaged   graduate   married   pregnant   retire
> separated

  1 My daughter's been studying history at university. It's her _____ ceremony next month.

  2 It's my grandparents' 50th anniversary today. They've had a long and happy _____ .

  3 My son and his partner have just announced their _____ . They're getting married in June.

  4 It was quite a difficult _____ , so it was a huge relief to finally give birth.

  5 After my parents' _____ , I lived with my mum and my sister lived with my dad.

  6 It's lovely to see my parents enjoying their _____ . They deserve it.

b Choose two of the topics in the box. Work in pairs. Take turns talking about your topics.

> the secret to a happy marriage   an anniversary
> how to really enjoy retirement   an engagement
> why marriages end in divorce
> your graduation ceremony

6 Choose the correct alternatives.

  1 I'll come and help you once I *finished/have finished* doing this.

  2 I'll call you as soon as I *get/will get* to my hotel.

  3 I'm going to finish that report after the kids *went/have gone* to bed.

  4 She's only got five more years to go until *retire/retirement*.

  5 After I *have left/left* home, I started working in a bank in the capital city.

Reflect

How confident do you feel about the statements below? Write 1–5 (1 = not very confident, 5 = very confident).

- I can speak in general terms about environmental problems.
- I can talk about a variety of relationships.
- I can talk about big events in my life.
- I can make calls and leave messages.

Want more practice?

Go to your Workbook or app.

9A Quality of life

> **Goal:** conduct a survey
> **Grammar:** patterns after *wish*
> **Vocabulary:** quality of life

Reading and vocabulary

1 **Look at the photos and discuss the questions.**

1 What are the people doing?
2 What things do you think contribute to the happiness or unhappiness of an individual person, a local community, a country?
   I think the main thing that makes us happy is family.

2 **Read the article and answer the questions.**

1 What is the Gallup World Poll?
2 How large is it?
3 What are five aspects of life that the poll asks about?
4 What are the main reasons for unhappiness according to the poll?

3 **Choose the best conclusion for the article.**

a The government shouldn't try to increase wealth.
b It's essential to improve people's environment and reduce working hours and stress levels.
c Poorer people are usually happier than rich people.

4 **Work in pairs. Check you understand the words in bold. Then complete the sentences with the nouns in the box.**

anxiety	charity	community	equality	faith
purpose	spaces	tolerance	violence	wages

1 We have a **strong** _____ and neighbours really support each other, which is great.
2 There are a lot of green _____ where kids can play.
3 Life's stressful and the **pressure** to be successful **causes** a lot of _____ and depression.
4 Lots of people can afford to **work part-time** because _____ here are generally quite high.
5 People are **generous** with their time and money. I do work for a _____ myself.
6 Many people have been unemployed for a long time, which makes them feel they have no _____ **in life**.
7 We haven't achieved full _____ yet. Women don't get paid as much as men and disabled people still **face** quite a lot of **discrimination** when looking for work.
8 Generally, people **trust** doctors and nurses and also still have _____ in politicians.
9 Unfortunately, crime and _____ are just **facts of life** here. I know lots of people who have been robbed.
10 Our society is much more mixed these days and in general there is more _____ of different lifestyles.

5 **Work in pairs. Which of the sentences in Exercise 4 are true for your country or region?**

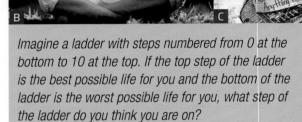

Imagine a ladder with steps numbered from 0 at the bottom to 10 at the top. If the top step of the ladder is the best possible life for you and the bottom of the ladder is the worst possible life for you, what step of the ladder do you think you are on?

Over recent years, it has often been argued that it would be better to measure a country's progress not simply in terms of wealth, but by thinking about what an economy should provide: good quality of life and happiness. The Gallup World Poll tries to measure this. The survey is done in over 160 nations and asks around 1,000 people in each country questions such as the one above.

Similar questions are asked about the situation of the country in general and about how those interviewed see their own lives in the past, present and future. The poll also has a wide variety of other questions which explore people's feelings about life. The questions not only ask about finance, but also cover mental and physical health, how strong people's local community is, social experiences and people's purpose in life.

In explaining why they are unhappy with their lives, people do sometimes say they wish they had a higher income or that they could afford a car. However, more often the reasons are not to do with money: mostly people complain about the environment they live in, lack of time with family and friends or anxiety and depression. The results of the survey suggest that societies might be better dealing with these reasons for unhappiness rather than only trying to increase wealth and wages. The results may also explain why Costa Rica is much happier than richer countries like the US and Singapore.

10 9 8 7 6 5 4 3 2 1 0

6 **Work in pairs and answer the questions.**

1 What things make a **strong community**?
2 Who else might **face discrimination**?
3 What **charities** do you know? What work do they do?
4 What else might **cause anxiety**? How can you **reduce anxiety**?
5 What else, apart from a job, might give someone a **purpose in life**?

Go to page 164 or your app for more vocabulary and practice.

D

E

8 a Complete the sentences with one word.

1 I wish I _____ quit my job.
2 I really wish people _____ stop complaining about it.
3 I wish there _____ more people like her.
4 I wish they _____ do more to support local communities.
5 I wish I _____ a bit more free time.
6 I wish I _____ what to do about it, but I have no idea.

b 🔊 9.2 Listen and check your answers.

9 Work in pairs. Write one *wish* sentence for each situation.

1 Pollution is just a fact of life here.
   I wish the government would create more green spaces./I wish it wasn't so polluted here.
2 My job is depressing. It's just the same thing every day.
3 It takes me ages to get to work. Public transport here is just so slow!
4 My neighbours just never stop arguing. It's so annoying.
5 I'd love to be able to play the guitar, but I'm not sure I'm patient enough.

10 a Write five *wish* sentences about the topics in the box that are true for you. Use the different patterns in the grammar box.

> your job/life   money   your family   your town/city
> the government   the world

b Work in groups. Compare and explain your answers.

📱 Go to page 152 or your app for more information and practice.

Grammar

7 a 🔊 9.1 Listen to three people answering different questions from the Gallup Poll. Match speakers 1–3 with questions a–c.

a Do you feel you have enough holidays/free time?
b Is the government doing enough to protect the environment?
c Are you happy with your job? How could it be better?

b Read the replies 1–3. Do the underlined phrases refer to a present, past or future situation?

1 I wish <u>I could work fewer hours</u>.
2 I wish <u>they would ban cars from the city centre</u>.
3 I sometimes wish <u>I earned a bit more money</u>.

c Read and complete the grammar box with *could*, *past simple* and *would*.

Patterns after *wish*

Use *wish* to say what you'd like to change, but probably can't change.
There are common patterns after wish:
Use *I wish* + **1** _____ to say how you want a present situation to be different.
I sometimes wish I earned a bit more money.

Use **2** _____ to say what you want to be able to do now.
I wish I could work fewer hours.

Use **3** _____ to say what you want someone/something else to do now or in the future.
I wish they would ban cars from the city centre.

Speaking

PREPARE

11 Turn to page 172. Read the survey. Choose the six questions you like the most. Add two more questions of your own.

SPEAK

12 a Conduct your survey round the class. When you answer questions, give some detail about how you would like things to be different. Try to use *wish*.

b Work in groups and compare your findings. Use the Useful phrases to help you.

Useful phrases

Almost everyone I spoke to (was happy with their job).
The majority of students in the class (had learnt something interesting in the last few days).
I'd say about half the class (had faith in the media).
Only one or two people (were happy with healthcare).
No one I asked (felt they had enough free time).

Develop your listening
page 126

9B An ideal society

> **Goal:** take part in a discussion
> **Grammar:** second conditional
> **Vocabulary:** society

Reading and vocabulary

1 What books, TV series or films do you know that are about imagined societies in the future?

2 a Read the summaries of five books quickly. Is each author describing:
   1 an ideal society?
   2 a nightmare society?

Dream worlds or nightmares?

Thomas More's book *Utopia* describes a perfect society where everyone in need receives a basic income so there's no **¹poverty/wealth** and no one is ever **homeless** because the **²state/democracy** provides a free place to live.

Suzanne Collins's book *The Hunger Games* describes a country called Panem, which is **³ruled/owned** by a terrible leader called President Snow. People in the countryside pay a lot of tax to **⁴fund/pay** the expensive lifestyle of people in the capital city.

In Malorie Blackman's series *Noughts and Crosses*, society is built on **⁵racism/the majority**. The wealthy black 'noughts' are in power and the poor white 'crosses' are fighting for **⁶rights/votes**, such as having a vote in elections and being able to access education and **healthcare**.

Ada Palmer's *Terra Ignota* books describe Earth in 2454, when people can travel freely to any part of the world in two hours and they have **⁷got rid of/put up** the idea of separate countries. There is complete **⁸peace/chaos** in the world as there have been no wars for over three hundred years.

In the book and TV series *The Handmaid's Tale*, the United States has been **⁹taken over/lost power** by the Republic of Gilead. Gilead has lots of laws that **¹⁰control/free** what women can do.

b Choose the correct alternatives to complete the text.

3 Work in pairs and answer the questions.
   1 What other **rights** can you think of?
   2 Do you know any other 'isms' like **racism**?
   3 Apart from **healthcare**, what else might taxes **fund**?
   4 How could a government **lose power**?

4 Do you know any of the stories in the text in Exercise 2a? Do you know any other stories about ideal or nightmare societies? What happens in them?

📱 Go to page 164 or your app for more vocabulary and practice.

Listening

5 🔊 9.6 Listen to a podcast about art and society called *Free Comment*. Choose the best summary of Rita de Longhi's arguments.
   1 We need more positive stories so people feel happier.
   2 We need more stories about nightmare societies to warn us of what can go wrong.
   3 We need more stories about ideal societies to help us aim for a more perfect world.
   4 Nightmare stories show us how good our life is now.

6 Listen again and answer the questions.
   1 Which of the stories in Exercise 2a do the speakers mention?
   2 What kind of stories does Rita think we need?
   3 What three things does Rita think we all want?
   4 And what would happen if you wanted to move or relocate?

Grammar

7 a Try to complete the sentences from the podcast with the correct form of the verbs in the box.

~~create~~ fund have have need tax

   1 If you *could create* a new world, what would it look like?
   2 What would you do if you _____ a completely free choice?
   3 Maybe if there were more robots in the workplace, we _____ more free time.
   4 R: How about Thomas More's idea of a basic income for all?
      L: And how _____ we _____ that?
   5 R: I don't know. What if we _____ robots?
   6 Maybe if we just bought less stuff, we _____ so much money?

b 🔊 9.7 Listen and check your answers.

8 a Work in pairs. Are the sentences true (T) or false (F)? Use the sentences in Exercise 7a to help you.

1 Conditional sentences have two clauses: the condition and the result.

2 Where the condition is clear or has already been stated, we can leave it out.

3 The condition clause always comes before the result clause.

4 We use the past simple/continuous in condition clauses to talk about past events.

5 *Would* shows you're certain about a result, *might* shows you're less certain.

b Read the grammar box and check your answers.

Second conditional

Use second conditionals to talk about imaginary or unlikely situations now or in the future.

The sentences have two parts: a condition clause and a result clause. Either can follow the other.

Maybe if we just bought less stuff, we wouldn't need so much money.

What would you do if you had a completely free choice?

- In the condition clause, use *if* + the past simple/continuous or *could*.

  If you created a new world …

  If you could create a new world …

- In the result clause, use *would* to talk about certain results, and *might/may/could* to talk about less certain results.

  If we used robots, we would/might have more free time.

Often, questions are either only about the condition or only about the result.

(If a basic income was introduced) How would we fund that?

What if we taxed robots? (We might be able to fund a basic income.)

9 a 🔊 9.8 Listen and notice the pronunciation of *would*.

1 If they made a few small changes, it'd work.

2 It'd help if they spent more on schools.

3 I wouldn't ask if I didn't have to.

4 There'd be less poverty if we weren't so selfish.

b Listen again and repeat.

10 Complete the sentences with the correct form of the verbs in brackets. You will need to use some negatives. Use *might/could* instead of *would* if you think it is more appropriate.

1 A: In a perfect world, they'd just _____ (close) all town centres to cars.

   A: What if an ambulance or something _____ (have to) get somewhere?

   B: I don't see why that would be a problem.

   A: And what about the traffic outside of town centres? It _____ (cause) chaos.

2 A: They should give waste food to homeless people.

   B: I know. It _____ (make) a real difference and it _____ (cost) them anything.

   A: It'd be better if people _____ (be) homeless at all. If I was President, I'd give everyone a free house.

   B: So how _____ that _____ (work)?

3 A: If I _____ (rule) the world, I would ban all guns.

   B: What if people _____ (want) to go hunting?

   A: I _____ (make) everyone become a vegetarian!

   B: But then some animals _____ (take over) the countryside and cause problems for farmers!

11 Work in pairs and discuss three of the questions.

What would you do if …

1 you could travel through time?

2 you found a million dollars?

3 you ran your school, university or company?

4 you ruled the world?

5 you owned a sports team?

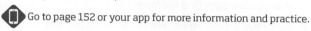 Go to page 152 or your app for more information and practice.

Speaking

PREPARE

12 a 🔊 9.9 You're going to discuss your ideal society. First, listen to three people doing the same. Which of the ideas do they discuss? Do they agree?

- a three-day working week
- everyone has a free home
- equal rights for children and adults
- you can live to 150
- no taxes
- no unemployment
- no wars
- free super-fast transport everywhere

b Read the list in Exercise 12a. Choose four ideas that you think would be good for your ideal society. For each idea, think about:

- any possible consequences (good or bad).
- how you might achieve it.

SPEAK

13 a Work in groups. Discuss your ideas and try to agree on four. How might you achieve them? Use the Useful phrases to help you.

Useful phrases

Wouldn't it be great if (there were no taxes)?

It'd be great/better if (there were no wars).

How would that work?

What if (we had a three-day working week)?

I can see how that might work, but I'd worry that (people wouldn't earn enough money).

b Report back to the class. Which do you think is the most achievable idea?

Develop your reading
page 127

73

9c Great sporting moments

> **Goal:** talk about a sporting event
> **Grammar:** past modals of deduction
> **Vocabulary:** sport

A

Reading

1 a Look at the photos and answer the questions.

  1 Do you recognise any of these people?

  2 How many great sporting moments can you think of?

  3 When and where did they happen?

  b Work in pairs and compare your ideas.

2 a Read the article about Devon Loch. Why is this a memorable sporting moment?

  b Read the article again. What do the dates and numbers refer to?

seven	half a billion	1956	two	fifty	1839
half a million	nine	three	six		

THE MYSTERY OF DEVON LOCH

The Grand National in Liverpool, where horses race 7 km and jump over 30 huge fences, is one of the most famous horse races in the world. It started in 1839 and is now watched by around half a billion people in 140 different countries, with the winner earning over half a million pounds. Over the years, the race has seen terrible accidents, incredible excitement, and slow horses surprising everyone by finishing first. However, the story of Devon Loch and his rider, Dick Francis, remains one of the strangest moments in the race's history.

Devon Loch was a nine-year-old horse owned by the Queen Mother, which competed in the 1956 Grand National. Early in the race, the two biggest favourites to win the race fell, leaving Devon Loch with a great chance. Dick Francis must have thought it was his lucky day, and with only three fences remaining, Devon Loch went into the lead. Victory seemed certain, but disaster was going to strike!

With less than fifty metres to reach the finish line and well ahead of the other horses, Devon Loch suddenly did a little jump and fell to the ground. The other horses raced past him and Devon Loch failed to finish. At first, people in the crowd thought he must have had a heart attack, but he recovered soon afterwards. Francis himself believed the horse might have just reacted badly to a loud noise from the huge crowd of 250,000 people, though no one remembers hearing anything unusual. To this day, the reasons for the jump and fall are unexplained.

Devon Loch went on to race again and lived for another six years. Dick Francis never won the Grand National, which can't have been easy to accept after being so close in 1956. However, he did go on to become a best-selling thriller writer, so there was a kind of happy ending for him.

Grammar

3 a Read the sentences from the article in Exercise 2. What structure follows the modal verbs *must*, *might* and *can't*?

  1 Dick Francis must have thought it was his lucky day.

  2 Francis believed the horse might have just reacted badly to a loud noise.

  3 Dick Francis never won the Grand National, which can't have been easy to accept.

  b Match sentences 1–3 in Exercise 3a with meanings a–c.

  a The writer is almost certain this didn't happen.

  b The writer is almost certain this happened.

  c The writer thinks it's possible this happened.

  c Read the grammar box and check your answers.

Past modals of deduction

To make deductions and guesses about the past, use *must*, *might* and *can't* + *have* + past participle.

Use *must* when you are almost certain something was true (based on the evidence).

*Something **must've scared** him.*

Use *might* when you think it's possible that something was true.

*He **might** just **have been** exhausted.*

Use *can't* when you are almost certain something wasn't true (based on the evidence).

*The Queen Mother **can't have been** very pleased about it!*

You often use these structures to make comments about people or situations. You sometimes respond to these comments as if they were questions:

A: He must've been very disappointed.

(= Do you think he was disappointed?)

B: Yeah, I guess so.

B

C

Vocabulary

8 a Work in pairs. **What sport is each sentence about? Which sentences describe sporting successes and which describe failures?**

1 I really thought I was going to **drown**, but I managed to finish, even though I **came last**.

2 I was **in the lead** for most of the race, but then I **fell over** and ended up coming fifth!

3 I **missed a penalty** in the first half and was then **sent off** in the second half.

4 He was going to **break the record time** for the race, but then the engine exploded.

5 It wasn't **a fair contest**. He was **knocked out** in the second round.

6 I **trained** for years and became **a black belt**.

7 I **represented my country** in my teens, but broke my leg on a **slope** a few years ago.

8 She was **the favourite**, she **got to the quarter-finals**, but then she **got beaten**.

b Work in pairs. **Choose some of the phrases in bold from Exercise 8a and make them true for you.**

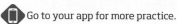 Go to your app for more practice.

Speaking

> **PREPARE**

9 a 🔊 **9.11 You're going to talk about a great sporting moment. First, listen to two people doing the same and answer the questions.**

1 Which sport are they talking about?

2 Was it a positive or negative experience?

b **Prepare to talk about a great sporting moment. Think about:**

• when it happened.

• whether you were watching or taking part.

• what the best/worst part was.

• how you felt.

> **SPEAK**

10 a Work in pairs. **Take turns talking. Make deductions about what your partner tells you. Use the Useful phrases to help you.**

> **Useful phrases**
> That must've been amazing/awful.
> You must've felt amazing/awful.
> It might've been worse!
> That can't have been much fun.
> That can't have been easy.

b **Report back to the class. Which are the greatest sporting moments of all time?**

---

4 a 🔊 **9.10 Listen and notice the weak form of** *have*.

1 You must've been really pleased.

2 That must've hurt.

3 Things might've been so different!

4 They can't have been very happy about it.

b **Listen again and repeat.**

5 **Rewrite the deductions underlined using** *must have*, *can't have* **or** *might have*.

1 A: I bet you were annoyed. *You must've been*
  B: Honestly! I was so angry!

2 A: I'm sure it wasn't easy doing that kind of training.
  B: No, I don't suppose it was.

3 A: I'm not sure, but I think it happened when I was at the gym last week.
  B: So quite recently then?

4 A: I suppose it's possible he was 40 when he played in that final, but I'm sure he wasn't older than that.
  B: Let's look online and find out.

5 A: I bet it was very different there when you were a kid.
  B: Yeah, absolutely!

6 A: I'm sure she wasn't very happy about that.
  B: She was actually OK about it.

7 A: I'm sure you enjoyed that a lot.
  B: Yeah, I did, but it was a lot of work!

6 **Work in pairs. Choose four of the deductions from Exercise 5. Write a sentence to come before the deduction to explain the situation. Then write a different response to come after the deduction.**

  B: I spent £100 on tickets but the game was cancelled.
  A: Oh no! You must've been annoyed!
  B: I was, but I complained and got my money back.

7 **Work in groups. Look at the photos on page 174. What do you think happened? How do you think each person felt? Use** *must/might/can't have*.

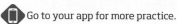 Go to page 152 or your app for more information and practice.

> Develop
> your
> writing
> page 129

9D English in action

> **Goal:** interrupt politely

1 Look at the picture opposite and discuss the questions.

  1 Have you ever felt like the woman on the left? When? What happened?

  2 In what situations do you find it easy/difficult to interrupt?

2 Work in pairs and discuss the situations 1–4. Would you interrupt? If not, why not? What would you say?

  1 You're in a meeting with colleagues and clients. A more senior manager is giving a presentation and you notice a couple of mistakes on one of the PowerPoint slides, including a factual mistake.

  2 You're on a train and a couple of people are loudly discussing politics. You can see one or two other passengers are uncomfortable. You strongly disagree with what they are saying.

  3 You're on a coffee break at work and you hear your name mentioned by other people in your team who are sitting at another table.

  4 You've met up with an old friend. Your friend is funny, but tends to talk a lot about themselves and doesn't ask much about you. They start to tell you a story they have told you before.

3 🔊 **9.12 Listen to three conversations. In which conversation is someone:**

  a giving a lecture?

  b planning a forthcoming event?

  c having a serious discussion?

4 Listen again. Complete the sentences with two words.

  1 a Yeah, sorry, but before you move on, could I just _____ here, if I may?

    b Yes, OK. That's a _____ , I guess. Anyway ...

  2 a I didn't quite follow that last part. Would _____ just repeating it?

    b Got it. Thank you. Sorry about that. Please _____ .

    c No worries. So anyway, to _____ to what I was saying ...

  3 Hi, Abbs. I'm really sorry _____ you, but ...

5 Read the Useful phrases box and check your answers.

Useful phrases

Checking it's OK to interrupt

Can I just say/add/ask something there?

Could I just say something here/stop you there for a moment (if I may)?

Do you mind if I come in here?

I'm really sorry to interrupt/bother you, but ...

Explaining why you're interrupting

Sorry, but could you just go over that again?

I didn't quite follow that last part. Would you mind just repeating it/that?

Repeating the apology

Anyway, sorry to interrupt. You were saying?

Sorry about that. Please go on.

Continuing

No worries. So anyway, to get back to what I was saying.

Yes, so as I was saying ...

Thanks for pointing that out/letting me know.

That's a fair point (I guess). Anyway, ...

6 a Complete the conversation with one word in each space.

  A: Sorry, could I just _____ you there for a _____ ?

  B: Yeah, sure. What's up?

  A: Would you _____ repeating that?

  B: Of course. I said that I think forcing people to vote would improve the economy.

  A: OK, thanks.

  B: No worries. So as I was _____ , the more voters, the better it would be for the country.

b 🔊 **9.13 Listen and check your answers. Notice the intonation. Practise reading out the conversation.**

7 a Work in groups. Choose three topics from this unit to discuss, e.g. a sporting success or failure, a story you have read/seen about an ideal world or what things would improve your life or where you live.

b Work on your own and think about what you will say about each topic. Make notes.

c Discuss the topics. Use the Useful phrases to interrupt politely.

Go online for the Roadmap video.

Check and reflect

1 a Complete the sentences with the best word. The first letter is given.

1 We used to have a strong c_____ . Everyone supported each other, but it's all changed.

2 There's a lot of crime and v_____ . I don't feel safe on the streets.

3 All the pressure on young people c_____ anxiety and depression.

4 Sadly, high unemployment is just a f_____ of life here.

5 Women still face real d_____ at work. Most top jobs still go to men.

6 A lot of people around the world have basically lost f_____ in their governments.

b Work in groups. Choose four sentences from Exercise 1a. Discuss the possible cause of each situation and what can be done to improve things.

2 Complete the sentences with the correct form of the verbs in brackets.

1 This weather's awful. I wish it _____ raining! (stop)

2 I wish I _____ you, but I'm much too busy at the moment, I'm afraid. (help)

3 I wish I _____ a bit more support from my boss and the people at work. (get)

4 I wish I _____ a bit more free time. I feel like I'm working all the time. (have)

5 I really wish you _____ that! It's really annoying. (not / do)

6 I wish I _____ in time to when I was 12 or 13. I'd certainly do things differently. (go back)

3 a Complete the sentences with the nouns in the box.

chaos	healthcare	poverty	state	tax	wealth

1 There's still too much _____ and there are still too many people becoming homeless.

2 The traffic in the capital is awful. It's total _____ on the roads.

3 Too much of the country's _____ is in the hands of a small number of people.

4 I think everyone should have free access to basic services like _____ .

5 If we all just paid a bit more _____ , we'd have more money for schools and hospitals.

6 The TV companies are still run by the _____ , not by private companies.

b Work in pairs. Give your country a mark from 1–10 (where 1 = awful) for each of the areas in the box. Explain your answers.

access to healthcare access to education
the number of people who pay tax
the quality of state-run companies
amount of traffic in the capital   levels of poverty

4 Find the four sentences with a mistake and correct them.

1 How would we pay for everything if access to healthcare was free?

2 If I would have a bigger place, you could stay with me.

3 If you worked harder, you'll earn more money.

4 I might feel differently if I wasn't working right now.

5 If they'd build more roads, it'd make life better.

6 Things improved if more companies were state run.

5 a Complete the sentences with *must, might* or *can't* and the correct form of the verbs in brackets.

1 They don't know exactly why Devon Loch fell, but he _____ a loud noise that scared him (hear).

2 You _____ hard to do that marathon. I know I could never do it! (train)

3 She _____ my message. She'd be here otherwise. (get)

4 You went to the final? Wow! That _____ exciting. (be)

5 She didn't play well. I guess she _____ an injury or something. (have)

6 He started young. He _____ more than 16 when he played his first game. (be)

b Think of two surprising or unusual things you have seen. Work in pairs. Take turns explaining what you saw and speculate about what happened. Use *must've, might've* and *can't have.*

6 Match verbs 1–6 with endings a–f.

1 train	a a penalty
2 come	b your country
3 become	c for years
4 break	d second
5 represent	e the world record
6 miss	f a black belt

Reflect

How confident do you feel about the statements below? Write 1–5 (1 = not very confident, 5 = very confident).

- I can discuss what makes a good quality of life.
- I can share ideas and make suggestions about ideal societies.
- I can describe amazing sporting moments.
- I can politely interrupt.

Want more practice?
Go to your Workbook or app.

10A A huge influence

> **Goal:** talk about an influential person
> **Grammar:** third conditional
> **Vocabulary:** influential people

A

B

Vocabulary

1 **Look at the photos and discuss the questions.**

1 How many of these people do you know?

2 What do you know about them?

2 **Work in pairs. Check you understand the words in bold. Then complete the sentences with the words in the box.**

> activist architect athlete explorer lawyer
> military leader painter philosopher poet
> trade union leader

1 She was a famous _____ . She **designed** lots of amazing buildings.

2 He was a very famous _____ . His best **works** are in the National Gallery.

3 He was a famous _____ , who led our army to **victory** in several important battles.

4 She was a famous _____ , who fought hard for **women's rights**.

5 He was a famous _____ , who fought all his life for **the rights of workers**.

6 She was a famous _____ . She won three **gold medals** at the Olympics.

7 She was a famous _____ . She's still very popular and very **widely read**.

8 She is a famous _____ . She was the first woman to **sail** round the world on her own.

9 He was a famous _____ , who wrote about power, freedom and human rights.

10 He was a famous _____ , who chose to **defend** poor people for free!

3 **Work in pairs. Use words from Exercise 2 to talk about the people in the photos.**

> *Martin Luther King was a famous activist, who fought for the rights of black people.*

 Go to page 165 or your app for more vocabulary and practice.

Reading

4 a **Work in pairs. Student A: Turn to page 172. Student B: Turn to page 173.**

b **Take turns telling your partner about your famous person. Ask questions to find out more details.**

> *A: Was Simón Bolívar married?*
> *B: Are there still problems in the southern states of the US today?*

Grammar

5 a **Read the sentences from the articles in Exercise 4a and answer the questions.**

1 None of his achievements would've been possible if the French army hadn't entered Spain in 1808.

a Did the French army enter Spain?

b Did this make independence for Venezuela possible?

2 If Rosa Parks had done as she was told, modern American history might have been very different.

a Did Rosa Parks do as she was told?

b Did American history definitely change because of this?

3 If she'd been paying attention, she would never have got on that bus!

a Did she get on the bus?

b Was she paying attention at the time?

b **Read the grammar box and check your answers.**

Third conditional

Use the third conditional to talk about imaginary or unlikely situations in the past.

The sentence has two parts: a condition clause and a result clause.

- In the condition clause, you often use *if* + past perfect simple or continuous.
- In the result clause, use *would* (*not*) + *have* + past participle to talk about certain results and *might* (*not*)/*may* (*not*)/*could* + *have* + past participle for less certain results.

The condition clause can come before or after the result clause, or it can be left out if you feel the condition is clear from the context.

If I'd known, I would've done something about it.

It would never have happened if it hadn't been for you, so thank you!

It might not have happened if I'd been paying more attention.

6 a 🔊 **10.1 Listen and notice the pronunciation of the underlined phrases.**

1 If I'd stayed there, things might've been very different.
2 I wouldn't have gone if she hadn't persuaded me to.
3 It would never have happened if you'd been listening!
4 If I hadn't been staying there, we'd never have met.

b Listen again and repeat.

7 Complete the sentences with the correct forms of the verbs in brackets.

1 Steve Jobs left Apple in 1985 and if he _____ (not return) in 1997, he might _____ (never invent) the iPhone.
2 If Nelson Mandela _____ (not be) released from prison in 1990, the situation in South Africa might _____ (become) violent.
3 Marie Curie would _____ (not make) her discoveries if she _____ (be) scared of being wrong.
4 If Leonardo da Vinci _____ (not have) rich friends who paid for his work, he could easily _____ (be) just another struggling artist!
5 I'm lucky! If I _____ (not work) late that day, I would _____ (be) on the train that crashed!
6 If it _____ (not be) for my English teacher, I would probably _____ (leave) school at 16.
7 I would _____ (never go) to university if my maths teacher _____ (not encourage) me to.
8 If she _____ (not work) in the shop the day that I went in, we might _____ (never meet) and the next part of our lives would _____ (be) very different!

8 Work in pairs. Make sentences about some of the people in the photos in this lesson. Use third conditionals.

📱 Go to page 154 or your app for more information and practice.

Speaking

PREPARE

9 a 🔊 **10.2 You're going to talk about an influential person. First, listen to someone doing the same. Who are they talking about? Why are they important to the speaker?**

b Think of a person who has had a big influence on the world, on your country or on you personally. Think about:
• when they lived.
• why they were important and how they changed things.

SPEAK

10 a Work in groups. Take turns talking about your influential person. Use at least one third conditional. Then ask and answer questions about each person. Use the useful phrases to help you.

Useful phrases

Asking questions
I wanted to know a bit more about (what she did).
I was wondering why (she was so important to you).
Could you just say a bit more about (her influence on you)?

Responding
That's a good question!   I wish I knew!
Can I get back to you on that one?

b Report back to the class. Who is the most influential person of our time?

Develop your listening
page 131

79

10B Interviews

> **Goal:** talk about successes and failures
> **Grammar:** *should have*
> **Vocabulary:** successes and failures

Reading

1 **Look at the photos and answer the questions.**

1 When was the last time you had an interview? What was it for?
2 How can you prepare for an interview?
3 What things can go wrong in an interview?
4 Do you think interviews are a good way to see if someone is the right person for a job?

2 a You're going to read an article about competency-based interviews. Have you heard about them? What do you know about them?

b Read the article again and answer the questions.

1 How are competency-based interviews different from other job interviews?
2 Why is this kind of interview good?
3 What steps should you follow in a competency-based interview when giving an example of an event?

A different kind of interview

Competency-based job interviews are becoming more and more common. Rather than asking people simply to list their achievements and previous jobs, interviewees are asked about events, for example:

1 Describe a time you successfully used your communication skills.

2 Tell us about when someone challenged a decision you had made and how you managed the situation.

3 Describe a failure you had at work or in education.

Using this technique, employers can match your answers to specific skills (or *competences*) such as how well you communicate, and find out more about your performance in a job.

When it comes to answering these questions, you should start by explaining the **situation** you were in and the **task** you had to complete. You should then talk about what **action** you took and what the **results** were.

It is important to be positive even when describing a failure. Do this by showing you understand why you failed and then giving an example of how the lesson you learnt has improved your performance. Follow these steps to be sure of success in your next job interview!

Vocabulary

3 a Complete the answers to interview questions. Use the correct form of the words in the boxes.

| attract   gain   evidence   persuade   introduce |

a In my last company, as the HR manager I **1**_____ a new working day – having a shorter lunch break and finishing the day earlier. At first, it **2**_____ **opposition**, so I had a meeting to explain how it would be better and **presented** **3**_____ from other companies. I then agreed to **delay** its introduction and asked people to **volunteer** to try it. The volunteers found several benefits and then they explained to colleagues what they'd **4**_____ from the change. In the end, I managed to **5**_____ almost everyone and only had to **force** the change on one or two people.

| achieve   disagreement   extend   force   grade |

b When I was at university, we were doing a group project and two of the team weren't getting on. I was worried we would miss our **deadline** and we wouldn't **6**_____ the mark we all wanted. I **7**_____ them to sit down and sort out their **8**_____ , which they did. I also talked to our tutor to explain the situation and I managed to get the deadline **9**_____ . In the end, we got a B+ **10**_____ for the project, which was good.

| manage   deadline   standard   responsible   rush |

c I worked for a printing company before, where I was **11**_____ for sales. One time, I agreed to a job, but I quickly realised it was too much work and I'd set the price far too low. In order to meet the **12**_____ , we had to pay people to work weekends. We **13**_____ to do the work, but it was still a **14**_____ , and the client said they expected **a higher** **15**_____ . So, we lost money and a future customer!

b Match answers a–c with questions 1–3 in the article in Exercise 2.

4 **Work in groups and answer the questions.**

1 Have you ever needed to **delay** something? Why?
2 Do you ever have **deadlines**? What for?
3 Do you ever have **disagreements**? Who with?
4 Have you ever been **forced** to do something? What?
5 Have you ever **volunteered** to do something? What did you **gain** from it?
6 Do you think you have **high standards**? Give examples.
7 When was the last time you did something **in a rush**?

Go to page 165 or your app for more vocabulary and practice.

Listening

5 🔊 **10.6 Listen to four more answers to job interview questions. Three speakers are answering the same question from the article in Exercise 2. Which question?**

6 **Listen again and answer the questions. Who …**

1 wanted to sell more than they did?
2 improved the company's yearly sales?
3 annoyed a client?
4 didn't do the work on time?
5 explained how their performance improved?

7 **Work in groups and discuss the questions.**

1 Which speaker(s) followed the model for answering competency-based questions described in the article?
2 Which speaker(s) talked about a positive outcome to their experience?
3 How do you think the speakers could have improved their answers?

Grammar

8 a 🔊 **10.7 Listen and complete the sentences from the interviews in Exercise 5.**

1 I _____ been more careful to begin with and shouldn't have been in such a rush.
2 I _____ immediately denied making the mistake.
3 I _____ number one.
4 Secondly, I _____ to finish the project at least a day before I needed to hand it in.
5 I should've at least spoken to the tutor to see if I could hand it in a little later and, if that wasn't possible, I _____ handed in the unfinished work.

b **Read the sentences in Exercise 8a. Then read the grammar box and choose the correct alternatives.**

should have

Use *should(n't)* + *have* + past participle to talk about regrets about ¹*past/present* events and actions. You can also use it to criticise other people (or yourself).

I should've started work on the project earlier.
You shouldn't have told her about it.

You use it to imagine ²*better/worse* alternatives than what actually happened.

I shouldn't have forced them to do it. I should've solved the problem another way.

When you use adverbs like *probably* and *just*, you usually put them ³*after/before* the word *have*.

*I should **probably** have told them earlier.*

However, you can also put them in a different position depending on what you want to emphasise.

I probably should have told them earlier.

9 a **Complete the sentences with the words in brackets and *should* or *shouldn't have*.**

1 We _____ this earlier. We're not going to meet the deadline. (start)
2 He _____ better with all the time he had. (do)
3 You _____ to do that. It's not part of your job. (agree)
4 I _____ that there would be problems. (know)
5 I _____ so worried about what people thought. (be)
6 I'm sorry. I _____ my manager sooner. (probably / ask)
7 We _____ their first offer, but we really needed to sell it quickly. (really / accept)
8 We _____ to get a discount. (at least / try)

b 🔊 **10.8 Listen and check your answers. Notice the pronunciation of *should have* and *shouldn't have*.**

c **Listen and repeat.**

10 **Work in pairs. Describe three things you *should've* or *shouldn't have* done in the last month, the last year or your whole life.**

I should've worn a coat today. It rained and I got really wet.

📱 Go to page 154 or your app for more information and practice.

Speaking

PREPARE

11 **Read the questions and plan your answers. Remember to explain the situation and the task, the action you took and the result.**

1 Describe a failure you had and what you learnt from it.
2 Describe a big change you experienced and how you coped with it.
3 Describe a time you made a positive contribution to a team.

SPEAK

12 a **Work in pairs. Take turns asking and answering the questions. Use the Useful phrases to help you and try to use *should have* and *shouldn't have*.**

Useful phrases

Looking back on it now, I can see that I (shouldn't have agreed to the deadline).
It was my own fault.
I learnt a lot from the experience. Firstly, (I should've thought of a better solution).
It was bad at the time, but I'm glad it happened.
It taught me that I (shouldn't do things in a rush).

b **Which do you think were the best answers? Why?**

Develop your reading
page 132

10C ⟩ Describing things

> **Goal:** describe possessions
> **Grammar:** adjective word order
> **Vocabulary:** describing things

Vocabulary

1 **Look at the photos and discuss the questions.**

1 Which of these things do you own?

2 Are you happy with them? Why?/Why not?

3 Do you ever read reviews before you buy things? Why?/Why not?

2 a **Complete the reviews with the pairs of words in the box.**

> automatically/last   leather/bargain
> reasonable/battery   tough/feature   designed/value
> decent/set up   room/stylish   ideal/complicated

1 Beautifully _____ and very easy to use. Heats up frozen food in super-fast time – and at only £300, it's excellent _____ for money.

2 It looks and feels OK, and it comes at a very _____ price, but the _____ life is terrible. It usually only lasts a couple of hours!

3 Surprisingly light, but _____ enough to take on even the longest journeys. My favourite _____ is the zipper, which never lets you down no matter how many clothes you pack!

4 I mainly ride out in the countryside and the tyres are _____ for that. However, when the bike arrived, I had to put it together myself, which took longer than I expected as the instructions were quite _____ .

5 Comes in black, grey or yellow _____ and looks great, but not quite as comfortable as I'd hoped. Still, it fits perfectly in my living room and for the price, it's a real _____ . Recommended!

6 Doesn't have quite as much _____ as you'd expect for a family vehicle, but the new design is very _____ and it's incredibly smooth to drive.

7 I was a bit worried as the main speakers are underneath, but the sound quality is actually pretty _____ . Had a few problems when I tried to _____ the system, but it was worth the effort!

8 Looks good, and turns on _____ if you go near it, which is great, but it could be brighter. The bulb doesn't _____ that long, either. Otherwise, no complaints.

b **Match reviews 1–8 in Exercise 2a with photos A–H. How many marks out of five do you think each reviewer gave? Why?**

Go to page 165 or your app for more vocabulary and practice.

A

B

C

D

E

Listening

3 🔊 10.9 **Listen to three conversations. In which conversation 1–3 does someone …**

a warn a friend about something? What?

b recommend something? What?

c worry? Why?

4 **Listen again. Are the sentences true (T) or false (F)?**

1 a Jim's old car has always worked very well.

  b He has been thinking of buying an electric car.

  c There are financial advantages to going electric.

2 a The ring used to belong to Tanya's grandmother.

  b She dropped it when she took it out of her bag.

  c It's a plain gold ring.

3 a James needs to get a new microwave.

  b He was thinking of getting a Tappan.

  c The Tappan microwave cooks things quite quickly.

Grammar

5 a Work in pairs. Underline the adjectives in sentences 1–3, then discuss questions a–c.

1 I've been driving this stylish little Japanese car for ages.
2 It's a beautiful small gold ring with a stone in the front.
3 It just sits there in the middle of the kitchen – this useless ancient white piece of junk.

a Which usually come first: adjectives describing facts or adjectives giving opinions?
b In spoken English, what's the maximum number of adjectives we usually use together?
c There are two fact adjectives in each of sentences 1–3. Which questions do they answer? In which order?

> What colour is it?   How big is it?   What's it made of?
> How old is it?   Where's it from?

b Read the grammar box and check your answers.

Adjective word order

Sometimes two or more adjectives are used together. As a general rule, opinion adjectives (adjectives which tell you what the speaker thinks of something) come before fact adjectives (adjectives that describe age, size, colour, etc.)

If you use two or more fact adjectives, you usually put them in this order (though you don't usually have more than three):

how big? how old? what colour? where from? what's it made of? + noun

It's a small old red Italian leather handbag.
I've got a big old black and white Persian cat.

Notice how to describe something with two colours:
a black and white cat; a green and yellow cotton T-shirt

Remember that compound nouns can be formed by putting two nouns together:
table lamp, sports car, walking boots

Always keep the two nouns together when you add a description:
a lovely wooden table lamp; a new red sports car; good strong walking boots

6 a 🔊 10.10 Listen and notice the way some adjectives are stressed.

1 He was wearing this ugly green and purple coat!
2 I lost my lovely old black leather boots.
3 She was driving this amazing old Italian sports car.
4 We found this beautiful little Danish table lamp.

b Listen again and repeat.

7 Put the adjectives in brackets in the best position.

1 a fur coat (warm / black)
2 walking boots (leather / brown)
3 a new restaurant (Japanese / cheap)
4 a(n) old movie (funny / French)
5 a new café (little / lovely)
6 a(n) ancient pot (white / Italian)
7 a(n) old necklace (silver / Mexican)
8 a Swedish table (old / wooden / small)
9 a chair (red / leather / horrible)
10 a spider (black / big / scary)

8 Work in pairs. Look at the photos in the coursebook and at objects in the classroom. Choose ten things and think of two or more adjectives to describe each one. Put the adjectives in the best order.

📱 Go to page 154 or your app for more information and practice.

Speaking

PREPARE

9 a 🔊 10.11 You're going to describe three objects. First, listen to someone describing an object and answer the questions.

1 Which category a–g are they talking about?
a a product you'd really recommend
b a product you reviewed because it was so bad
c the most important thing you have ever lost
d something that's very precious to you
e the first object you'd save in a fire
f an object that you've always wanted
g the worst present you've ever received

2 Which adjectives do they use to describe the object?

b Now choose three objects from categories a–g to talk about. Make notes about each object. Think about:
• how to describe it.
• why you like/don't like it.
• any other important details.

SPEAK

10 a Work in pairs. Take turns describing your objects. Ask questions. Use the Useful phrases to help you.

Useful phrases

How long have you had it?
Where did you get it from?
What's it like?
What do you like most about it?
How much did it cost you?

b Report back to the class. Which objects are the most interesting?

Develop your writing
page 134

1 Work in pairs and discuss the questions.

1 When was the last time someone offered to do something for you? What was it? Did you accept? Why?/Why not?

2 When was the last time you offered to do something for someone? What happened?

2 🔊 10.12 Listen to four conversations. Match conversations 1–4 with situations a–d.

a a host and a guest

b two complete strangers

c a teacher and a student

d two business people

3 a Listen again and complete the sentences with two or three words.

1 Could you give me a bit longer? _____ try and do it myself, if that's OK.

2 B: Hi. Thanks.
A: _____ you a hand with your suitcase?
B: It's OK. I can manage.
A: If you're sure. _____ take your coat?

3 A: I've made some soup if you'd like some.
B: Oh. _____ kind, but I had something to eat on the plane.

4 Well, if you're hungry later, _____ help yourself from the fridge.

5 A: Absolutely.
B: _____ a list of the action points.

6 Would you _____ give you a lift?

7 Are you sure? _____ happy to take you.

8 A: No thanks. I don't drink coffee.
B: _____ get you a fruit juice.

b Read the Useful phrases box and check your answers.

Useful phrases

Offering

Would you like me to (give you a lift)?
Do you want me to (help you with that)?
Can I give you a hand with (your suitcase)?
Need any help?
Shall I (take your coat)?
I'd be happy to (take you), if you like.
You're welcome to …
Feel free to (help yourself from the fridge).
Let me (get you a fruit juice).
I'll (make a list of the action points).
Are you sure you don't want me to (give you a clue)?

Accepting

Please.   That'd be lovely/great.
Would you mind?

Declining

Don't worry. I'm OK.   I'm fine. Thanks.
It's OK. I can manage. Thanks.
It's OK. There's no need – really.
That's very kind, but (I had something to eat on the plane).
Thanks for the offer, but I'm fine.
I'd rather (try and do it myself).

4 a 🔊 10.13 Listen to ten phrases from the Useful phrases box. Tick the ones you hear.

b Listen again and repeat.

5 a Work in pairs. Take turns reading out one of sentences 1–6. Your partner should make an offer. Respond and continue the conversation.

1 Oh, I haven't got my glasses!
A: Oh, I haven't got my glasses!
B: Would you like me to read it for you?

2 Oh no! I'm late.

3 I'm starving.

4 I don't feel that well.

5 This is a nightmare.

6 The car won't start.

b Take turns making offers 1–4. Your partner should decline the offer with a reason.

1 Would you like some more?

2 Let me do that for you.

3 Feel free to use my computer if you need to.

4 You're welcome to stay the night here, if you like.

6 a Work in pairs. Turn to page 173.

b Prepare your roleplays. Think about what you're going to say. Roleplay the situations.

Go online for the Roadmap video.

Check and reflect

1 a Match people 1–8 with descriptions a–h.

1 athlete
2 explorer
3 architect
4 military leader
5 activist
6 poet
7 trade union leader
8 lawyer

a fought hard to protect the environment
b first person to reach the North Pole
c won a silver medal
d designed one of my favourite buildings
e led the army to a famous victory
f defended the boss of a criminal gang in court
g is still widely read today
h fought hard to get the best deal for workers

b Work in pairs. Think of at least one more thing that the people in Exercise 1a often do. Give examples if you can.

2 a Complete the second sentence so that it means the same as the first.

1 His dad was a friend of the boss. Maybe that's why he got the job!
   He might _____ the job if his dad _____ friends with the boss.

2 I'm lucky I went to university because I almost left school at 16. I'm glad I didn't!
   If I _____ school at 16, I may _____ to university.

3 I only got the opportunity because I was working in Fez at the time.
   If I _____ in Fez at that time, I _____ the opportunity.

4 I didn't study very hard at school. Not speaking good English made it harder to travel.
   I could _____ more if I _____ harder at school.

5 I only met Marco because I was studying abroad that year.
   I _____ Marco if I _____ abroad that year.

b Think of three big moments in your life. Work in groups. Use third conditionals to explain to the group why they were important to you.

3 a Match verbs 1–8 with endings a–h.

1 attract
2 miss
3 force
4 persuade
5 sort out
6 achieve
7 present
8 volunteer

a people you're right
b a change on people
c your disagreements
d the grade you want
e to try the new system
f a lot of opposition
g a deadline
h evidence

b Work in pairs. Who or what might do the things in Exercise 3a? Explain your ideas.

4 Complete the sentences with *should have* or *shouldn't have* and the correct form of the verbs in the box.

be	complain	eat	listen	say	take	train

1 I didn't finish the race. I just wasn't ready for it. I _____ harder, I guess.
2 I _____ anything about it. She got really angry when I did!
3 I feel sick. I _____ that last piece of cake.
4 I can see now that I _____ never _____ the job. What was I thinking?
5 I don't know why I let him talk to me like that. I _____ to the manager about it.
6 It's my own fault. I _____ so stupid. I _____ to what everyone was telling me.

5 Complete the sentences with the best word. The first letter is given.

1 It's excellent v_____ for money.
2 I can't believe how cheap it is. It's a real b_____ .
3 It's beautifully d_____ and very easy to use.
4 The battery life is terrible. It only l_____ two hours.
5 The instructions that come with it are quite c_____ .
6 I love it. It's i_____ for long journeys.

6 Find the four sentences with a mistake and correct them.

1 He's got a job with an amazing big new French company.
2 She lives in a Greek little lovely village.
3 I bought a red old coat in the market.
4 Use that small blue plastic box to keep your pens in.
5 She was wearing a lovely black white dress.
6 For his birthday, I got him some leather big black walking boots.

Reflect

How confident do you feel about the statements below? Write 1–5 (1 = not very confident, 5 = very confident).

- I can explain why someone had a big impact.
- I can talk about successes and failures.
- I can describe objects, possessions and products in detail.
- I can offer, decline and accept with a range of expressions.

Want more practice?
Go to your Workbook or app.

1A Develop your writing

> **Goal:** write emails arranging a party

> **Focus:** making requests in emails

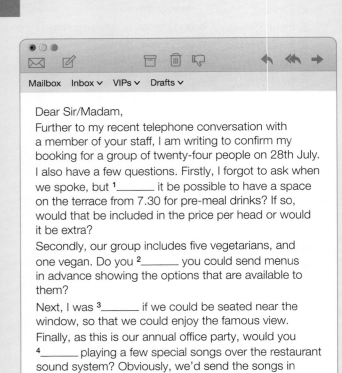

Dear Sir/Madam,

Further to my recent telephone conversation with a member of your staff, I am writing to confirm my booking for a group of twenty-four people on 28th July.

I also have a few questions. Firstly, I forgot to ask when we spoke, but **1**_____ it be possible to have a space on the terrace from 7.30 for pre-meal drinks? If so, would that be included in the price per head or would it be extra?

Secondly, our group includes five vegetarians, and one vegan. Do you **2**_____ you could send menus in advance showing the options that are available to them?

Next, I was **3**_____ if we could be seated near the window, so that we could enjoy the famous view.

Finally, as this is our annual office party, would you **4**_____ playing a few special songs over the restaurant sound system? Obviously, we'd send the songs in advance, and this would ideally happen near the end of the meal.

If these requests are possible, I would be most **5**_____ if you could let me know when you email confirmation of our booking.

I look forward to hearing from you soon.

Best regards,

Ahmed Rafiq

Hi everyone

Hope this finds you well.

Not long now till our office dinner and a chance to say thank you to everyone for all their hard work throughout the year.

Just a very quick email to say I've booked a table for everyone at Strofi on 28th July. The booking's for 8.15, so if any of you can no longer make it for whatever reason, then **6**_____ email me back asap and **7**_____ me know.

Oh, before I forget, I've also asked if the restaurant can play some of our music at the end of the evening. If you've got any special requests, **8**_____ you send them over to me this week so I can get a final list to the restaurant ahead of time. Nothing too crazy, obviously!

Cheers,

Ahmed

1 Work in pairs and discuss the questions.

  1 How often do you write emails in your own language?

  2 Do you write more personal or work-related emails?

  3 Who do you write to most often? What about?

  4 When was the last time you wrote an email in English? Who to? Why?

2 Work in pairs. Think of two different requests you might make in an email to:

  1 your boss

  2 a friend

  3 a hotel

  4 a language school

  5 a restaurant

3 Read the two emails quickly. Answer the questions.

  1 Who are the emails to?

  2 How well does Ahmed know the person/people he's writing to?

  3 What requests does he make?

4 Complete the emails with the words in the box.

> could   grateful   let   mind   please   think
> wondering   would

5 Work in pairs. What would you write in the subject line for each email?

6 a Read the emails again. Underline the phrases used to make requests.

b Work in pairs and compare your answers. Is each phrase more formal or informal? What features of the phrases help you decide? Then read the Focus box and check your ideas.

Making requests in emails

When you ask for things – or ask people to do things for you – in more formal emails, you tend to use longer phrases.

Would it be possible to stay an extra night?

I would be (most) grateful if you could email me the details.

Do you think you could (possibly) send me written confirmation of my booking?

I was wondering if we could have our own private room.

Would you mind moving us to a bigger table?

In more informal emails, you can just use *could* or *can*.

Could/can you (please) let me know if you can make it?

You can also use imperatives. Make imperatives sound softer by adding *please*.

(Please) call me as soon as you hear anything.

After requests, you often explain why you were asking.

If you've got any special requests, could you send them over to me this week **so I can get a final list to the restaurant ahead of time**.

---

7 Rewrite the requests using the words in brackets.

1 I was wondering if you could check there are no nuts in any of the dishes. (mind)

2 Please put some red roses on the table before we arrive. (could / please)

3 I would be most grateful if you could give us a room facing away from the road. (possibly)

4 Could you cook a special dish if we send the recipe in advance? (possible)

5 I was wondering if you could check that everyone knows about the meeting tomorrow. (can)

6 Would you mind providing a high chair for our two-year-old son? (grateful)

7 Can you please write 'Happy Birthday' on the cake before bringing it out? (think)

8 Do you think we could possibly have a room at the back of the restaurant? (wondering)

8 Match explanations a–h with requests 1–8 in Exercise 7.

a It's our son's sixteenth, and it would be a wonderful surprise for him.

b He's still too small for adult seating, but too independent to sit on my knee.

c One member of our group is highly allergic to them, so this is very important.

d Last time we stayed with you, we were unable to sleep because of the traffic.

e They are my wife's favourite flowers, and it would add to the romantic atmosphere.

f We would like to be able to have a private discussion.

g I realise this is an unusual request, but it's a family favourite our grandmother used to make.

h I am slightly worried that some people did not receive the initial email about it.

9 a Look at your answers to Exercise 2. Write three more requests. Use different language.

b Work in pairs and compare your answers. Write an explanation for each request.

10 Read the emails again and complete the table.

	More formal	More informal
Phrase used for greeting		
Phrase used to explain why writing		
Is small talk included? If so, what?		
Are contractions (*I'm, you're,* etc.) used?		
Phrase used to end the email		

Prepare

11 a You're organising a surprise party and need to write two emails to make requests – one to the venue for the party, the other to the guests. Decide ...
- who the party is for.
- where it is going to be.
- what you would like to happen.
- what requests you will make of the venue/the guests.

b Work in pairs and compare your ideas.

Write

12 Write your emails. Use the Focus box and Exercise 10 to help you.

> **Goal:** understand a biography
> **Focus:** noticing collocations

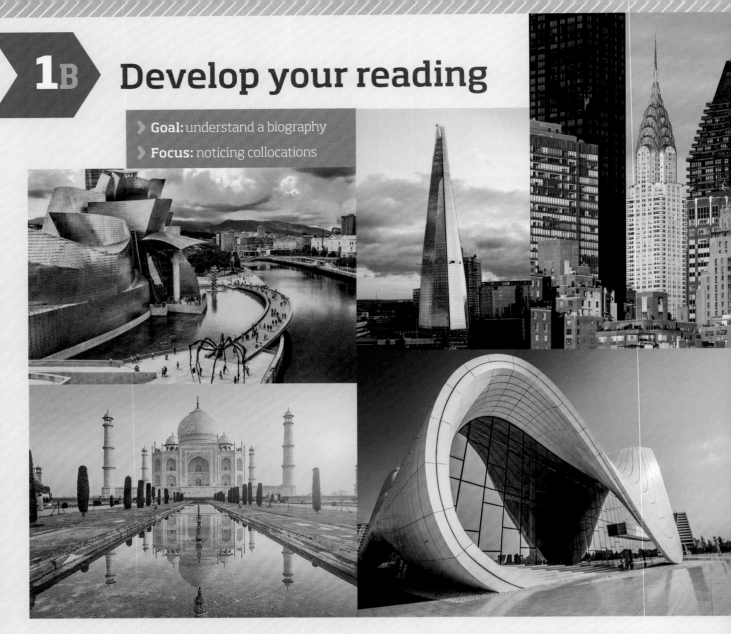

1 **Work in pairs and discuss the questions.**

  1 What are your favourite buildings in your town/city? In your country? In the world?

  2 Are there any buildings you really don't like? Why not?

  3 Do you know any famous architects (people who design buildings)? Do you like their work?

  4 Which of the buildings in the photos do you like most/least?

2 **Read the biography of the architect who designed one of the buildings in the photos. Are the sentences true (T) or false (F)?**

  1 She became famous while at university.

  2 Very few new buildings were built in Baghdad in the 1950s.

  3 She was mostly educated outside of her home country.

  4 Her early designs were impossible to build.

  5 For a long time, people saw her designs as art, not as designs for real buildings.

  6 She became famous for her use of straight lines.

  7 Some of her designs were built outside Europe.

  8 Some of her designs will be completed after her death.

3 **Read the Focus box. Then work in pairs and discuss the strategies you already use.**

Noticing collocations

When a word is often used with another word, it forms a collocation. The most common kinds of collocations are:
verb + noun: *rent a house, design a building*
adjective + noun: *a tall building*
One of the best ways to get better at reading is to learn more collocations. If you learn words which go together, it will help you read more quickly (and use words correctly, too). Here are some things you can do:

• When you read something, underline the adjective + noun and verb + noun collocations you notice (even if they contain words you already know).

• Keep a list of common nouns and add new verb/adjective collocations when you meet them.

• Make flashcards (on paper or online) with nouns on one side and verbs/adjectives on the other.

• Use a good dictionary to find collocations of new words you meet.

• Think about which collocations are the same in your language and which are different.

• Write example sentences that contain new collocations. Try to make them true for you.

Queen of the curve

Marjorie Zemach looks at the life of a famous female architect.

Born in Baghdad, Iraq, in 1950, Dame Zaha Hadid went on to become perhaps the most famous female architect in the world. In 2004, she was the first woman to win the important Pritzker Prize and her beautiful buildings can be seen in cities all over the world. What makes her story really <u>amazing</u>, though, is the fact that none of her designs were actually built for many years after she finished **university**. During that time, she was just seen as an interesting 'paper architect', whose designs were thought to be too difficult and unusual to make.

The daughter of a politician father and an artist mother, Hadid grew up in both a family and a city that was relaxed, modern and confident. Many famous foreign architects were working in Baghdad in the 1950s, and many exciting new universities, cultural buildings and sports centres were built during this time. In the 1960s, she was sent to schools in England and Switzerland, and then got **a degree** in mathematics from the American University of Beirut. In 1972, she moved to London, where she studied at the Architectural Association School of Architecture.

While studying in London, Hadid's skill and ideas started attracting attention and she developed the **style** she later became famous for. She loved the Russian artist Kazimir Malevich and wanted to make buildings that looked like his paintings. This meant creating a feeling of movement and using space in <u>new and different</u> ways.

In 1979, she opened her first **office** in a small room in East London, and spent much of her **time** doing drawings and paintings of the buildings she wanted to create. She became much better known in 1983 when one of her drawings won a **competition** in Hong Kong. The engineer Peter Rice, who had worked on the Pompidou Centre in Paris, said the design could be built. However, in the end, it wasn't as there wasn't enough money.

It is common for architects to find that their original ideas are developed and adapted when their designs are actually built. However, Hadid's problem was more <u>serious</u> – her ideas were not being built at all. **Plans** to use her designs in Berlin, Düsseldorf and Cardiff all failed, and many people felt her ideas only worked on paper. The problem was made even worse when her **pictures** were shown in museums as works of art themselves.

However, all this changed in the 1990s, when some of her most interesting designs were finally built. Before long, her work was everywhere: the Olympic swimming pool in London and a university in Vienna; offices in Beijing and the Heydar Aliyev Center in Baku, Azerbaijan; bridges in Abu-Dhabi and museums in Denmark. Her work rarely used <u>straight</u> lines, and always looked for ways of bringing different spaces together.

Although not loved by everyone – some said her **work** cost too much and others didn't like her <u>strong</u> personality – her buildings were generally <u>very popular</u> and in 2012 Queen Elizabeth II gave her a special title – Dame – for her services to architecture. Hadid died of a heart attack in 2016, aged 65, but her work remains and her designs continue to be built. This Iraqi-British woman will be remembered for many years to come.

Girls in the field by Kazimir Malevich

4 Look at the nouns in bold in the biography. Complete the collocations with the correct verbs.

1 She _____ **university** and then later _____ her first **office** in London.
2 She _____ **a degree** in mathematics from the American University of Beirut.
3 While studying in London, she _____ her own **style**.
4 She _____ a lot of **time** drawing and painting.
5 In 1983, she _____ **a competition** in Hong Kong.
6 **Plans** to use her designs in Berlin, Düsseldorf and Cardiff _____ .
7 Her **pictures** were _____ in different museums.
8 Some people felt that her **work** _____ too much.

5 Find the underlined adjectives 1–6 in the biography. Match them with the nouns a–f they describe.

1	an amazing	a	personality
2	new and different	b	problem
3	a serious	c	building
4	straight	d	story
5	a strong	e	lines
6	a very popular	f	ways

6 Complete the collocations with one noun from Exercises 4 and 5.

1 go to .../study at .../a top .../a private ... = *university*
2 damage a .../build a .../an empty .../a public ...= _____
3 tell a .../read a .../a true .../a love ... = _____
4 paint a .../draw a .../a beautiful .../a colourful ...= _____
5 make .../change your .../new .../big ... = _____
6 waste .../have .../a short .../ free ...= _____

7 a Write four sentences that are true for you. Use collocations from Exercises 4, 5 and 6.

*I **got a degree** in Law from Charles University in Prague.*
*In **my free time**, I usually just watch TV and sleep.*

b Work in pairs. Compare and explain your sentences.

1c Develop your listening

> **Goal:** understand a radio programme
> **Focus:** recognising sounds and words

1 **Work in pairs and answer the questions.**

1 Do you know anyone who works nights? What do they do? Do they like it?

2 What might be good or bad about working during the night?

2 **Work in pairs. Read the Focus box and tick the strategies that you already use.**

Recognising sounds and words

Listening usually involves recognising sounds and words first and then using your understanding of grammar and how words connect to build up the meaning of a whole text. You can develop this skill by working with a short text or on short parts of a longer text.

• Note any words you hear - especially nouns and verbs.

• Discuss what you heard with someone who was also listening (if possible).

• Try to reconstruct the whole text.

You can also improve by:

• listening several times (if possible).

• reading the text while you listen.

• hearing how the same word sounds different in different contexts.

• listening again to hear how new words are said in real situations.

3 a **Read the words noted by a student after listening to the introduction to a radio programme. What do you think the presenter said in the introduction?**

• in 1667 – Paris – first – light – night
• popular – how long – slept – choice
• getting up – sun – bed – dark – 24 – divide – night owls – shifts – sleep less

b 🔊 1.7 **Now listen to the introduction. Add any words you hear to the lists in Exercise 3a.**

c **Work in pairs. Compare the extra words you noted. Try to say the whole introduction.**

d **Turn to page 166. Listen and read the introduction. How close was it to what you said?**

4 🔊 1.8 **Listen to the sentences from the rest of the radio programme. They all contain *as*. Notice that it sounds different in different contexts. Complete the sentences with three or four words.**

1 _____ in eight adults now work nights.

2 We may see this 24-hour culture _____ progress.

3 On average, night workers age quicker and don't _____ .

4 In stressful areas _____ , ...

5 I think my brain _____ anyone's!

6 But, _____ , the evidence is really very strong.

5 **What do you think the radio programme is about? Choose from 1–4.**

1 A city where nightlife is creating problems for its people.

2 Working as a doctor at night.

3 Whether night working is good or bad for people.

4 The benefits of a 24-hour culture.

6 a 🔊 1.9 **Listen to the rest of the programme. Note down as many content words as you can.**

b **Work in pairs and compare your answers. What is the answer to Exercise 5?**

7 **Work in pairs. Which sentences are exactly what you heard? Then listen again and correct anything that was not exactly what you heard.**

1 Recent research suggests nightlife and reduced sleep is not a problem for us.

2 I was always late for school and struggled there.

3 They get fatter, have higher rates of heart disease and suffer from colds more.

4 You use 50 percent less energy sleeping during the day.

5 Weight is a problem for me.

6 We're talking about the heart aging an extra six years for every ten years people work nights.

7 There are three times more errors on night shifts than there are during the day.

8 I don't have all the answers – which is why I'm a scientist and not a politician!

Develop your listening

> **Goal:** understand a radio phone-in programme

> **Focus:** identifying details that support key ideas

1 Work in pairs and discuss the questions.

1 Do you do any sport/physical activity?

2 What things do you think might be good for your mental and/or physical health?

2 2.3 **Listen to the beginning of a radio programme and answer the questions.**

1 What kind of programme is it?

2 What is the main topic being discussed?

3 Read the Focus box. What do supporting details do? What phrases do people use to give details?

Identifying details that support key ideas

When listening, it's important to first identify the key ideas, and then listen for details. Think of a key idea as an 'umbrella' idea with supporting details under it.

Supporting details may describe or explain a key idea. They can include examples, reasons, results and other facts. Speakers sometimes show listeners they are going to give examples or give reasons by using certain phrases.

We should spend less money on Olympic sports and more on general public sports ... (= key idea)

*... **like** park football or providing free gym membership.* (= example)

*... **For example,** you could build a swimming pool in every neighbourhood.* (= example)

***Look at** people's level of fitness – we all spend too much time sitting down.* (= reason)

***In fact,** we spend almost the same on a few Olympic athletes as we do on all school sport.* (= fact)

***It's the kind of thing** that would win votes in an election.* (= result)

*And **another thing** is, if people were fitter we could save money on healthcare.* (= result)

However, speakers often assume that listeners understand why details are being given, and so don't always draw attention to them like this.

4 2.4 **Listen to the rest of the programme. Number the key ideas in the order that you hear them. One of the ideas is not discussed.**

a having Olympic sports that are based on jobs

b having Olympic motor sports

c having Olympic sports that are connected to parenting

d having Olympic sports that are only played in one country

e having Olympic sports that aren't physical, e.g. card games

5 Work in pairs and answer the questions. Then listen again and check your answers.

1 Which of these arguments are given to support the idea of making the card game, bridge, an Olympic sport?

a My gran plays with her friends.

b There aren't enough Olympic sports for older people.

c It's good for people's mental health.

d The winner doesn't rely on a judge's score and can't cheat.

2 Which of these are suggested by the presenters as examples of new Olympic sports that would 'broaden the Olympics for our times'?

a an event involving fire

b buggy pushing

c ice cream throwing

d tug-of-war

e American football

6 Work in pairs and discuss the questions.

1 Do you watch the Olympics when it's on? Why/Why not?

2 What do you think of the selection of sports mentioned in the listening? Would you consider all of them sports? How would you decide the winner in each case?

3 What new 'sports' can you think of to add to the Olympics? Think of connections to jobs, parenting, different age groups, etc. and how they might be judged.

4 Have you heard of any examples of cheating connected to the Olympics? How could it be stopped?

5 Did you ever have 'sports day' at school? What are your memories of it?

7 Work in groups and decide on the best new Olympic 'sport' from the 'sports' that you discussed in Exercise 6, Question 3.

Develop your writing

> **Goal:** write an informal email
> **Focus:** linking words and questions in informal emails

1 a Look at the photos and answer the questions.

    1 What are the people doing?

    2 How do you think they are feeling?

    3 What jobs do you think they are doing?

    4 How are their jobs going at the moment?

b Work in pairs and compare your ideas.

2 Read sentences 1–8 from emails about work. Match the words in bold with definitions a–h.

    1 They're **expanding** our department. We're going to have five more people working with us.

    2 She's only been a manager for six months, but she's already **had a promotion**. They've made her the head of department. She'll be running the whole business soon!

    3 He's quite new and hasn't done this kind of thing before, so he's **struggling** a bit. I'm having to help him a lot.

    4 Our website won the best travel site of the year **award**. It's nice to have your work recognised.

    5 I'm going to **be made redundant**. The company has been losing money and needs to cut staff, and unfortunately my job is one they're cutting.

    6 We are going to **be taken over** by a bigger company, HDC. Apparently, they are paying $3 billion to buy us.

    7 They're introducing a new **admin system** so all our forms and records will be in one place and can be accessed through an app.

    8 His boss is basically **bullying** him. He's always telling him to work late and saying bad things about his work – often in front of other people.

    a frightening and hurting

    b be bought and controlled

    c moved to a higher level in a company

    d prize

    e lose my job because I'm no longer needed

    f increasing in size

    g trying hard to do something difficult and not doing very well

    h way of organising and arranging the operations of the company

3 Work in pairs. Do you know anyone who has experienced any of the things in Exercise 2? What happened?

> *I was made redundant a few years ago. I worked for a small computer company and we were taken over. Most of us lost our jobs.*

4 Read Saroj's reply to an email from her friend, Keisha. Answer the questions.

    1 Which things from Exercise 2 are mentioned?

    2 What questions do you think Keisha had asked Saroj?

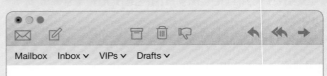

Mailbox   Inbox ∨   VIPs ∨   Drafts ∨

Hi Keisha,

Thanks for the email. It was lovely to hear from you. Hope all is well your end. How's work going?

Here, the kids are great – they're growing up fast! Alisha started school last month and is doing well. It only seems like yesterday that I was changing her nappies. Dele's really happy because he's just got into the school football team.

Gabby's been really busy. He's travelling quite a lot with work, but on the whole he enjoys it. It means it's a bit difficult for me to come and visit at the moment, though, but I might be able to come in November. Mum might be able to come and look after Alisha and Dele.

Things are a bit strange at work at the moment, though I'm doing really well myself. We heard a few weeks ago that we're being taken over by a Chinese company. They're a social media company, so it does make sense for them to buy a games company. They've said that there won't be any changes in staff, and they are hoping to expand, but you know what can happen when companies get taken over. It often results in people getting made redundant. It would be really annoying if they do, because I've just been promoted to head of marketing after all my work on *Drone Strike*. I'm really proud of how well it's done! It's the second best-selling product they've ever had and it's just won two industry awards as well, so that's all great.

Anyway, fingers crossed everything will be fine at work and that we can meet in November. If not, let's Skype sometime and have a catch-up – it's been far too long since we had a good long chat.

Lots of love,
Saroj

B

C

5 Read the Focus box. How are informal emails different from formal emails?

Linking words and questions in informal emails

Informal emails and letters are often more like a conversation. You tend to use short sentences and simple linking words like *and, so, but, though, because*. You might just use a dash to show a connection or to make clear that information is not central to understanding the rest of the sentence. You also often include questions as if you are talking to someone face to face. Sometimes these questions will be rhetorical, i.e. they don't require an answer.

6 a Where would you put these questions in Saroj's email? There may be more than one possible answer.
 1 Have you seen the adverts for it?
 2 When's the best time to call?
 3 Did I tell you she's retiring next month?
 4 Would that work for you?
 5 Did you see his photos of Shanghai on Facebook?
 6 Can you believe it?
 7 How's Fina? Is she still working too hard?

b Which of the questions in Exercise 6a might Keisha reply to? Which questions are rhetorical?

7 Match sentences 1–5 with follow-up questions a–e.
 1 We're struggling, to be honest. Sales have really fallen badly.
 2 I'm going to see Stefania next week.
 3 You were still unsure when we spoke last week. It's a great opportunity, but I can understand why you might not want to move the family or travel so far to work.
 4 I'm busy all next week. But I am a bit freer the week after that.
 5 The new admin system is amazing. It's so much easier to find things and it doesn't crash as often!

 a How did we ever live without it?
 b Would one day then be OK for you?
 c How are things with you?
 d Have you seen her at all recently?
 e Have you thought about it any more since then?

8 Underline in the email the linking words in the box and any dashes (–).

and because but so though

9 Complete the sentences with the linking words in Exercise 8 or a dash.
 1 My boss has been bullying me _____ it's starting to make me hate my job!
 2 They're introducing a new system _____ the one we're using now is ancient!
 3 Lots of people in my department were made redundant, _____ I managed to keep my job.
 4 Apparently, they spent a huge amount on the takeover _____ over a hundred million, I heard.
 5 She got a pay rise _____ she got promoted, _____ she's obviously happy about all that.

Prepare

10 a Choose one of the tasks.
 1 Think of a person you could write to to tell them about your work or studies. You can say something true or invent it.
 2 Imagine you are Keisha and reply to Saroj's email.

b Before you begin to write, think about:
 • an event or news related to your work/studies that you'll tell them about.
 • other questions you might ask and answer in the email.
 • how you will start and end the email.

Write

11 Write your email. Use the information in the Focus box to help you.

> **Goal:** understand an article
> **Focus:** using affixation to recognise new words

1 Discuss the questions.

1 Which social media platforms/apps do you use (e.g. Facebook, WhatsApp)? What for?
2 How often do you post things on social media?
3 How often do you update your profiles on social media?
4 Are there any social media tools you have stopped using? If so, why?

2 Complete the sentences with the words in the box.

broadcasting	content	likes	message
platforms	post	profile	registered

1 WeChat is one of China's biggest social media _____ . As well as using it to _____ people and share photos, articles and other _____ , users can also order taxis and pay for things through the app.
2 Netflix is taking business from traditional _____ companies like the BBC.
3 I _____ with Twitter, but I've never really used it. My _____ still says I'm single, but now I'm married.
4 We have a Facebook page for our company and try to _____ something on it every day. The last video we put up had 20,000 _____ , which isn't bad.

3 Read the title and subtitle of the article. How might 1–5 be connected to the reasons young people stop using certain social media tools?

1 a photograph and a grandmother
   Maybe a grandmother saw a photograph that her grandchild didn't want her to see.
2 employers, universities and banks
3 body image
4 sleep
5 panic attacks

4 Read the article and check your answers to Exercise 3. Can you explain the title?

5 Read the article again. Which of ideas 1–7 are mentioned? Underline the parts of the article that support your answers.

1 Being friends on social media with older relatives can be a bad idea.
2 Users of social media should learn more about the settings for each tool.
3 Failure to manage your online image could affect your career.
4 The design of some tools encourages you to spend more time on them.
5 It can be very hard to stop using social media.
6 Younger users of social media are sometimes believed to be easier to sell to.
7 The move towards narrowcast tools may put some social media companies out of business.

A ROOM OF MY OWN

Kate Jenkins asks why young people are leaving the wide open spaces of open social media.

'I first started thinking about quitting when I woke up one morning and found my grandmother had liked one of my photographs during the night – and not just any old photo either, but one that I really wouldn't have shown her in any other circumstances!' Almir Amsellem is explaining why he stopped using Facebook, the world's most popular social networking site. 'Like most of my friends, I used to post all the time,' he continues, 'but then I suddenly realised how many people could see what I was putting up, and I was just really **uncomfortable** with that idea.'

Almir is one of tens of millions of young people who over recent years have made the move from the more open public broadcast spaces like Facebook to more private 'narrowcast' tools. 'These days, I'm all about messaging apps and **auto-deletion**', he reveals, 'so what I share goes no further than a small group of friends, and often ceases to exist after a minute or two anyway.' In fact, one of the main reasons why many young people are leaving open platforms is that they are becoming more and more aware of the way that past posts may come back to bite them in the future. The knowledge that everyone from **employers** to universities to banks now look at social media profiles has resulted in more **self-censorship** and far safer and more boring public images, with more personal thoughts and pictures being shared in private elsewhere.

6 a Complete three of the sentence starters so they are true for you.

1 One problem with the article is that it doesn't mention …
2 A major advantage of open social media that wasn't mentioned is …
3 Another reason for quitting open social media tools is …
4 One problem with leaving open social media is that you then …
5 The best thing that could happen to social media in the future is …

b Work in pairs. Compare and explain your ideas.

There may also be **psychological** benefits to spending less time on open social media. Recent research suggests that spending large amounts of time on some of the most popular platforms can have a negative effect and lead to increased worries about body image, sleep problems as well as increased anxiety, **loneliness** and **depression**, all problems that Karen Roach, 21, recognises. 'I used to be totally addicted to social media,' she admits. 'I'd wake up and the first thing I'd do was check all my pages to see what I'd missed. I'd post my carefully selected selfies and then check back every minute or so to see how many likes I was getting! It was crazy. I started having panic attacks and in the end, it got so bad that I just decided enough was enough. That was about six months ago and I've felt far less stressed since then. I've learnt that sometimes it's nice to be unreachable, away from technology.'

However, despite such developments, there may be problems ahead. If fewer people provide shared content and like their friends' posts, then social media companies receive less income from advertising. **Advertisers** are particularly keen to target young people as they feel young people's tastes are more easily influenced, but in return for placing adverts, advertisers want access to as much data as they can get. Less data equals fewer opportunities to sell, and this is the real issue with the move to closed 'narrowcast' platforms: it's much harder to sell to their users. While this may not worry Almir as he chats and sends photos to his closest friends, for the narrowcast companies themselves it's a threat to their **existence**. How can they keep going without advertising revenue? And what will happen if they can't?

Using affixation to recognise new words

Many words are made up of smaller elements:

root – *reach*

suffix – reach**able**

prefix – **un**reachable

Knowing the most common prefixes and suffixes – and how to combine them – can help you deal with new words when you are reading. Prefixes usually change the meaning of a word. Suffixes usually change the word class (the type of word it is), e.g. from a verb to a noun or from a noun to an adjective.

For example: *unreachable* is based on the root word *reach*, which is a verb. Adding the suffix *-able* makes it an adjective, and adding the prefix *un-* changes the meaning to *not*, so the word describes something you are not able to reach or get to.

7 Read the Focus box, then work in pairs. Read sentences 1–8, which all contain a word in bold from the article. For each word, decide:

  a what kind of word it is (adjective, verb, noun, etc.) and how you know.

  b what the root word is.

  c what prefixes (if any) are attached.

  d what you think it means.

  1 I'm really **uncomfortable** with the idea that my phone knows where I am all the time.
    a adjective: -able
    b comfort
    c un-
    d not feeling good about something

  2 I wouldn't rely on **auto-deletion** myself. People can still copy what you send them.

  3 It's fine for **employers** to look at your social media profiles.

  4 **Self-censorship** on social media isn't necessarily a bad thing.

  5 There are plenty of **psychological** benefits to spending less time on social media.

  6 Spending time online can actually help people deal with **loneliness** and **depression**.

  7 **Advertisers** are slowly killing the internet!

  8 Social media is a threat to the **existence** of newspapers.

8 Choose the correct alternatives.

  1 Social media can help maintain old *friendly/ friendliness/friendships*.

  2 With social media, I have no *self-/auto-/pre*-control. I'm constantly checking for new posts and changing my profiles and I spend far too much time on it.

  3 A lot of photos on social media are *nature/natural/ unnatural* because people use Photoshop. I think it creates false *expectations/expects/unexpected* for young people.

  4 Businesses need to check what employees put on their social media. One bad post can damage the company's *repute/reputation/reputable* and can *redo/undo/self*-do all the work they've put in to building their brand.

9 a Give the sentences in Exercises 7 and 8 a mark from 1–5 (where 1 = I completely disagree and 5 = I completely agree).

  b Work in pairs. Compare and discuss your ideas.

> **Goal:** understand a newspaper article

> **Focus:** understanding cause and result

1 Work in pairs and discuss the questions.

  1 Which cities/towns/areas in your country attract the most tourists? Why?

  2 What might be the effect of tourism on a place?

2 a You're going to read an article about tourism in Barcelona. What do you know about the city? Why is it popular with tourists?

  b Read the article and complete it with sub-headings a–f. There are two extra sub-headings you don't need.

  a The fight for a better future

  b The power of art

  c The wrong type

  d Six stages of tourism

  e Choice for tourists, less choice for locals

  f Building the Barcelona brand

3 a The article includes many examples of ways to express cause and result, e.g. *Having millions of tourists each year has led to rising rents.* Can you think of other words and phrases that are used to talk about cause and result?

  b Read the Focus box and check your ideas.

Understanding cause and result

You can make clear the connection between the cause and the result by using linking words:

so/such

It was so hot (that) we stayed indoors during the day.
We had such a good time (that) we're going there again next year.

because/as

We're going there again next year because/as we had such a good time.

because of

During the day, it can reach 45 degrees. Because of the heat, most people stay indoors.

as a result

During the day, it was 45 degrees. As a result, most people stayed inside with the air-conditioning on.

We also often use these verbs: *lead to, mean, result in, create, cause, make.*

Tourism in Barcelona

Sam Garcia reports from a city that may have become a victim of its own popularity.

1 _____

'It's so crowded, you can hardly walk down the street, but what's worse is how the character of the neighbourhood has changed.' So says Amparo Peris, owner of the last shoe shop in her part of Barcelona, a shop which is now closing down. 'This isn't just where I ran my business; it's where I used to do my own shopping, too. There was a fruit and vegetable store, a baker's, a pharmacy. My kids went to the nearby sweet shop and played in the street, but now that's just impossible. It's all just restaurants and bars.' Forty-five restaurants and bars, to be exact, serving everything from traditional paella to sushi, in a pedestrianised street only 600 metres long. Of course, all of this means more choice for the tourists who visit the city, but many locals are now starting to feel that it also means they now have fewer choices. Having millions of tourists each year has led to rising rents, the loss of normal day-to-day services, increased noise and other problems. In the last few years, there have been a number of protests by people who live and work in the city.

2 _____

Even those working in the tourist industry are worried. Luis Perreira, a human statue working in the city centre, says that the city is now attracting a different kind of tourist. 'They are less polite now. You get big groups and sometimes someone tries to push me – for a joke. They don't appreciate my art.'

3 _____

Tourist numbers in Barcelona have increased 500 percent in 25 years and it seems the city has reached what the academic Richard Butler calls 'stagnation'. Butler

suggests that tourism typically goes through six stages. First is the 'exploration' stage, where a few artists and explorers look for something new and 'discover' a place. Next comes 'involvement': tourism begins to increase as the early explorers talk about their experiences. As a result, local people start providing basic tourist services and the local government begins to get involved with marketing. Butler calls the stage that follows 'development'. Large numbers of tourists from around the world are persuaded to visit and tourist services grow very quickly, which leads to locals losing control over how tourism develops. During the fourth stage – 'consolidation' – tourism becomes the strongest part of the economy. By now, it's mainly run by national or international companies, which build big hotels and tourist attractions like theme parks or golf courses that spoil the original beauty of the place. The hotels and attractions often take space, water and other resources from locals and they can often cause damage to the environment. This results in complaints from local people and this anger grows during the fifth stage, as has been the case in Barcelona. Because of protests, no new facilities are developed, and 'stagnation' is reached. The question is what happens next. Butler suggests different possibilities for the sixth stage. The first possibility is that war or disaster could suddenly end everything. Another is that nothing is done. This leads to a drop in tourist numbers as visitors don't like either the local protests or the crowds. Alternatively, action may be taken to reduce tourist numbers, attract a different type of visitor and improve the situation for locals.

4 _____

It seems Barcelona is taking the last option. As a result of all the protests, the local government has introduced controls on people renting flats to tourists and increased punishments for bad behaviour. They have also banned performers from certain areas to reduce crowds. Will it work? For Amparo, it has already come too late, but she sees some hope. Her friends have organised a closing down party. 'I didn't really want to retire now, but seeing all these people, I know I still have my friends and we can fight this situation together.'

4 Match causes 1–6 with results a–f. Underline the parts of the article that helped you decide.

1 It's so crowded
2 There are forty-five restaurants and bars, which means
3 Having millions of tourists each year has led to
4 As tourism slowly increases,
5 Hotels and attractions often cause
6 As a result of all the protests,

a the local government has introduced controls.
b more choice for tourists.
c environmental damage.
d you can hardly walk down the street.
e rising rents.
f local people start providing basic tourist services.

5 Read the article again and answer the questions.

1 Why is Amparo Peris sad about the changes to her street?
2 According to Butler's model, what starts tourism in an area?
3 What leads to environmental problems?
4 Why does a tourist industry stop growing?
5 Why has the local government in Barcelona stopped some people doing shows in the street?
6 Why is Amparo positive about the future?

6 Complete the sentences with the words in the box.

anger   attractions   basic   crowded   explore
punishment   services   spoilt   unspoilt

1 It became the Capital of Culture, which led to more tourism, but it's still not too _____ .
2 It's full of cheap souvenir shops and tourist _____, which have _____ the place.
3 There's been no tourism there so the facilities are very _____ but the area is also totally _____ .
4 It used to be well-known for its wild nightlife. The local government increased the _____ for bad behaviour, but this has meant tourist numbers have fallen.
5 It's a lovely area, but there are plans to make the local airport bigger, which has caused _____ and protests among locals.
6 These days, there are a few more _____ provided like car hire and guided tours so it is easier to travel around and _____ the countryside.

7 Work in pairs and discuss the questions.

1 Do you know any places that fit the descriptions in Exercise 6?
2 What stage of Butler's model do you think each place in Exercise 6 is at? (Use the graph to help you.)
3 Do you know any other places that are at different stages of tourist development?
4 How would you like to see tourism in your country develop?
5 What do you think of the solutions that Barcelona is trying? Can you think of any other ways the city could tackle the problem?

3B Develop your writing

> **Goal:** summarise an article
> **Focus:** writing a summary

1 a Work in pairs. Read the news headlines and match them with photos A–D.

1 ## Getting up early causes increased stress

2 ## Social media is bad for your health

3 ## DRINKING COFFEE MAKES YOU SMARTER

4 ## DOING EXERCISE REDUCES THE RISK OF HEART DISEASE

b Work in pairs and discuss the headlines.

    1 Which do you think are true? What proof is there?

    2 What other news stories have you heard about food, drink or activities that are supposed to be good/bad for you? Do you know any details about them?

2 Read the summary of an article. Match with the correct headline in Exercise 1a. Is the story true or not?

> The article *I've got coffee on my mind: What do we really know from the most recent scientific study?* by Marina Hindle, published online recently, argues that a lot of media reports about scientific research are wrong or presented in a way that's not totally truthful. She gives the example of headlines that claim drinking coffee is good for the brain. She explains how the research had found a possible link, but it was only a possibility at best. Hindle goes on to list all the extra information that would be needed to show that the link was real, including the strength and type of coffee, how much to drink each day, and brain tests before and after. Hindle emphasises that this was a standard scientific study and that the researchers were clear about the limits of what it showed. She ends by saying that the media then made incredible claims, and that the research had never intended such claims to be made.

3 a Read the Focus box. What are the different parts of a summary? What should you remember when you write a summary?

Writing a summary

When you write a short summary of an article, use this structure:

1 Say who the article is by, what it's called and where it's from.

2 Give the overall point/argument/theory the article puts forward.

3 Give the first or main example the author uses to explain the point.

4 Give one or two more details about the example or introduce another point that the article makes.

5 Explain how the article ends.

A summary doesn't always follow the same pattern as the original article, because an article often starts with an example or background information, and the main point the author is making may only become clear later in the article.

As well as thinking about the structure, remember that:

• when you summarise, you need to paraphrase (i.e. explain ideas in your own words, rather than copy from the article).

• it's a good idea to make notes on the key ideas/ examples from each paragraph of the original article while you're reading. This will help you structure your summary.

• there are useful summarising verbs and phrases you can use, e.g. *claim, goes on to (discuss)*, etc.

b Circle six summarising verbs and phrases in the text in Exercise 2. There is an example to help you.

4 Complete the sentences with the phrases in the boxes.

> argues that   describes recent research
> explores how

1 The article _____ into possible solutions to climate change.

2 Bee Wilson _____ we come to prefer some foods more than others and what happens as a result of those choices.

3 In the article, Jonathan Safran Foer _____ it is wrong to eat meat if you can avoid it.

> states that   gives the example   emphasises the fact

4 The article talks about a theory from Nobel-Prize winner Daniel Kahneman that _____ there are two kinds of mind and two kinds of thinking.

5 To illustrate the point, the article _____ of China, which has grown very fast.

6 The report then _____ that being a journalist can be very dangerous.

> goes on   ends with   ends by

7 The author _____ to list several other events that cannot be easily explained.

8 Finally, the article _____ suggesting a number of ideas for further research.

9 It _____ a quote by Margaret Mead: 'Never doubt that a small group of committed people can change the world.'

5 Read the summary of the article on page 94. Divide the summary into the five sections listed in the Focus box. The first one is done for you as an example.

1 *A Room Of My Own* is an article by Kate Jenkins. // It discusses the trend of younger people leaving open social media because of issues such as privacy, companies looking at profiles and addiction. It gives the example of a twenty-one-year-old girl, who has recovered from panic attacks after giving up social media. The article goes on to suggest that while the trend is healthy for users, it may be a problem for companies like Facebook as they rely on money from advertising. The writer ends by asking what will happen if these companies can't survive.

6 Put the sentences in the correct order to make a summary of the article on page 96.

a To illustrate this, it gives the example of Barcelona, where tourism has grown 500 percent over the last 25 years.

b It then goes on to explain action that the local government has taken to improve the situation.

c The article *Tourism in Barcelona* by Sam Garcia describes the process that leads to places becoming popular with tourists and …

d It reports how local people there are angry about problems such as rising rents and loss of services.

e Finally, it ends by suggesting that protests against tourism can be a way to bring communities together.

f how it almost always leads to problems for local communities, which can cause anger and protests.

Prepare

7 a **You're going to summarise an article. Either:**

1 summarise the article about Zaha Hadid on page 89.

2 think of an article that you have read recently. It doesn't have to be in English.

b **Work in pairs. Tell your partner what you chose and what the article was about.**

Write

8 **Write your summary. Use the structure suggested in the Focus box and the language you have learnt in this lesson.**

3c Develop your listening

> **Goal:** understand a podcast
> **Focus:** understanding attitude

1 **Look at the photos and discuss the questions.**

1 What do you think is happening in the photos?
2 How do you think the people feel? Why?
3 Have you been to any formal ceremonies like these? What for? What did you think of them?

2 a 🔊 3.10 **Listen to four people give their opinion of a ceremony. Who enjoyed it?**

b **Work in pairs. Try to recreate what each speaker said. Use the adjectives.**

1 terrible
2 good
3 bad
4 great

c **Listen again and check your answers.**

3 **Read the Focus box. In what different ways can you show your attitude to something?**

Understanding attitude

When people talk about what they think, they often use quite direct language:

I thought it was terrible.

However, people sometimes do not want to be direct in case they appear rude or too negative, so they use softer or more subtle language to express what they mean.
You can use a negative form with a positive word to say something negative. Compare:

I thought it was really bad.

with

I didn't think it was that good.

You can use a type of double negative to say something a bit more positive:

It wasn't bad. (= It was quite good.)
It's not unusual. (= It happens quite often.)

You can also use intonation to express your attitude. You generally use a rising voice to suggest something is good, and a falling voice to suggest something is bad. For example, *It was just great!* can be said to mean simply *It was great!*, but with a falling voice, it can also mean *It was terrible!*

When you are listening, you should also pay attention to what else the speaker says. The surrounding language may help you decide if their attitude is positive or negative.

4 🔊 3.11 **Listen to nine sentences. Do you think the speaker's attitude is positive or negative?**

5 🔊 3.12 **Listen to the sentences from Exercise 4 in short conversations. Use the extra context to check your answers to Exercise 4.**

6 🔊 3.13 **Listen to a podcast where two people talk about moving to another country. Answer the questions.**

1 Which country did they come from?
2 Where did they move to?
3 Are they happy where they live?

7 a **Listen again. Are the sentences true (T) or false (F)?**

1 Brad enjoyed travelling between Australia and Canada.
2 Brad likes the weather in Canada.
3 Brad enjoyed his first ice hockey game.
4 Brad was surprised he enjoyed the ceremony.
5 Brad is a good singer.
6 Casho liked the place she stayed in when she arrived.
7 Casho liked the snow.
8 Casho is happy with what she's achieved.
9 Casho's dad is from a more middle-class background in Somalia.
10 Casho's mother is feeling a bit lonely.

b **Work in pairs. What did Brad and Casho lose and gain from moving countries?**

8 a **Make a list of anyone you can think of who:**

• has moved from your country to live somewhere else.
• has moved from somewhere else to your country.

b **Work in pairs. Take turns talking about the people on your list. Say as much as you can about:**

• where each person moved to/from.
• why they moved.
• what their experience of moving was like.

Develop your listening

> **Goal:** understand informal conversations

> **Focus:** recognising rhetorical questions

1 a **Work in pairs. Choose three things from the box and think of a problem you might have with each.**

You could order some bad seafood at a restaurant that makes you ill.

> a hotel room   some clothes you bought   a computer
> one of your neighbours   food   your parents
> money   a flatmate

b **Work with another pair and compare your ideas. Discuss which problem is the worst and why.**

2 🔊 **4.3 Listen to four conversations between two friends. Answer the questions.**

   1 What's the problem?

   2 What possible solutions are mentioned?

3 **Read the Focus box. Why do we use rhetorical questions?**

Recognising rhetorical questions

Rhetorical questions are questions that you don't want or expect an answer to. Use them to encourage the person you're speaking to to agree or answer in the way you want them to.

If you can recognise rhetorical questions in informal conversation, it can help you understand the particular point a speaker is making. For example:

Why bother doing that? I've tried that already. It didn't make any difference!

Here, *Why bother doing that?* means I don't think there's a good reason to do that.

You often add comments after rhetorical questions to explain or expand on the point you're making.

Unlike questions that you ask because you want an answer, rhetorical questions don't usually have rising intonation at the end. The intonation may even fall.

4 🔊 **4.4 Listen to Conversation 1 again. What comment is added after the rhetorical questions 1–3?**

   1 Who needs that?

   2 It's not good, is it?

   3 What else can you do?

5 a 🔊 **4.5 Listen to Conversations 2–4 again. Which of the questions are rhetorical and which are real?**

   1 It's the arms, isn't it?

   2 That's the problem with not trying things on first, isn't it?

   3 Well, what would be the point of keeping it?

   4 Any idea what I've done to it?

   5 When did it start acting strangely?

   6 What are friends for?

   7 Really? Would you be OK to do that?

   8 What would I do without you?

b **Work in pairs and compare your answers.**

6 a 🔊 **4.6 Listen and repeat the rhetorical questions.**

   1 Why on earth would I want to do that?

   2 Go on, then. Why not?

   3 What's the point of trying?

   4 Did you really expect anything else from him?

   5 Do you want to teach the class today?

   6 What have they ever done for us?

b **Work in pairs. Choose at least two of the questions from Exercise 6a and write a short conversation.**

   A: Why don't you try swimming? It might help you relax.

   B: Why on earth would I want to do that? You know I hate exercise!

   A: Well, you never know, you might enjoy it.

7 **Work in pairs. Take turns talking about the problems.**

- a problem with a neighbour
- an online purchase that turned out to be a big mistake
- a problem with money
- a problem with a computer
- a problem with a meal you ordered
- a problem with a friend

4B Develop your writing

> **Goal:** write a story

> **Focus:** creating interest in stories

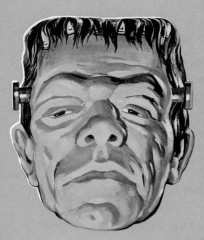

1 **Look at the pictures and answer the questions.**

   1 Do you recognise the characters?

   2 Which stories do they come from?

   3 Do you like the stories? Why/Why not?

2 **Work in pairs. Discuss two of the following in as much detail as you can.**

- a story you loved as a child
- a story that used to scare you
- a memorable story that a friend told you
- a true story that's hard to believe
- a film/book that has an amazing story

3 **Work in pairs. What makes a story interesting? Make a list. Then decide on the two most important things.**

4 a **You're going to read a short story that starts with the line *Just after midnight, there was a knock on the door*. The story includes the words in the box. What do you think might happen in the story?**

> basement   fire   memories   pet   to put out
> uncle

b **Now read the story and check your ideas.**

Just after midnight, there was a knock on the door. With only the orange light from the fire to guide us, we quickly made our way through the fields to the house our uncle had lived in for years. **¹***By the time/When* we arrived, it was already burning **²***just like/just as* someone had poured petrol on it! The firefighters made us stand back **³***during/as* they tried their best to put the fire out, **⁴***but/despite* it was too late. **⁵***As/While* I stood there watching, lots of old memories started coming back to me: hiding from my brother in the cool, dark basement; cooking steaks outside on hot summer nights; listening to my uncle tell stories of all the things he had done in that house as a boy. Before I knew it, I was crying. The saddest thing of all, **⁶***though/however*, was when my 75-year-old Uncle Bill, who was standing next to us by now, suddenly asked if Shep was OK. His old pet dog Shep had died more than ten years earlier.

c **Cover and try to retell the story. Use the words in the box in Exercise 4a.**

5 **Read the text again. Look at the linking words and phrases in italics. Cross out the alternatives that are not possible.**

6 **Look at the text again and find:**

   1 four linking words/phrases which show a time relationship between two events.

   2 three linking words/phrases which show contrasting ideas.

   3 one linking word/phrase that shows one thing is similar to another.

7 **Complete the sentences with the linking words and phrases in the box.**

> by the time   despite   during   however   just as
> just like   though   while

   1 It was dark, it had started snowing, and we were lost. _____ , we still had hope.

   2 We only met once _____ my time in Rome, but it's a meeting that I'll never forget.

   3 When he turned to face me, I was shocked to see that he looked _____ my brother.

   4 My hands were shaking _____ my efforts to control them.

   5 I found some old, black and white photographs _____ I was cleaning out the garage.

   6 It started to pour with rain _____ we were leaving for the park.

   7 The traffic on the motorway was terrible and _____ we arrived, most of the other guests had already left.

   8 It was an amazing experience, _____ not one I'd like to repeat any time soon!

8 **How many marks out of ten would you give the story? Why? How well does it meet your definition of an interesting story from Exercise 3?**

9 Read the Focus box and find an example of each feature in the story in Exercise 4b.

Creating interest in stories

You can make a short story more interesting by:
- starting or ending with something surprising.
- quickly introducing the location and/or the main characters.
- adding descriptive adjectives and adverbs.
- using similes (phrases that describe something by comparing it to something else).
- describing how people in the story feel.

10 a Add adjectives and adverbs to make the sentences more interesting.

1 There was snow on the streets as the car drove into town.

There was deep snow on the quiet streets as the old car drove slowly into town.

2 I closed the door and walked away from the house for the last time.

3 As I opened the book, a photograph dropped onto the floor.

4 He moved his face near to mine and started shouting.

5 The birds were singing outside the window as the sun came up.

6 When we came in, a man with a suitcase was looking around the store.

7 The train stopped inside the tunnel and we all heard a noise outside.

8 The rain was falling as I walked along the street.

9 The woman turned and smiled. Her face brought back memories.

10 As I walked down the corridor, I had no idea what my boss might want.

b Work in pairs and compare your ideas. Which sentences are most interesting?

11 Work in pairs. Make similes to complete the sentences.

1 I lay down on the floor, feeling like …
I lay down on the floor, feeling like I could sleep for a month.

2 I was so scared that my hands were shaking like …

3 I got home that night and started crying like …

4 I ran home across the fields like …

5 When he finally spoke, his voice was like …

6 I fell into my bed and slept like …

7 Our taxi driver drove along the narrow mountain roads like …

8 The noise that came from the forest behind our house was like …

9 We followed him through the streets like …

10 He had eyes like … and skin like … . When he spoke, his voice sounded just like …

Prepare

12 a Choose one of the tasks.

1 Write a story beginning with the line *I had never felt so nervous before in my life*.

2 Write a story about something interesting that happened to you or someone you know.

3 Write a story based on one of the ideas you discussed in Exercise 2.

b Plan your story. Think about:
- the main characters and the location.
- the main action you will include in your story.
- how the story could surprise the reader.

Write

13 Write your story. Use the ideas in the Focus box to add interest and try to use a range of past tenses.

Develop your reading

KEEPING THE CUSTOMERS SATISFIED

Karen Brady travels to Oman to find out what it takes to keep the bad reviews away.

For some companies, complaints don't seem to matter much. People regularly have conversations about their **disastrous** experiences with certain low-cost airlines, but these companies continue to do **incredibly** well because, in the end, the most important thing for customers is how cheap the service is. It's different for higher-class products and services, though. When you're selling luxury to people, complaints can **seriously** damage your business. So how does a five-star company keep the customers happy and the bad reviews away? I **set off** for Oman's latest luxury resort, Jewel in the Mountain, to find out. It was a **tough** job but someone had to do it!

The resort immediately has one advantage when it comes to getting its five-star reviews and that is its **spectacular** six-star location. The Jewel in the Mountain hotel resort is on the edge of a cliff 2,000 metres high with amazing views of the valleys and mountains of Northern Oman. However, the hotel does not charge up to £6,000 a night for the view alone. It also provides incredible service, a wonderful mix of relaxation and adventure, modern design and an introduction to Omani culture. Guests can have a yoga lesson on the absolutely **stunning** viewing platform or they can **scramble** down part of the cliff and fly on a zip wire high above the valley below. They can eat **delicious** Middle Eastern food in the Al Qaiaa restaurant or order a private dinner cooked especially for them by top chefs and served under the stars of the Arabian night sky.

Guests are welcomed by a group of staff playing traditional Omani music before being given a guided tour of the hotel and its facilities by their personal assistant, who will look after all their needs during their stay. While the tour takes place, staff carry the guests' luggage from the car to their private villa and then disappear. When the guests **step** through the door, their things are there and they feel as if they are entering their own home. Towels have been left on the beds in the shape of elephants or flowers and the air is filled with the sweet smell of rose water, which is produced in a nearby village. From the **spacious** living room of each villa, you go out onto a terrace with a luxurious private swimming pool next to the cliff edge – no one, apart from perhaps a mountain goat, is able to walk past and **peer** at the guests.

It is this care and attention that is so essential to achieving top-level service. The hotel is run by general manager Darren Darwin, an ex-army officer. Each morning, he checks the hotel staff's uniforms are perfect before they start work and looks round the hotel to list the tiniest problems that need to be sorted out. And Darren is **extraordinarily** careful. He notices everything from a candle that has fallen down to a plant that has been put in the wrong place or a small mark left on the glass of the viewing platform. Yes, we're back to that view again, but Jewel in the Mountain is so much more and it's the service and the staff who make the difference.

1 **a** Have you ever ...
- flown with a low-cost airline?
- flown business class?
- stayed in a cheap hostel?
- stayed in a luxury hotel?

b How was your experience? Discuss your answers.

2 Read the introduction to an article quickly. What is the main point?
a Luxury services get more complaints than services that are cheap.
b Luxury brands have to work harder to keep customers happy than low-cost brands.
c People like to complain and it doesn't matter how much they have paid.

3 a Match the words in bold in the first paragraph with their essential meaning in the box.

> bad   hard   really   went

b Read the Focus box and check your answers.

Guessing meaning

Rather than use simple words like *bad, really* or *go*, writers often use more descriptive language, which you may not completely understand:

bad - *terrible, disastrous*   **go** - *set off*
good - *amazing, incredible*   **hard** - *tough*
really - *incredibly, seriously*

Some of these words are not very common. However, you can often get the general meaning by thinking about the kind of words they are. Once you know this, you can look again at the context and think about:

Adjectives: are they generally positive or negative?
Adverbs: does it mean 'a lot' or 'a little'?
Verbs: is it a way of going, a way of looking, etc?

4 Read the rest of the article. Which of 1–7 does the author mention as reasons why Jewel in the Mountain gets excellent reviews and few complaints?

1 Where it is.
2 The people who work there.
3 They drive guests from the airport.
4 The variety of activities the hotel offers.
5 How they make people feel at home.
6 The hotel is run by the army.
7 They deal with even very small problems quickly.

5 Find the words in bold in the article and choose the correct essential meaning.

1 spectacular and stunning
  a very beautiful   b very ugly   c very bad
2 scramble
  a walk   b fall   c climb
3 delicious
  a tastes very bad   b tastes quite nice
  c tastes very nice
4 step
  a take   b look   c go
5 spacious
  a very big   b very small   c very
6 peer
  a take   b look   c go
7 extraordinarily
  a really   b slightly   c quite

6 Complete the sentences with the adjectives in the box.

> amazing   awful   boiling   delicious   exhausted
> freezing   huge   tiny

1 The room in the hotel was _____ . There was room for a bed and a cupboard and almost nothing else!
2 The view of the lake and mountains from our room was absolutely _____ . I'll never forget it.
3 The food at breakfast was absolutely _____ and they had a huge choice, too.
4 It's a lovely area, but unfortunately the weather was absolutely _____ . We couldn't really go out.
5 The weather is really _____ in the summer, so people usually stay in during the day and go out at night when it's cooler.
6 I went into the pool once, but I got out straight away. It was absolutely _____ .
7 The apartments in the resort were _____ ! Most of them were bigger than my home!
8 We were absolutely _____ after the flight so we just went straight to bed when we got there.

7 Work in pairs. Take turns talking about things or experiences. Use the adjectives in Exercise 6.

8 Work in pairs and discuss the questions.
• Would you like to stay in a hotel like this? Why?/Why not?
• Which of the activities mentioned in the article would you do?
• What's the best view you have seen? What could you see?
• What's the best service you have ever experienced? Why was it so good?

▶ **Goal:** write an essay

▶ **Focus:** using supporting examples

1 Look at the photos and discuss the questions.

1 Match photos A–C with the areas:
- robots
- social media
- medicine

2 What technological changes are happening in these three areas? Try to think of specific examples.

3 Which of these changes do you think are positive and which are negative?

2 Read the essay and answer the questions.

1 How far do you agree with the writer?

2 How many of the changes that you thought of in Exercise 1 are mentioned in the essay?

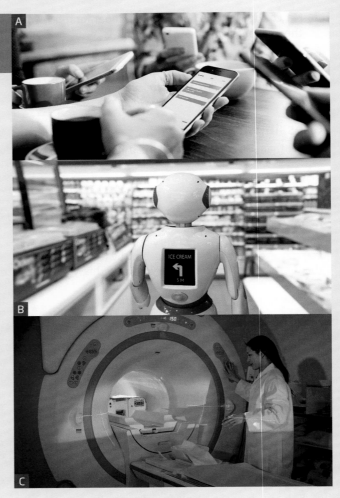

Should we be concerned about the effects that changes in technology will have on society? Discuss the question with reference to one of the following areas:

- robots - social media - medicine

One of the areas of technology that is developing most quickly is robots. Robots are now able to do more things and can learn from experience. Some people argue this offers enormous possibilities as robots are cheaper and more reliable than humans. However, ¹ <u>I would argue that the effects could be very bad in terms of jobs and social relationships</u>.

² <u>While robots have been used in factories before, the number of different jobs that robots could soon do is huge</u>. There are already driverless cars, which may replace taxis and lorries. Soon, there may also be robots for nursing and farming, robots working as shop assistants and even robots offering basic legal advice. One report has suggested that 50 percent of all jobs will soon be lost in some countries.

³ <u>As well as the social problems caused by unemployment, greater use of robots damages social relationships in other ways</u>. While having a robot nurse may be cheap, it cannot chat or share emotions. There is plenty of evidence that human contact improves our health and well-being. Robots could mean humans have less contact with each other and start feeling lonely.

⁴ <u>In short, I think we should be very concerned about the use of robots</u>. They will cause unemployment and could make people feel less connected to others.

3 Read the essay again. Match underlined sentences 1–4 with functions a–d.

a introduces the second main point

b summarises and repeats the writer's main opinion

c introduces the first main point

d states the overall opinion of the writer

4 Read the Focus box. Where can we get ideas for examples from?

Using supporting examples

When writing an essay, it is usual to support opinions with examples. These examples may be from your general knowledge and can include stories in the news, reports, statistics or quotes from experts. You can introduce these supporting examples with the phrase *for example*, but often you don't use a linking word or phrase.

The power of social media is growing all the time and many of the effects it has are positive. For example, people from anywhere can connect with anyone and share thoughts, feelings, ideas and opinions.

5 a Read the essay in Exercise 2 again. Underline an example that supports an opinion in each of paragraphs 1–3.

b Work in pairs and compare your answers. Do you think they are good examples? Why?/Why not?

6 Read another essay on the same topic. Does the writer have the same opinion as the first writer?

Technology is progressing rapidly, especially robotics. Soon, many jobs could be replaced by robots and some argue it will result in a huge increase in unemployment. ¹_____ . However, I would argue that, firstly, the rise in unemployment is exaggerated and, secondly, robots are an opportunity for a better life.

It is clear that robots will replace some jobs done by humans. However, based on what has happened in the past, unemployment on the whole will not increase. ²_____ . New jobs are created to support new technology. ³_____ . Something similar will probably happen in the case of robots.

While it is possible that unemployment may increase, there are still things we can do to reduce the effects and improve our lives. ⁴_____ . As a result, we may need more money to live, but we could raise this through taxes. ⁵_____ . Moreover, these changes could create more leisure time, which in turn could create new jobs.

In short, the impact of robots on unemployment will probably be smaller than people think. Furthermore, if the money from taxes is used to pay for more research, robots will bring great benefits to everyone.

7 Complete the essay with the examples a–f. There is one extra example you do not need.

a For example, millions of farming jobs have gone, but general employment is now much higher

b For example, tech companies are spending a lot of money on drones and on driverless cars

c Bill Gates has suggested we could tax robots in the same way we tax workers

d We could reduce working hours and lower the age people retire, so that work is shared out more

e Thirty years ago, there were no website designers and fewer computer programmers

f Some studies have suggested that 35-50 percent of current jobs are at risk

8 Find and underline *however* and *while* in the essays. Then complete the definitions with the two words.

1 Use _____ when you are adding a new sentence or a comment that contains surprising information or that contrasts with what came before. If it begins a sentence, it is followed by a comma.

2 Use _____ at the start of a clause that introduces information that contrasts with information in the main clause.

9 Complete the sentences with *however* or *while*.

1 _____ some argue that the effects of advances in technology are all positive, it seems to me that there will clearly be a number of negative effects.

2 I understand that the growing population is a concern. _____ , the negative effects are often exaggerated.

3 Many internet companies are huge multinational organisations. _____ this gives them some power, it doesn't mean we have no control over them.

4 Some diseases will no longer be a problem for us, _____ new diseases will probably appear.

5 In the future, more and more robots will be used in hospitals. _____ , _____ they may be useful, robots will not replace humans completely.

10 a Read the statements. How could you argue against them? Write sentences using *however* and *while* to show your contrasting ideas.

1 New technology allows people to have more leisure time.
   While new technology allows people to have more leisure time, it can also make them more lonely.

2 Some have argued that we need more laws to control tech companies.

3 An increase in the population can help an economy to grow.

4 People spend a lot of time on social media and it may affect the economy badly.

b Work in pairs and compare your ideas. Think of examples to support your contrasting ideas.

Prepare

11 a Choose one of the tasks.

1 Write an essay using the title of the essay in Exercise 2.

2 Write an essay using the title:

Should we be concerned about the power of big technology companies? Discuss the question with reference to one of these areas:
• work and daily life
• smaller businesses
• social life and privacy

b Prepare for writing:
• Choose the essay area you are going to write about (task 2).
• Do you feel generally positive or negative about the question in the essay title?
• Think of two main points to support your opinion.
• Think of one example to support each of those points.
• Think about how to structure your essay. Use the two essays in this lesson to help you.

Write

12 Write your essay.

> **Goal:** understand a blog
> **Focus:** recognising attitude

1 Work in pairs. You're going to read a blog about self-help business books. First, discuss the questions.

1 Do you ever read blogs or watch talks on YouTube, etc.? What are they about?

2 Do you know anyone who is well-known for giving their opinions in the media on the topics in the box?

fashion   sport   politics   film

3 Have you ever read a self-help book? Which self-help books would you recommend to the people in the pictures?

2 a Read the title of the blog post. What do you think the author's attitude is?

b Read the introduction to the blog and check your answer. Were you correct?

The key to success?
Ignore key-to-success books!

Yesterday I read something that suggested that delaying decisions is the key to being successful. Basically, if you avoid making a decision until later then the problem may go away or a better option may appear. As someone who never does anything today if I can do it tomorrow, I'm attracted to this idea. <u>Apparently</u>, it means that even if I am lazy and prefer thinking to doing, I too can become a <u>millionaire!</u> <u>Obviously</u>, though, that's <u>*not*</u> going to happen because – like almost every other idea I've ever read in key-to-success books – it's <u>complete NONSENSE!!</u>

1 Read enough of these books and you realise they basically contradict each other. *One* book says quiet people are best, but then *another* says success comes from being an extrovert; *one* book claims you just have to keep going; but *another* says you need to know when to quit; *one* writer talks about the importance of 10,000 hours of practice to be an expert, but *another* says being lazy is the key! I mean, they can't all be right, can they?! Some must be nonsense.

3 Read the Focus box and match the underlined words and phrases in the introduction with techniques 1–5. Not all the techniques are used.

Recognising attitude

Blogs are often written with a particular attitude or only show one point of view. They do this to get a reaction from the reader or to try to persuade them. Some common techniques writers may use are:

1 'Extreme' words: emphasise you like or don't like something
It's completely crazy. (= very silly)
It's a total failure. (= It doesn't work.)

2 Attitude adverbs: show your attitude to what you're going to say next
Actually, it's fantastic. (= Others are wrong to say it's bad.)
Apparently, it's fantastic. (= It's what people say, but maybe it isn't!)

3 Comment clauses: show your attitude to what you've just said
They made $1million in a day, which is amazing.

4 Rhetorical questions/tag questions: show you think something is obvious and no one should disagree.
Who wouldn't want a million dollars?
Everyone would want a million dollars, wouldn't they?

5 Punctuation
Italics and CAPITALS emphasise a point. Capitals can look like you are shouting! Exclamation marks can show you think something is surprising or crazy.
He spent $1 million dollars on a watch! A WATCH!!!

2 Most of these books start with a personal story: I delayed decisions/practised a lot/quit something (choose the one you like), and I'm rich and successful. Therefore, they are saying, 'The thing I did is what can make anyone successful,' which is nonsense! Actually, what they're saying is, 'If only everyone was like me, life would be better.'

3 Obviously, because it's all about them, these writers ignore how their behaviour affects others. So it's fine for them to delay their decision, say, but do they think about the people who have to wait for them to decide? Absolutely not! And they don't care, either! It's great to work 20 hours a day and never quit, but what about the friends and family you never see?! That seems selfish to me and basically … nonsense!

4 Of course, putting something off can bring benefits – sometimes. But what about those times when it leads to nothing happening or worse: losing money, divorce, death!? Writers usually ignore these exceptions or try to explain how they are examples of the wrong kind of delay, etc., but we know it's total nonsense!

5 It's nonsense, because it's basically impossible to apply the advice in these books. If I have a decision to make, is the right time to decide, delay or quit NOW? Or in one month's time? Or two? If you actually spoke to the writers, they couldn't tell you, either! That's because they never test their theories on people starting a business and continue studying those people to see if their advice works. That would be scientific, and take far too long! They can't wait that long to sell their ideas!

6 Talking of money, these writers ignore the biggest factors in business success. I mean, who would buy a key-to-success book which said you not only need to be rich already, but you also need a lot of luck?! I'll give you that advice for free – the rest is nonsense!

Comments

seethelight – one week ago
You think ALL these books are rubbish? That's nonsense! Just because some may be wrong, it doesn't mean they *all* are! It's easy to find examples of bad advice, but why be so negative about everything?

4 Read the rest of blog. Match paragraphs 1–6 with summary sentences a–f.

  a The advice the writers give is difficult to use and has not been tested.

  b The ideas are often based on the writers' personal experience.

  c The writers don't mention very important things most people need for success.

  d They ignore examples which do not fit the advice.

  e Different books and writers often give the opposite advice.

  f The advice might be good for one person, but bad for someone else.

5 a Complete the sentences from the blog with one or two words and any punctuation.

  1 Read enough of these books and you realise they _____ contradict each other.

  2 They can't all be right, _____ Some must be nonsense.

  3 They are saying, 'The thing I did is what can make anyone successful,' which _____

  4 _____ , what they're saying is, 'If only everyone was like me, life would be better.'

  5 Do they think about the people who have to wait for them to decide? _____

  6 What about the friends and family you never see?! That seems _____ to me and basically … nonsense!

  7 That would be scientific, and take _____ too long!

  8 You think _____ these books are rubbish? Just because some may be wrong, it doesn't mean they _____

  b Work in pairs. Which techniques from the Focus box are used in the sentences in Exercise 5a? Some sentences show more than one technique.

6 a Complete three of the sentence starters so they are true for you.

  1 I like the post because …

  2 I don't really like the post because …

  3 The point about …. is very true.

  4 I don't really agree with the point about …

  5 I don't exactly get the point he's making when he says …

  6 I'm not sure what the word …. means in this context.

  7 I'd like to find out more about …

  8 I agree with the comment that …

  b Work in pairs. Take turns using your sentences from Exercise 6a to discuss your views of the blog.

> **Goal:** understand a lecture

> **Focus:** understanding explanations

1 Read the explanation of PISA and discuss the questions.

> How do governments make decisions about education systems? An international project called PISA can help as it compares education around the world. Every three years, around half a million 15-year-olds from 72 countries take a two-hour test in the areas of reading, maths and science. The results are then put in a chart showing how each country performed.

1 Have you heard of PISA?

2 Do you think your country would be near the top of the PISA chart? Why?/Why not?

2 ◀ **5.8 Listen to the introduction to a lecture and answer the questions.**

1 Which two countries have experienced PISA shock in the last few years?

2 Why do people visit Finland?

3 What is the lecture going to be about?

3 Listen again and complete the definitions with one or two words.

1 Over recent years, some countries have suffered a _____ PISA shock. PISA shock _____ rich countries _____ Japan and the US perform surprisingly badly in the PISA tests, which then causes a lot of debate about the education system. _____ , Japan changed its education policies because of their lower scores in 2003.

2 In fact, so many people have been to Finland to study the education system, it is _____ PISA tourism!

4 Read the Focus box and underline the phrases in Exercise 3 used to define and clarify terms.

Understanding explanations

Lectures often contain specialist terms. The lecturer sometimes signals a specialist term by using the adjective *so-called* or the verb phrase *is sometimes/often called.* If you don't understand a term immediately, you may get further opportunities because the lecturer will often do one of the following:

• give an alternative name: *It's also known as ..., it's very similar to ...*
*Structured play **is also known as** 'play with a purpose'.*

• define the term: *X is where/when ..., X is a kind of ..., The idea (of X) is that ...*
***The idea is that** the children learn without realising.*

• give an example of the term: *So, for example, ..., An example of this might be..., ... such as ...*
***An example of this might be** doing jigsaw puzzles, which helps us develop problem-solving skills.*

5 Read the PowerPoint slides from the lecture. Do you think any of the terms will be defined? Which ones?

A **Trust**
• Little homework
• Government test to check general standards
• No comparisons between schools
• Teacher qualifications

B **Mixed-level groups**
• Benefits weaker students
• Many students get some individual teaching
• Narrow gap between best and worst students

C **Equal opportunities**
• Free education
• Mix of rich and poor
• Similarity in standards
• No streaming

D **Phenomenon-based learning**
• Topics, e.g. sound
• Students choose topics

E **Learning for life**
• Encouraging young children to enjoy learning
• Free books
• Free nursery education
• Primary school and lessons from 7

6 ◀ **5.9 Listen to the rest of the lecture and number the slides in the order that you hear them. Which two terms on the slides are defined and clarified?**

7 a Work in pairs. Try to explain the two terms that were defined. Use the Focus box to help you.

b ◀ **5.10 Listen and compare your answers to Exercise 7a.**

8 a ◀ **5.9 Listen again and make notes. Use the slides to help you structure your notes.**

b Work in pairs. Compare your notes and discuss what you understood from the lecture.

9 Discuss how the Finnish system is different from the education system in your country.

Develop your reading

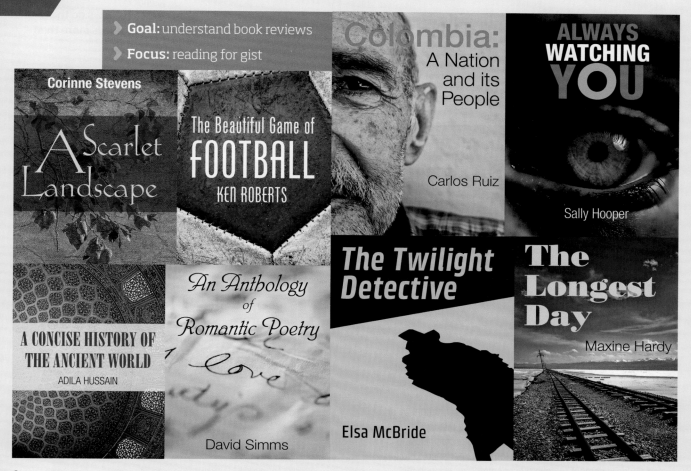

1 Look at the book covers and answer the questions.

   1 What kind of books do you think they are?
   2 Which kind of books do you read the most, e.g. detective story, love story?
   3 Which do you like the least? Why?

2 Read the Focus box. Which advice do you already follow?

Reading for gist

When you're choosing what to read or when you're in an exam, it's often helpful to have a 'light' read of the text as quickly as you can. This will help you:

- decide if the text is relevant or at the right level for you.
- get the general idea of the content.

To read for gist:

- focus on any titles or subtitles and on words you understand.
- move your eyes quickly over the text to get an idea of any main content words that are repeated.
- ignore any words you don't know.
- time yourself when you read texts to see if you can improve your reading speed.

If you're choosing what to read and there seem to be a lot of words that you don't know, try to find an easier text.

3 a Read two short book reviews for gist. What kind of books are they? Give yourself four minutes, but time yourself and see if you can do it more quickly.

b Compare your ideas with a partner. Which words helped you decide?

A

> ***A Head Full of Ghosts* by Paul G Tremblay: Winner of the Bram Stoker Award**
>
> *A Head Full of Ghosts* tells the terrifying story of 14-year-old Marjorie's developing madness. Doctors fail to make her better, and her family have huge medical bills. Marjorie's worried parents agree to take part in a reality TV programme called *The Possession*, hoping for an alternative solution. The result is an awful event. Years later, Marjorie's younger sister, Merry, is interviewed and as she retells what she remembers, she reveals new deeper fears that raise questions about memory, religion and science, as well as the nature of evil. It's a clever, scary book. You won't want to turn the lights off after reading it!

B

> ***The Mark of the Meridian* (La Marca del Meridiano) by Lorenzo Silva: Winner of the Premio Planeta**
>
> Lorenzo Silva was the surprising winner of one of the world's greatest book prizes when he won with the seventh book in his Bevilacqua and Chamorro series. The story follows two police officers trying to find out about a death in Logroño. The dead man was a friend and colleague and as they try to find the murderer, they have to examine events from the past that they were trying to forget. The book touches on some serious issues, but not in a deep way. It was quite tense at times, but this reader found the ending rather dull and undramatic.

4 Read two more reviews quickly. Then answer the questions for each review.

1 What's the basic story?
2 How many stars – one, two or three – do you think the reviewer gave?

C

Honeybees and Distant Thunder by Riku Onda: Winner of the Naoki Prize

Riku Onda is a multi-award-winning writer, who has previously written fantasy and crime fiction. This brilliant novel won one of Japan's most important prizes for literature and shows all of Onda's skills. The story follows four main characters in an international piano competition. It is told through the different points of view of the people involved – judges and news reporters as well as the pianists themselves. The novel is a bit like a sports movie in terms of type of characters and plot. There's a young unknown taught by an expert, and an older competitor having one last try. There's also a wealthy 'prince' and a beautiful young pianist who is returning to competition after a terrible experience. Onda brings excitement to each player's progress through the competition. However, more than anything, her book explores in wonderful detail the nature of music and human beings, and she manages to bring the music to life through her words.

D

Miracle on 5th Avenue by Sarah Morgan: Winner of the RITA Award

Sarah Morgan's third book in the *From Manhattan with Love* series opens with Eva Jordan on her way to look after an empty apartment for a few days and get it ready for the owner's return. It's Christmas and it's snowing. Eva is working too hard and she's single – still. But then she discovers the flat isn't empty after all. The best-selling crime writer Lucas Blade is finding it hard to write as he struggles to recover from his wife's death. The last thing he wants is to celebrate Christmas or spend time with anyone … until Eva arrives! Will his heart melt as the snow falls outside? Of course, we know the answer, and although there's some decent humour along the way, this is really only a book for fans of the genre. Personally, I lost interest towards the end.

5 Read reviews A–D again. Which reviews do the sentences refer to? Sometimes there is more than one answer.

1 The writer has won many prizes.
2 People didn't expect the writer to win the prize.
3 The book probably contains characters from a previous novel.
4 Several different characters tell the story.
5 The book is funny.
6 The book makes you think about serious themes.
7 Characters have money problems.
8 A family has to deal with a terrible crisis.

6 Complete the sentences with one word. The first letter is given.

1 The book t_____ the story of a family in Baltimore.
2 The book begins with a terrible e_____ that changes the lives of everyone involved.
3 The novel manages to r_____ difficult questions about how far we are responsible for our actions.
4 The story f_____ the lives of the couple as they go through a divorce.
5 It's actually quite funny, although it also looks at some quite serious i_____ .
6 I quite enjoyed most of the book, but I didn't really like the e_____ .
7 The book e_____ the changing nature of family life.
8 She really brings the characters to l_____ . You really believe in them.
9 However, he then d_____ she has a secret past and has to reconsider their relationship.
10 I lost i_____ halfway through the book.

7 a Order the books in reviews A–D from 1–4 (where 1 = the one you would most like to read). Think about your reasons.

b Work in pairs and compare your answers.

Develop your listening

> **Goal:** understand a technical support line

> **Focus:** dealing with technical terms

1 How good are you at dealing with technical problems? What do you usually do when you have a problem?

2 🔊 6.4 Listen to a recorded message about technical support. Match sentences a–e with the options 1–5 that you hear.

a I'd like to buy a new laptop.

b I'd like to speak to Fatima Hanif, please.

c The keyboard on the laptop I ordered recently has stopped working.

d I ordered a tablet online, but have been sent the wrong size.

e I ordered a tablet this morning, but have actually decided I want to cancel my order.

3 Read the Focus box. What techniques can help you deal with technical phone calls?

Dealing with technical terms

When you get technical support, the person helping you might use technical terms that you do not know. However, they will often explain what they mean by:

• using a synonym.

Enter the URL – that's the address of the web page.

• describing what something looks like.

Look for the Bluetooth symbol. It looks a bit like the letter B, but with two lines coming out of the left-hand side – one pointing up, one pointing down.

• explaining what you should do with something.

So basically, it's a small gadget about the size of a memory stick and you plug it in to your computer and it connects you to the internet.

You can help yourself in these situations by:

• stopping the person and saying that you do not understand and want more information. Use questions like, *Sorry, but what does that mean?* or *Do you mean the little icon at the top?*

• preparing for technical support phone calls by learning relevant technical terms. Predict before the call what words you might need and look them up in a dictionary.

4 Work in pairs. Match icons A–H with descriptions 1–8.

1 It's a kind of three-part symbol. There's an arrow on it with two other bits coming off.

2 It looks like a multi-coloured beach ball and it just goes around and around and around.

3 It's like a circle, but not a complete one. It doesn't join up at the top. Instead, there's a line coming down into the circle. You press it to shut the computer down.

4 It's round with little bits sticking out around the edge – and an empty circle in the middle.

5 It's a security icon. It means you're protected against computer viruses.

6 It's a warning sign.

7 It's a folder icon – like a yellow rectangle. It's where your folders and files are organised.

8 It looks like a window. Well, four little windows, really. If you click it, you get the start menu.

5 🔊 6.5 Listen to a conversation between a customer and a technical support adviser. Tick the icons in Exercise 4 that they mention.

6 Listen again and complete the sentences.

1 So Loretta, can you see the little window icon in the _____ corner?

2 It's the cog icon – it's like a little circle _____ .

3 Can you click on where it says 'devices' for me? It's about _____ the list.

4 Is there a warning sign by it at all? Like a yellow sign with _____ ?

5 It's the shield thing with _____ . It should be at the bottom of the screen.

6 The last thing you could do is just check the battery, which is inside the computer _____ .

7 Then put it back in and reboot it – just turn it _____ .

7 🔊 6.6 Listen to the final part of the conversation. Did the advice work?

8 Work in pairs and discuss the questions.

1 When was the last time something went wrong with your computer or another gadget? How did you solve the problem?

2 Have you ever had to phone a technical support line? What happened?

> **Goal:** write a report
> **Focus:** organising information

1 a Read the survey and answer the questions.

Media survey

1 How many hours a week do you spend following the news?

A 0–2   B 2–5   C 5–10   D 10–15   E 15+

2 What is your main source of news?

A TV   B radio   C newspaper (print)
D newspaper (online)
E social media   F blogs   G other

3 How much of the news you read/listen to do you believe is completely true?

A 0–20%   B 20–40%   C 40–60%
D 60–80%   E 80–100%

4 In your opinion, which source of news in Question 2 tells the truth the most?

5 In your opinion, what areas of the news are covered too much (TM), just enough (E) or too little (TL)?

politics	TM	E	TL
business	TM	E	TL
sport	TM	E	TL
science	TM	E	TL
weather	TM	E	TL
celebrities	TM	E	TL
positive stories	TM	E	TL
negative stories	TM	E	TL

6 What other areas of news would you like to hear more about, if any?

b Work in pairs. Compare and explain your answers.

2 Work in pairs. Look at the graphs that show responses to Questions 1 and 2 in the survey. What findings do you think are interesting/surprising?

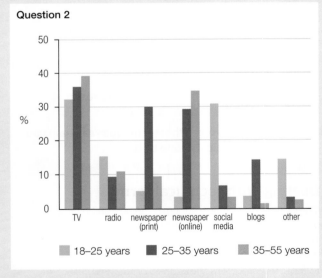

Question 2

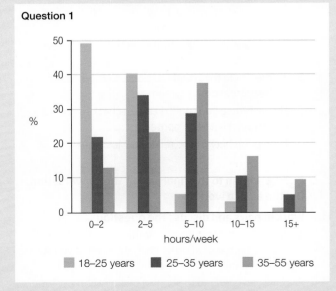

Question 1

3 You're going to read a report based on Questions 1 and 2 of the survey in Exercise 1a. Under which heading in the box would you find the answers to questions 1–6?

Introduction   Main findings   Conclusions

1 Which age group reads printed newspapers the most?
2 What is the most popular source of news overall?
3 Who took part in the survey?
4 Do people of different ages have the same news habits?
5 What might the results mean for the future of newspapers?
6 When did the survey take place?

4 a Read the report and answer the questions in Exercise 3.

> ## Report on news habits
>
> ### Introduction
> This report describes the results of a survey of people's news habits, which was conducted in March of this year. One thousand people between the ages of 18 and 55 [1]_____ and asked how much they followed the news and what their main source of news was.
>
> ### Main findings
> The survey found significant differences in the habits of younger and older people. Only 11 percent of people under the age of 25 followed the news for more than 5 hours a week, whereas almost [2]_____ of people over 35 did, and nearly 10 percent of over-35s followed the news for more than 15 hours.
>
> While TV was the most popular news source for all age groups, there was [3]_____ between age groups for other sources. Perhaps unsurprisingly, only those over 35 gave printed newspapers as their main source of news. However, interestingly, [4]_____ 4 percent of under-25s said online newspapers were their main source. This is compared to around a third of over-35s. [5]_____ , the majority of people who mainly used social media for news were under 25.
>
> ### Conclusions
> The survey results suggest that while TV will probably continue to be an important source of news, traditional newspapers may die out. Furthermore, [6]_____ social media will become more important, which might be a problem as news on social media is often less reliable.

b Complete the report with the words and phrases in the box.

> a clear difference   it appears that   two-thirds
> were interviewed   in contrast   only

5 Read the Focus box. What's the best way to organise a report? What information goes into each section?

Organising information

To write a simple report about a survey, use headings to organise it:

Introduction
- Explain what the survey is about, who conducted it and when.
- Use the passive to do this:

the survey was done, people were interviewed

Main findings
- Say what the most important finding is in the first sentence, but don't give reasons for it.
- Give one or two statistics to support this finding. You don't have to quote them all.
- If there is more than one topic in the survey, discuss each one in a different paragraph.
- To describe a contrast, use words like *while, in contrast, whereas, compared to.*
- To describe statistics, use a variety of language: *20 percent, the majority, almost two-thirds.*

Conclusions
- Explain what you think the survey results mean. Use words such as *suggest ..., it appears that.*
- Sometimes you might want to make a recommendation:

This suggests newspapers should do more to attract younger readers.

6 Work in pairs and discuss the questions.

1 Do you think the findings in the report would be similar for where you live?
2 Do you agree with the writer's conclusions? Can you think of any different conclusions, based on the survey results?
3 Can you think of any recommendations that you might make to newspaper owners?

7 Read the sentences and replace the words in bold with the phrases in the box.

> nearly all   a large majority   significant
> one out of every five   a tiny percentage
> almost a third   a quarter   just over half

1 **Thirty-two percent** of all those who were interviewed said they thought there was too much negative news.
2 **Twenty-five percent** of people below the age of 35 said they trusted TV news the most.
3 There was a **40%** difference between TV and radio as a main source of news.
4 Only **0.5%** of 18-to-25-year-olds read a printed newspaper regularly.
5 **Fifty-three percent** of all those questioned followed the news for five or more hours a week.
6 **Seventy-four percent** of older people said there was too much about celebrities in the news.
7 **Twenty percent of** people said there wasn't enough news about science.
8 Only a small number of people thought **80-100%** of the news was untrue.

Prepare

8 You're going to write a report based on two questions from the survey in Exercise 1a. Use either the survey results on page 171 or conduct the survey in your class. Do the following:

- Make a note of what the survey is about, when it was done and who was interviewed.
- Decide what the most important finding is.
- Choose one or two statistics to support this finding. Or what contrast can you show?
- Discuss one or two conclusions you could make from this finding.
- What recommendation could you make about the future?

Write

9 Write your report.

> **Goal:** understand a written interview
> **Focus:** recognising pronoun referents

1 **Look at the photos and discuss the questions.**

1 Have you ever had a pet? If not, why not?

2 What animals do you think make good pets? Why?

2 **You're going to read an interview with a vet. First, read the extract. Do you agree with the vet's answers? Why?/Why not?**

What animal makes the best pet?

It really depends on the person [1]_____ . The whole point of a pet is to reduce stress, [2]_____ ! I personally love dogs – they're so intelligent and friendly – but I don't actually own one. I work such long hours, I simply don't have the time to give a dog the attention it needs. [3]_____ . I actually have some fish. If you have a good tank for them, they look after themselves and it's very relaxing to watch them swim around. [4]_____ .

So, what makes a good pet owner?

Well, it kind of depends on the pet, [5]_____ ! Whatever animal you have, you need to care about their health [6]_____ .

3 **Complete the text in Exercise 2 with phrases/ sentences a–f.**

a and how much time they want to spend looking after <u>it</u>

b and not allow <u>them</u> to suffer unless you absolutely have to

c not add to <u>it</u>

d <u>They</u> get lonely at home and you need to take them for regular walks

e <u>That</u> makes them the best pet for me.

f but as a general rule, I'd say <u>someone</u> with pet insurance

4 **Read the Focus box. Then match the underlined pronouns in Exercise 3 with the nouns in the box. There is one underlined pronoun that does not have a matching noun.**

a pet   a pet owner   dogs   pets   stress

Recognising pronoun referents

Writers use pronouns to take the place of nouns and avoid repetition. These are called pronoun referents. If you can recognise what they refer to, you will become a better reader.

Writers use pronoun referents like *it, they, them, someone/-thing*, etc. to refer back to nouns that have already been mentioned.

They also use *it, this* or *that* to refer back to the previous sentence or a list of several ideas.

To work out what a pronoun referent refers to:

• pay attention to the verb the referent goes with. (What normally goes with that verb?)

• look back at previous sentences and find a noun that might match the pronoun.

• look back at previous sentences and find an idea that might match *this/that*. (Note that it might be used with a similar verb.)

A vet's life

Continuing our series on medical careers, we interview vet Celine Swartz, and find there's no escaping the people.

1 Well, I was shy as a kid and my family life was complicated. The pets I had offered easier relationships, which is why I prefer the phrase 'animal friends' to 'pets'. Anyway, because of that, I decided this was what I wanted to do.

2 Be prepared for the people. I probably spend 70 percent of my time with the owners. I have to make them feel better when pets die, argue with them, train them. It's difficult sometimes. The other thing I'd advise them to do is take seriously any business training at college. It's a big part of the job.

3 Well, to be honest, it's the owners! We see a lot of cats and dogs that are overweight because they're fed too much. People are under pressure at work and in a way, they need their pets more than ever, but they don't know how best to show their love. You know, they'll give their dog a biscuit without thinking that it's actually like us eating a whole packet! And with long work hours, dogs especially don't get enough exercise. This leads to obesity, which can then cause heart disease, breathing difficulties, problems with knees and even psychological issues like depression.

4 Depression in dogs? Of course! There's an enormous amount of evidence that animals experience emotions. Why wouldn't they? Take elephants – they live in close family groups all their lives. Mothers and daughters may stay together for 40 years. When a family member dies, they suffer sadness as we would – obviously! We also know animals suffer stress and pain and that can cause very strange behaviour.

5 Well, there are sprays that can help calm pets and also drugs similar to Prozac that can treat symptoms, but I think they avoid the real issues and can sometimes cause other problems, too. My partner is a pet psychologist and she runs courses to actually change behaviour. We also have to train owners, which can be hard. They often don't want to accept that their own behaviour isn't helping their pet. In some ways, they'd rather see it as a medical problem.

6 Well, they're not very helpful. I mean, of course training is more expensive than drugs in the short term, but it actually solves problems, so is cheaper in the end. Sure, vet bills have gone up, but that's not because we're greedy. We used to earn extra from people buying food and pet toys and so on, but big superstores and the internet have taken away a lot of that income. We've had to replace it by increasing fees. The other thing is, as medicine develops, there's a lot more we can do. In the past, if a dog lost a leg in an accident or had cancer, then we would put it down – which costs $100. These days, we can build a plastic leg and cure some cancers, so if owners have the money or insurance, $10,000 for a treatment is not unusual.

7 Well, we are a business so it varies from year to year, but $60,000–100,000 is fairly typical, which isn't that much when you think of all the training we have to do. Most vets leave college with a $100,000+ debt. Then there are the hours we work and the risks of having a business.

8 The animals, of course!

9 Early in my career I would've said the people, but I've learnt to enjoy that side of things. I'd say it's money – worrying about it, talking about it, getting complaints about it.

5 **Read the rest of the interview with the vet. Match questions a–i with answers 1–9. The referents may help you.**

a How much do you earn, then?

b So how do you treat that? Can you treat it?

c What's the worst?

d Is that a real thing?

e Why did you become a vet?

f What's the best thing about the job?

g What is the biggest problem for pets that you see these days?

h What would your advice be for anyone thinking of becoming a vet?

i I'm guessing those training courses aren't cheap. How do you feel when you see media comments about rising vet fees?

6 **Read the interview again. What do the underlined words refer to?**

1 … because of <u>that</u>, I decided this was what I wanted to do.

2 <u>It</u>'s difficult sometimes.

3 <u>It</u>'s a big part of the job.

4 … <u>they</u> don't know how best to show their love.

5 … <u>it</u>'s actually like us eating a whole packet!

6 Why wouldn't <u>they</u>?

7 <u>they</u> suffer sadness as we would

8 … <u>that</u> can cause very strange behaviour.

9 I think <u>they</u> avoid the real issues

10 In some ways, <u>they</u>'d rather see it as a medical problem.

11 … but <u>that</u>'s not because we're greedy

7 **Work in pairs and discuss the questions.**

1 What do you think is the most interesting/surprising thing in the article?

2 Do you think being a vet is a good job in your country? Why?/Why not?

3 Do you think people spend too much time and money on their pets?

4 Do you know how animals are treated in other countries? Is it different from your country?

> **Goal:** understand a conversation

> **Focus:** understanding vague language

1 Discuss the questions.

1 Do you know anyone who you can describe in the following ways? Give examples of their behaviour.
- He's/She's very generous.
- He's/She's careful with money.
- He/She spends money very easily.
- He's/She's got more money than sense.

2 What different payment methods can you think of? Make a list.

3 Which payment methods do you use? What for? Which do you use most?

2 a 🔊 **7.7 Listen to two friends, Aiden and Burak, discussing cashless payments. Which topics are mentioned?**

1 homeless people taking cashless payments

2 the number of people in Sweden who use cash

3 the fastest way to shop online

4 Aiden's attitude to money

5 how big companies use the data they collect

6 psychological differences between paying by card and paying with cash

7 the reasons why there are homeless people in Sweden

8 why banks and tech companies prefer cashless payments

b Work in pairs and compare your answers. What do you remember about each topic?

3 Read the Focus box. Which words and phrases have you heard before? Do you use any of them?

Understanding vague language

Vague language is very common, especially in spoken English. You often add words and phrases like *sort of, kind of, about, that kind of thing,* etc. to make what you say less direct and factual.

You may hear vague language when speakers want to show that:
- they don't know the name of a thing or person.
- they aren't sure of the best way to describe something.
- they think the listener already has the general idea.
- something is part of a group or a category.
- they're being friendly and that it's not important to be precise.

Learning common phrases that are used to do these things will help you get better at understanding longer informal conversations.

4 a Listen to the conversation again. Complete the sentences with two or three words.

1 I was talking to a friend of mine in Sweden _____ .

2 Everyone he knows there has _____ stopped using cash altogether.

3 Maybe they carry _____ card reader around.

4 Actually, it all left me _____ feeling I was going to use cash more!

5 They don't have to pay people to count the cash and store it and move it around – like security guards _____ .

6 Not like a real physical pain _____ .

b Choose the best definition of your answers to Exercise 4a.

1 ⓐ sometime recently
   b the day before yesterday

2 a completely
   b almost

3 a a special kind of
   b it's not important what kind of

4 a feeling more like this than anything else
   b feeling exactly like this

5 a and other people who do similar jobs
   b and other similar activities

6 a and nothing similar to this
   b it's similar, but not exactly like this

5 a 🔊 **7.8 Listen to ten sentences. Which sentences contain vague phrases?**

b Listen again and write down the vague phrases.

6 Work in pairs and discuss the questions.

1 What are the advantages of having a cashless society?

2 What are the disadvantages?

Develop your writing

> **Goal:** give written directions

> **Focus:** adding supporting details

1 Discuss the questions.

1 When was the last time you gave someone directions to your home? Did they find it easily?

2 How good are you at giving directions in your own language? And in English?

3 When you are travelling in a car, do you prefer to use a map or GPS?

2 Read the messages and answer the questions.

1 Why was each message written?

2 What is the relationship between the writer and the other person?

3 How does the writer think the other person will be travelling?

1

Messenger

Hello again Leila,

It's now just two weeks until your stay with us in beautiful Wales and we're looking forward to meeting you and your family. Check-in is between 4 p.m. and 6 p.m., so if you think you'll be late for whatever reason, please call and let us know (05681 3779).

I'm guessing you'll be using GPS, but the last part of the journey can be tricky, so I thought it best to give you directions.

Once you've gone through Lampeter, take the A482 towards Aberaeron, and after passing through the village of Ciliau Aeron, continue for a quarter of a mile until you come to a crossroads. You'll see a brown sign for the Llanerchaeron National Trust property on your right, but you need to turn LEFT here.

You go up a steep hill and continue until the road bends round to the right. You should see a post box and a house called Parc Maw. Turn left here and One Cat Farm is the second entrance on the right, a few hundred yards along. We're actually a bit off the road, so if you reach a small cottage on the left, it means you've gone too far. Parking is right outside the cow shed!

Hope this helps.

Call me if you have any problems finding us.

All the best,

Sally

One Cat Farm Bed and Breakfast

2

Dear colleague,

We are all looking forward to our training event and team-building weekend next week. We will be providing coach transport on Thursday evening, but for those who are not joining us until Friday, please find directions below:

By Car

Postcode for your Sat Nav: LS78 5XX

Directions

- Take the M35 motorway and come off at junction 2.
- Follow signs to Barlow on the B3461.
- As you enter the village and *before* you reach the church, you should see a sign on the right to Heathcoat Lodge and Training Centre. The venue is about half a mile down the road.

We have spaces reserved in the car park. You will need to tell reception the registration number of your car.

By train

Take the train from Victoria to Kendal. There is a taxi office in the car park outside the station. We have set up an account with the company so you do not need to pay.

Remember there is coffee at 9.30 for a 10 o'clock start to the training event.

If you have any further queries, please do not hesitate to contact me.

Halle Simmonds

HR Senior Consultant (Training)

Extension 3672.

3

Hi Rika

Great to hear from you! Really looking forward to seeing you again.

Can't remember if I told you or not, but I've moved since the last time you were here. I finally managed to buy my own place last year (with a little bit of help from mum and dad!). It's lovely! I'm now at 57B Pemberton Road, London N4 1BJ.

Not sure if you're getting a cab from the airport or if you can access maps on your phone, so here are some directions for using the underground just in case.

Get the Piccadilly Line from Heathrow to Manor House – it's one line so you don't need to change. Come out of Exit 6 and at the top of the stairs there's a bus stop just ahead of you. If you have your back to the stairs, you should also see some shops on your right. Get the 29, 341 or 141 bus and get off at the third stop. You should hear an announcement saying Mattison Road. To your right, on the other side of the road, there's a big Turkish place called Gökyüzü. You want the second road on the left after the bus stop. I'm about halfway up the road, on the right. Oh, and make sure you ring the top bell.

If you get lost or have any problems, call me on +44-7791-7730167.

See you Saturday,

Tanya

3 Read the Focus box. What kind of extra details can writers add to help readers understand directions?

Adding supporting details

When you give directions, you often add extra details to make sure the reader doesn't get lost. You can give information about:

- local landmarks and easily recognised places.

As you're walking down the main road, you should see a clock tower on your right.

- distance.

It's about two hundred metres up the road from there.

- facing the right way.

If you're standing with your back to the station, turn left.

4 Work in pairs. Read each message again and find two examples of supporting details.

5 Complete the sentences with the words in the box.

approach	direction	exit	facing	fork
halfway	off	roundabout	side	subway

1 Keep going until you get to a big _____ . Take the third exit.
2 Once you get off, keep walking in the same _____ as the bus.
3 Come out of the main _____ of the station and turn right.
4 The farmhouse is a bit _____ the main road, so it's quite easy to miss it.
5 When you're coming along Rue Chapon, we're about _____ down, on the right.
6 As you _____ the village, you'll see a large cross at the side of the road. Take the next left.
7 Warren Mews is a tiny _____ street immediately after the supermarket on the right.
8 When you're walking away from the station, you'll see a _____ under the main road. Go down that and turn left at the other end.
9 If you're _____ the station, the bus you need leaves from the stop on the end.
10 After about 500 metres, you will reach a _____ in the road. Take the road on the left.

6 Complete the sentences with the correct preposition if one is needed.

1 If you have your back _____ the hospital, I'll be waiting for you in the car park to the left.
2 As you come _____ of the building, you need to go right.
3 Take exit 33 _____ the motorway. It should be signposted to Livorno.
4 As you approach _____ the beach, buy a ticket from the small wooden building by the side of the road.
5 Our house is about halfway _____ the hill.
6 The turning is immediately _____ the last house in the village.
7 As you walk _____ from the tower, you'll see a grand building on the left. That's the President's residence.
8 If you're facing _____ the lake, walk along the shore to the left.

7 Work in pairs. Choose two places you both know. How would you get there from where you are now? Which language from Exercises 5 and 6 could you use to describe the journeys?

Prepare

8 a You're going to write an email giving directions. Choose one of the tasks.
- A friend is coming to your house for the first time.
- A colleague from overseas is coming to your office for the first time.
- You are organising an event (e.g. a conference).

b Think about:
- the reason they are coming.
- where they are coming from.
- the best way to get to the destination.
- what they should look for on the way.
- what they should do if they have problems.
- whether your email should be formal or informal.

Write

9 Write your email. Try to use language from this lesson and remember to add supporting details.

8A Develop your listening

> **Goal:** understand a radio programme

> **Focus:** understanding new words

1 Look at the photo. You're going to listen to a radio programme called *Man-Made World*. What do you think it will be about?

2 a 🔊 8.3 Listen to the introduction of the programme. Can you work out the meaning of the words in the box?

> micro-plastics   the food chain
> sculptures   zero waste

b Work in pairs and discuss your answers to Exercise 2a. Can you improve your answers?

3 Read the Focus box. Did you use any of the techniques when you were doing Exercise 2a?

Understanding new words

When you listen to English, you will hear words that you do not know.

the dangers of them entering **the food chain**

You can improve your understanding of new words in different ways.

- Learn affixes: *micro-plastics* (*micro-* = very small), *reuse* (*re-* = again)
- Focus on the words you do know:

*micro-**plastics** in the **sea** and the **dangers** of them entering the food chain through **fish** and therefore ending up **in our own bodies***

- Notice surrounding definitions or examples:

*Martha follows a zero-waste lifestyle and she and other members of her online community **claim to throw away less than a shoebox of rubbish.***

- Learn collocations and chunks of words that go together: *recycle rubbish, throw away rubbish, take rubbish to the dump.*
- *Be* aware of collocations which use a pronoun instead of the noun: *throw it away, take it to the dump.*

4 🔊 8.4 Listen to the rest of the programme. Are the sentences true (T) or false (F)?

1 Zero waste basically just means recycling everything.

2 Recycling products isn't always better for the environment.

3 Martha first thought about unnecessary waste when her son got a lot of toys he didn't care about.

4 She first decided to try a zero-waste lifestyle because of a friend.

5 People who promote zero waste have been criticised.

6 A lot of people writing about zero waste are women.

5 a 🔊 8.5 Work in pairs. Listen to extracts from the programme and discuss what you think the words in the box mean.

> austere   bulk   clicked   come in for   disposable
> dump   flamed

b Match the words in the box with meanings a–g.

a suddenly make sense

b be criticised a lot – especially on social media

c describes something you only use a few times and can throw away easily

d describes something basic and uncomfortable

e very large quantities of something

f a place where rubbish is taken

g receive

6 a 🔊 8.6 Read five sentences from the interview that contain *it*. Listen and notice how the surrounding words in bold link with the pronoun.

1 He was surrounded **by it**.

2 I **used it to** make noises, I **made it into** a ball, you know, played **with it** a lot.

3 You **know**, **it's kind** of quite a shock.

4 Do you **think it has** anything to do with you being a woman?

5 I wouldn't **say it's a** woman's issue.

b Work in pairs. What does *it* refer to in the sentences in Exercise 6a?

7 You often add *re-* to verbs to mean 'again'. Complete the sentences with a common verb plus *re-*.

1 Don't throw that away yet. You can _____ it at least a couple more times.

2 I obviously missed something because the end of the film made no sense to me. I'll have to _____ it.

3 It's such a great book. It's definitely worth _____ . You enjoy it more the second time.

4 I thought it was a good idea, but maybe we need to _____ it.

5 The whole thing is a complete mess. I'm just going to have to _____ it from the beginning.

6 If the soup's gone cold, I can _____ it in the microwave.

8 Work in pairs and answer the questions. What could you do to reduce waste? Do you do any of these things? Why?/Why not?

Develop your reading

> **Goal:** understand a blog post

> **Focus:** using existing knowledge

1   Look at the photos and discuss the questions.

1   Where do you think the weddings took place?

2   Which looks most like the kind of wedding people have in your country? In what way/s?

2   Read the Focus box. Which things do you already do? Which do you think would work best for you?

Using existing knowledge

When you read a text in English about a familiar topic such as weddings and marriages, you can use your existing knowledge of the topic to help you understand the language.

Here are some tips:

• Think of words connected to the topic that might be used and look them up in a dictionary.

• Create a page in your notebook with topic words.

• Add to the list after you have read the text and when you read other texts on the topic.

• Don't just write single words, but pay attention to words that go together (also known as collocations) such as *a lovely bouquet/throw the bouquet, the beautiful bride/kiss the bride/the bride's dress.*

3 a   Work in pairs. Which of the things in the box can you see in the photos?

bouquet   ceremony   groom   guest

b   Work in pairs. Make a list of at least six more nouns connected to weddings. Use the photos to help you.

4   Read the blog post about a wedding between a British woman and a Colombian man. Which of a–i normally feature in 1–3? Match a–i with 1–3.

1   a Colombian wedding

2   a British wedding

3   both

a   money

b   a best man

c   a bouquet

d   candles

e   dancing

f   rings

g   shoes

h   singing to the bride

i   speeches

Tales from Colombia

The Big Day(s)

It's three months since the wedding and, as you will have noticed, I haven't been doing much to the blog! Hey, I've been busy. We had a perfect **honeymoon** – Vegas, LA, San Fran – then there was the move into the new apartment, and, well, just being in love! Sometimes blogging just has to wait. But now Camilo is away on business and I'm all on my own, so I thought I'd start writing again. And what better place to start than with the big day itself – or rather the big three days. The whole thing was a real mixture of British and Colombian traditions, with a few twists.

The Colombian part:

The *serenata*: The evening before the wedding, we met some friends and family for dinner and then I went back to the hotel where we were staying. I was just getting ready for bed when I heard this band playing. I went to the window and there was my Camilo. Anyone who's heard his karaoke may be surprised, but he seemed to have the voice of an angel to me – the whole thing was so sweet! But then it was quite hot and I felt a little dizzy looking down from the balcony!

The coins and candles: As well as exchanging the wedding **rings**, which they do here too, we followed the Colombian tradition of *las arras*. These are small coins that traditionally the groom gives to the bride. This symbolises that what's his is now also hers. But I have my feminist beliefs and so I gave Camilo some coins, too. We also did the candle ceremony, where you each light a small candle and then use those to light a larger one before blowing out the small ones. It's a beautiful **symbol** of marriage.

The shoes: In the UK, the bride throws her **bouquet** to a group of single ladies to catch to see who'll get married next. In Colombia, it's the single men that the tradition applies to. They all place a shoe under the bride's dress and she picks one out. We did both. It's only fair.

The dancing: My salsa dancing is basically at a similar level to Camilo's singing, but you can't have a wedding in Colombia – or, in fact, any celebration – without dancing. We had a fantastic band, which played till 4 in the morning – with a British part in the middle (see below).

The British part

The bridesmaid: Unlike in British weddings, there's no best man or bridesmaid in Colombian weddings. The tradition is to have an older godfather and godmother who support the happy **couple** in their marriage, but I had to have my best friend, Fi, as a bridesmaid, too.

The speeches: They aren't a big thing here in Colombia, but we had them. My dad gave one, translated by Fi – we studied Spanish together. And then because Camilo had no best man, and because I like to play with UK tradition too, my bridesmaid Fi gave a **speech**, which was hilarious.

The dancing: It's not that we never have dancing at a British wedding, it's just that there's usually a bad disco with even worse dancing – a tradition I am happily continuing! So, to make things a bit fairer for me, we had a break for a British country dance. My brother, Tom, plays fiddle in a folk band and he organised it with his mate, Hamish, who taught everyone the moves. I think the Colombians were a little confused at first, but then they realised most of the Brits were, too!! It was great fun and a great sharing experience.

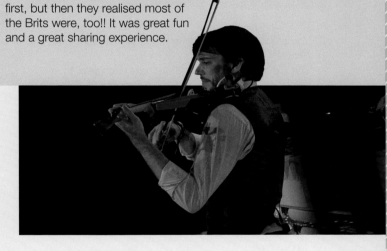

5 Read the blog again and answer the questions.

1 Why do you think she is writing the blog in general?

2 Why did she stop for a while?

3 Is Camilo a good singer?

4 What two traditions do they adapt? Why?

5 How does the candle ceremony symbolise marriage?

6 Is the writer a good dancer?

7 Do you think country dancing is a big tradition in the UK? Why?/Why not?

8 What's your overall impression of the writer? What words would you use to describe her?

6 Find the words in bold in the blog and complete the collocations.

1 We _____ a _____ honeymoon.

2 As well as _____ the _____ rings ...

3 It's a _____ symbol of _____ .

4 The bride _____ her bouquet to a group of _____ .

5 The godfather and godmother _____ the _____ couple.

6 My bridesmaid Fi _____ a speech, which was _____ .

7 Work in pairs and:

1 underline any other nouns in the blog that are connected to weddings.

2 underline any verbs, adjectives or nouns that go with these nouns.

3 think of other verbs, adjectives or nouns that go with these nouns.

8 Work in pairs. Take turns describing weddings you have been to. Which wedding was:

• the biggest?

• the smallest?

• the most traditional?

• the least traditional?

Develop your writing

> **Goal:** write invitations

> **Focus:** formal and informal language

1 a Match invitations 1–4 with the events in the box.

> a birthday   a launch party   an awards ceremony
> an engagement party   a conference   a wedding

b Discuss the questions.

1 Have you been invited to any of these events in the past? When was the last one?

2 Why were you invited?

3 How exactly were you invited?

4 How did the event go?

2 Read invitations A and B and answer the questions.

1 What kind of event is it?

2 Who is invited?

3 Is it the kind of event you would like to go to?

A

Invitation

Adrian Gooch CEO
Centaur Care Group
warmly invites you to the
5th Centaur Pride Awards

Dear Giorgio,
You are warmly invited to attend the Centaur Pride Awards.

The Centaur Pride Awards are held each year to celebrate the success and achievements of our staff across all our operations in ten different countries. All 16 finalists receive a cash prize of £200, with the winner receiving the Pride trophy. We wish all the finalists the best of luck.

<u>Find out more about the finalists.</u>

The winners will be announced at our gala dinner and awards ceremony held at The Markham Hotel, Birmingham. The event will be hosted by stand-up comedian and ex-Centaur employee, Jenny Jones.

Thursday, 23rd June
18.00–23.00
The Markham Hotel
20 St John St
Birmingham
B1 7JS
Dress code: formal

Should you have any special dietary or specific access requirements, please include this in your RSVP or contact <u>Belinda Fortova</u>.

RSVP by Friday, 10th May, Belinda Fortova, Marketing and Events.

Centaur
CARE GROUP

1
Roger
&
Marjorie Jones
would like to invite
Martha Green
to celebrate the marriage of
their daughter
Rachel Grace &
James Bentley
at The Royal York Hotel
on 4th April 2019 at 2 p.m.
RSVP by 4th February

2
Party!
COME AND CELEBRATE MY
50th
BIRTHDAY PARTY
on Friday, 12th December
from 8 p.m. til late
at The Grange Hotel
Dress: smart casual
No gifts!
RSVP

3
The Corner Bookshop
invites you to the launch of Sally Hooper's thrilling new novel, Always Watching You. 22nd October from 8 p.m. Author Q&A, and signed copies available.

4
Homestyle Kitchens
invites you to its annual sales conference
from 16th–18th February
at Millthorpe Hotel, Glasgow
Dress: smart casual
End-of-conference party
on the last night

B

Mailbox   Inbox ∨   VIPs ∨   Drafts ∨

Dear Monica,
As you know, it's Jie's first birthday in a few weeks' time. My parents are going to be there, but obviously not many of my friends and family from China can come. I'd really like it if you could, though. It would mean a lot to me as you've been so friendly and supportive since I've been here. For Chinese people, the first birthday is always a big celebration and we're having a big party with what's called 'the birthday grab'. It's a bit complicated to explain, but basically the baby chooses a present and that says something about their future. You'll see.

Anyway, the party is on Saturday, 16th Nov – from two o'clock onwards – and it's going to be at our apartment, 55 Johnson House, Amhurst Rd. Let me know if you need directions.

Obviously, bring little Asher and your husband, too. I've also invited Kath and her daughter from our mother and baby group.

Really hope you can make it.
Anqi

3 Read the invitations A and B again. Which of information a–h is in both invitations?

a reason for the event

b date and time

c the venue

d instructions for how to get there

e what you should wear

f an offer to provide special food

g a request to reply by a certain time

h the names of other people who are invited

4 Work in pairs. What features make invitation A formal and invitation B informal? Underline examples.

5 Read the Focus box. Are the features you underlined in the box?

Formal and informal language

Formal	Informal
Clear layout and design: headings underlining bullets (•)	Text (no obvious layout)
No contractions *I am We will*	Contractions *I'm We'll*
More passives (fewer *I / we*) *You are warmly invited.* *Winners will be announced.*	More direct (more *I / we*) *We're having a big party.* *I'd really like it if you could come.*
Other more formal grammar (*will / should*) *The event will be held at The Markham Hotel.* *Should you need any help, contact Nicola.*	More everyday grammar *It's going to be at our apartment.* *If you have any problems, phone me.* *Bring Asher, too.*
Formal words *receive an award* *I will be attending.* *RSVP*	Everyday words *I'm definitely going to come.* *Let me know if you can come.*

Replies usually reflect the same level of formality as the invitation.

6 a Complete the sentences with words from invitation A.

1 You are _____ invited to the wedding of Jane Smyth and Mark Saddleworth.

2 The reception will be _____ at the Bay Country Club.

3 You are invited to _____ the 35th Top Builder Awards.

4 The event will be _____ by Usain Bolt.

5 All the winners _____ a €1000 prize.

6 _____ you require transport to the venue, please contact Roger Blunt.

7 Dress _____ : black tie.

8 _____ by Friday, 10th May to the address below. Please include any dietary requirements.

b Work in pairs. How might you rewrite the sentences in Exercise 6a in a more informal way?

1 Mark and I are getting married and we'd really love it if you could come to our wedding.

7 Read the replies to the invitations. Can the people who were invited go? What extra information do they give?

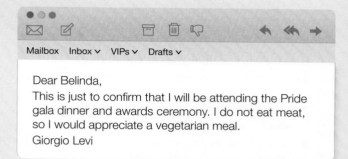

Dear Belinda,
This is just to confirm that I will be attending the Pride gala dinner and awards ceremony. I do not eat meat, so I would appreciate a vegetarian meal.
Giorgio Levi

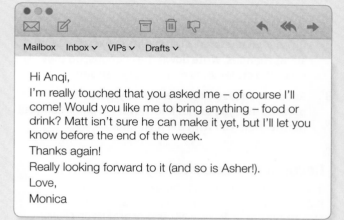

Hi Anqi,
I'm really touched that you asked me – of course I'll come! Would you like me to bring anything – food or drink? Matt isn't sure he can make it yet, but I'll let you know before the end of the week.
Thanks again!
Really looking forward to it (and so is Asher!).
Love,
Monica

8 Read the sentences from other replies to invitations A and B. Match 1–10 with A or B. Then work in pairs and compare your answers.

1 That's such a shame!

2 This is to confirm that I will be attending.

3 I feel really honoured that you've invited me.

4 I have a previous engagement that day.

5 I have a severe nut allergy, which requires food to be prepared separately.

6 I'll see if I can rearrange things.

7 This is just to inform you that I will be unable to attend.

8 I'm afraid I won't be able to make it.

9 What'll people be wearing? Is it going to be very formal?

10 I will require access for a large electric wheelchair.

Prepare

9 You're going to write an invitation, either formal or informal. Choose an event from the box in Exercise 1a or use your own idea. Include relevant details such as:

• the reason for the event.

• where and when it'll take place.

• other information about what will happen at the event.

• how to respond to the invitation and by when.

• other people who could come, too.

Write

10 Write your invitation.

9A Develop your listening

> **Goal:** understand a radio programme

> **Focus:** recognising uncertainty and opinion

1 How true do you think the statements are?

1 How happy you are depends on how you were brought up.

2 Research shows that people who speak a foreign language are happier and live longer.

3 Richer people are happier and healthier than poorer people.

4 Scientists claim that good health mainly depends on having good genes.

2 ◁)) 9.3 Listen to the statements in Exercise 1 with slight changes. Write down the changes. Do they make the statements more or less certain?

3 Read the Focus box. Underline any words and phrases that you do not know. Work in pairs. Can your partner help you with the meaning?

Recognising uncertainty and opinion

There are many words and phrases that show something is not certain or not always true. Some show that statements do not apply in all cases or are just opinions. Knowing – and being able to hear – these phrases will help you decide your own attitude towards the statements you hear.

Certain
Research **shows/proves** happy people live longer.
Psychologists **know** happy people live longer.
Happy people **will** live longer.
It has been shown/proven that happy people live longer.

Less certain
Research **suggests** …
Psychologists **argue/claim** that …
They **may (possibly)** …
It's possible that they …
It appears that they …
I'd suggest that they **might** …

Applies to all
Research **shows** happy people live longer.
Without exception, happy people live longer.

Doesn't apply to all
Some research shows that …
Research shows **most** happy people …
Research shows that, **on average**, happy people …
In general, happy people **normally** live …
Happy people **tend to** live …

4 ◁)) 9.4 Listen to the introduction to a radio programme. Which of points 1–3 does the presenter make?

1 People want to have a long and happy life.

2 People will tend to live for longer because of better healthcare.

3 People's levels of happiness are falling.

5 ◁)) 9.5 Listen to the rest of the programme. Which of 1–6 do we learn?

1 There's more research into depression because drug companies make a lot of money from it.

2 Positive psychology focuses on behaviour that will make people feel happier.

3 We can control our levels of happiness in several ways.

4 Smiling or laughing can make you feel better.

5 Several governments have invested in charities and 'Happiness Clubs'.

6 The economy benefits from having a happier society.

6 Listen again and complete the sentences with two or three words.

1 Until recently, research ＿＿＿＿＿ focus more on what causes depression.

2 However, research also ＿＿＿＿＿ about 40 percent of happiness is due to things we do in our daily lives.

3 Being kind to other people certainly makes people feel positive, so it's ＿＿＿＿＿ volunteering may be good for people.

4 Usually the simple act of laughing is enough to create more – and genuine – laughter. And ＿＿＿＿＿ that laughter has improved the health of those taking part.

5 However, these organisations are community projects with limited money and ＿＿＿＿＿ governments are not doing enough to increase people's happiness.

6 There is an economic benefit from investing in making society happier, because ＿＿＿＿＿ happy people are healthier.

7 Governments don't seem to see this benefit because, ＿＿＿＿＿ , many in power don't take the idea of positive psychology seriously.

7 Work in pairs and discuss the questions.

1 Did you learn anything new from the programme?

2 Do you do any of the activities that develop happiness?

3 Would you do any of the other activities? Why?/Why not?

4 Do you think governments should try to promote happiness?

> **Goal:** understand adverts
> **Focus:** recognising persuasive language

1 Look at the photos and discuss the questions.

1 What charities or non-profit organisations from your country do you know? What do they do?

2 Have you ever donated something to a charity, volunteered or raised money for one?

3 If so, which charity and why?

2 Read the advert for a charity and answer the questions.

1 What do they want you to do: donate something, raise money or do work for them?

2 How do they try to persuade you?

¹You're in a plane flying at over 3000 m. A door opens and your instructor tells you that this is your moment. This is your time to experience the magic of flying – falling through the clouds at ²nearly 200 km/hour – yet safe in the knowledge that you are attached to an instructor who has done this hundreds of times before.

You can get this once-in-a-lifetime feeling for free ³if you collect just $2,000 for our charity. And with that money, ⁴we'll make a wish come true for a child suffering from a serious illness, we'll help you live your dream and we'll change lives forever. ⁵Why wait till tomorrow? ⁶Call us today.

3 Read the Focus box and match the underlined examples 1–6 in the advert with a–f.

Recognising persuasive language

Adverts often use particular patterns and vocabulary to try to persuade you to do something. They usually include some or all of the following:

a words like *thousands, millions* or *nearly* and *over* to emphasise the size.
   help thousands of people; costs nearly a million dollars

b words like *just, only, simple* and *small* to show that an action is easy.
   It only takes five minutes to make a difference.

c *we/us/our* and *you/your* to make it feel as if you are in a personal conversation.
   We know you want to help. And we can show you how.

d rhetorical questions to encourage agreement.
   (Have you) ever wanted to save a life? You can.

e 'the power of three': a list of three points or similar sounding structures to emphasise a point.
   'Government is of the people, by the people, for the people.' (Abraham Lincoln)

f imperative at the end to encourage you to act.
   Do it now – before it's too late.

4 Read three more adverts for charities. Are the sentences true (T) or false (F)?

1 a The charity provides activities for young people.
 b You need experience to do the work.
 c The charity encourages people to work together.

2 a Vegans for Life want people to volunteer to work for their organisation.
 b You don't have to pay for the recipes and advice.
 c Most people had stopped being vegan three months after they started.

3 a *Straight Up* is a kind of newspaper on the internet.
 b Readers must give $3 a month to support the organisation.
 c Staff at *Straight Up* are volunteers.

5 Work in pairs and discuss the questions.

1 Which advert do you think is the most persuasive? Why?

2 Would you do what any of the adverts ask you to do? Why?/Why not?

6 a Complete the sentences from the adverts with two words.

1 This is also a great opportunity for you to learn _____ , give something back to your community and get valuable work experience.

2 Come on, _____ .

3 What if you could do that while also making life better for animals, reducing your impact on the environment and _____ ? _____ ? It isn't.

4 _____ people have already tried it and our surveys show 97% felt healthier, _____ had more energy and over two-thirds were still vegan after 90 days.

5 As you're here, we have a _____ to ask.

6 Yes, _____ the price of a cup of coffee you can get all the facts, so you can decide what to think.

b Match the sentences in Exercise 6a with a–f in the Focus box.

c Work in pairs. Find and underline in adverts 1–3 other examples of the persuasive language in the Focus box.

7 Work in pairs. Think of a slogan or hashtag for the four adverts. Then share your ideas with the class.

8 Work in pairs and discuss the questions.

1 If you had a million dollars to donate to charity, who would you give it to and why?

2 If you had ten hours a week of free time to volunteer for an organisation, who would you volunteer for and what would you do? Explain your answers.

3 What's your favourite charity and why?

1

ARE YOU OVER 18 YEARS OLD AND LOOKING TO GET MORE INVOLVED WITH YOUR LOCAL COMMUNITY?

THE GREEN PEOPLE

Do you enjoy working with young people and children?

The Green People charity needs bright, active volunteers like you to run weekly groups for children aged 4–16 years old. This is also a great opportunity for you to learn new skills, give something back to your community and get valuable work experience.

Training will be provided by us and there will be on-going support from current volunteers. We require just 1–2 hours of your time every week.

So if you want to make a difference and share our values of peace, equality and love of nature, then we are the organisation for you. Come on, apply today.

2

VEGANS FOR LIFE

Who doesn't want to feel lighter, healthier and fitter? What if you could do that while also making life better for animals, reducing your impact on the environment and saving money? Sounds impossible? It isn't. All of this comes from one simple thing: being vegan.

We at Vegans for Life know that being vegan is easy, but we also know that first step can be hard. People have questions: What can I eat? How do I cook without meat or dairy? Can I get everything my body needs from a vegan diet?

That's why we have the Vegan Promise. Promise to be vegan for 30 days here and we'll send you a daily email with easy recipes and loads of advice, all for free. Thousands of people have already tried it and our surveys show 97% felt healthier, almost 90% had more energy and over two-thirds were still vegan after 90 days. Join us and see the positive effects a vegan diet can have on your life.

3

As you're here, we have a small favour to ask. We need a little money, any amount you can afford will do. Unlike other online news services, we don't make you pay a monthly fee, we keep advertising to a minimum and any profit we make goes back into the business. We think real, fair, independent news is a right and should be free. But unfortunately, it still costs money: most of our reporters could earn more elsewhere, but they work here because they believe in our values. On average, our readers give around $30, but if everyone gave just $3, we could survive and achieve even more. Yes, for just the price of a cup of coffee you can get all the facts, so *you* can decide what to think. Click here to donate.

Thank you.

Develop your writing

1 Look at the photos and discuss the questions.

1 Have you ever been to any events like these? If so, when? What were they like?

2 Which would you like to go to in the future? Why?

2 Which event/s in the photos could the sentences describe?

1 They have the loudest **supporters** in the world!

2 Tickets **sold out** as soon as they went on sale.

3 It can **go on** for days.

4 We had to **queue** for ages to get in.

5 It rained, which really **ruined** things.

6 The **atmosphere** was amazing.

7 The security was really **tight**.

8 It was incredibly **stressful** to watch.

3 Read a post describing a visit to one of the events in the photos and answer the questions.

1 Which event did Marina go to? Why?

2 What was unusual about the visit?

3 What did she enjoy about it?

4 a Complete the comments with the adjectives in the box.

brilliant	disappointing	exciting	jealous	lucky
pleased	terrified	worried		

b Write a comment of your own to Marina. Ask at least one question.

Marina

As most of you know, I really wasn't looking forward to turning 30. In fact, I was so stressed about the idea that I'd decided to spend the day locked in my apartment crying and eating too much cake! Luckily, though, Johan had other plans for me. I knew he was planning a surprise for me, and he'd told me to be ready by 6.30, so I was up really early getting ready. He picked me up in his car and told me to close my eyes during the drive, which I more or less managed to do! When I was finally allowed to open them, you can imagine how excited I was to see we were at Wimbledon! Listening to me go on about tennis all the time has clearly had an impact on Johan!

He had tried to get tickets in advance, but it's a kind of lottery and since he didn't have any success we had to queue for one of the tickets they sell each day of the tournament. As it's such a popular event, I suppose that's fair and allows all the real fans to go. We had to queue for hours, but we got talking to the people around us and I loved the whole atmosphere. And luckily the tickets hadn't sold out when we finally got to the gate at midday! We saw two of the women's quarter-finals, which were both excellent and very close. They had to shut the roof at one point due to the rain, but we still had the traditional strawberries and cream – and I had the best birthday ever!

Anna

Wow! You ¹_____ thing! That sounds ²_____ . I actually tried to get into Wimbledon once, but we got there late and as a result missed out on tickets, so I'm super ³_____ . How much did you pay, btw?

Fernanda

I'm glad you had such a good time and that the matches were so ⁴_____ . I went to see Arsenal play Man United a couple of years ago. I had to pay extra for the tickets, we had to queue for ages because of the tight security and then it was just a very dull 0-0 draw with absolutely no atmosphere in the stadium. The whole thing was just really ⁵_____ and ruined my birthday!

Julian

Really ⁶_____ you had a good time, Marina, but 30? Don't know what you were ⁷_____ about! You're still just a kid! I turn 40 next month and I'm ⁸_____ ! Any thoughts on what kind of cake I should lock myself away with?

5 a Work in pairs. Choose the correct alternatives.

1 I was *so/very* stressed about the idea that I'd decided to spend the day locked in my apartment crying.
2 He'd told me to be ready by 6.30, *because/so* I was up really early.
3 *Since/Due to* he didn't have any success we had to queue.
4 *As/So* it's such a popular event, I suppose that's fair.
5 They had to shut the roof at one point *due to/because* the rain.
6 We got there late and *since/as a result* missed out on tickets.
7 We had to queue for ages *as/because of* the tight security.

b Read the post and the comments again and check your answers. What do the sentences have in common?

6 Read the Focus box and answer the questions.

1 Which phrase in bold is used to link two complete sentences?
2 Which words/phrases in bold are followed by a noun or a pronoun?
3 Which word is followed by an adjective?

Expressing cause and result

There are many ways you can express cause and result.

Cause	Result
The tickets were **so** expensive **(that)**	we decided not to go.
It's a very popular event,	**so** you should book soon.
Since I was working near the stadium,	I went to queue up for tickets.
Because/As it was so crowded,	we couldn't see a thing.
Due to the bad weather	they cancelled the match.
The crowds had become dangerous.	**As a result**, they moved the carnival out of the city.

Result	Cause
It was amazing	**because** no one expected her to win!
It was cancelled	**due to** a lack of interest.
I missed her wedding	**because of** illness.

---

7 Rewrite the sentences using the words in brackets so that they mean the same.

1 Because we really enjoyed it the first time we went, we started going every year. (so / that)
   We enjoyed it so much the first time we went that we started going every year.
2 I was really excited as it was the first time I'd seen them play live. (so)
3 They were so terrible that they ended up losing 6–1. (because)
4 The whole thing was a bit of a disaster because of the rain. (as)
5 The game was delayed as there was an accident in the crowd. (due to)
6 As it was my first time at that kind of event, I didn't know what to expect. (as a result)
7 They had very tight security because the president was attending the game. (since)
8 I had to leave before the end as the game went on really long! (so / that)

Prepare

8 You're going to write a post describing an event you went to. It can be a real event or you can invent one. Think about:

- where and when the event was, and why you went there.
- who you went with and what it was like.
- anything that was unusual about the event and why.
- what the best part of it was and why.

Write

9 Write your post.

Develop your listening

> **Goal:** understand a lecture

> **Focus:** taking notes

1 Work in pairs. Look at the photos and discuss the questions.

1 What do you know about each place?

2 Have you visited either of them? If yes, when? What were they like?

3 What do you think the places have in common?

2 ◁ 10.3 Listen to the introduction to a lecture about an amazing substance. Take notes on what you hear.

3 a Work in pairs and compare your notes. Discuss:

1 how similar your notes are.

2 what connects the places in the photos.

3 what main areas the lecture will cover.

b Read the Focus box. Which strategies for note taking did you use?

Taking notes

When deciding what to take notes about:

- use the introduction of the talk as a guide. As well as the main topic, it often explains the main arguments that will be given.
- listen for information or key words that are repeated or explained.
- listen for language that helps you understand the structure, e.g. *However, Let's not forget … , This leads to …*
- pay most attention to the nouns and verbs that are strongly stressed or said more loudly.

When taking notes:

- use headings to organise your notes.
- focus on writing down the key words only.
- don't write full sentences – omit 'grammar' words, e.g. pronouns, articles.
- use symbols and abbreviations like *e.g.* (= for example) and *i.e.* (= this means).
- underline, circle or highlight key points.
- note new vocabulary or concepts so you can look them up later.

4 ◁ 10.4 Listen to the last part of the introduction and the first part of the main lecture. Complete the notes with a number or a word.

Concrete
top material – use 2x other materials
History
1_____ yrs ago in Syria + Jordan
Romans big users, e.g. bridges
2_____ yrs nothing
Industrial Revolution: e.g. roads, 3_____
Reasons for 4_____
1) easy to make
2) flexible – easy to make into different 5_____
3) strong – gets 6_____ over time
4) doesn't 7_____ easily
5) 8_____

5 ◁ 10.5 Listen to the rest of the lecture and take notes.

6 a Are the sentences true (T) or false (F)? Use your notes to help you. Explain your answers.

1 Use of concrete in the home has reduced illness.

2 Concrete has made life easier for many women.

3 Concrete has allowed more children to get an education.

4 Concrete production has a negative impact on the environment.

5 Cheap forms of concrete last as long as more expensive ones.

6 Concrete always results in ugly architecture.

7 Governments should be stricter about what concrete is used.

8 Technology means concrete will be replaced by other materials.

b Listen again and check your answers.

7 a Complete the sentences about the lecture so that they are true for you.

1 I hadn't realised …

2 The thing that surprised me the most was the fact that …

3 I'm not sure I understand …

4 I'd like to know a bit more about …

b Work in pairs. Compare and explain your answers.

> **Goal:** understand a magazine article

> **Focus:** recognising referents

Regrets, I've had a few, but then again ...

Kieran Trippier finds comfort in stories of failure.

1 _____

Research at Cornell University has revealed some of the most common regrets that **pensioners** have – and the findings might surprise you: they wished that they hadn't worried so much.
5 Looking back on their lives, **the old people** felt that worrying was not only a waste of time in itself, but that it had often stopped them getting on with their lives and following their dreams. In general, **those interviewed** regretted *not* doing things and failing to take opportunities more than doing things that then went
10 wrong. Better to have tried and failed than never to have tried at all! So, for example, they were more likely to regret *not* leaving their job to follow a passion and create their own business than to regret setting up a company that then failed and went bankrupt. At the end of the day, they now realise losing money in such
15 a way isn't so bad. In fact, another common regret was giving money too much importance. Many felt they should've spent less time working and more time with family and friends.

2 _____

The Legacy Project, which is led by Professor Karl Pillemer, has
20 interviewed over 1,500 **retired people**, in order to learn lessons in life that might be passed on to younger generations. It has resulted in a website, where the pensioners' stories have been organised into a number of categories, and two best-selling books, which share their wise words.

3 _____

Professor Pillemer's work is part of a wider trend that sees **mentors** as an important source of learning. Schools now often get **older students** or **adult volunteers** to give one-to-one advice and encouragement to kids who are, say, having
30 difficulty with reading or maths. Workplaces increasingly pair up **experienced staff** with new employees or colleagues who are

---

1 Look at the photos and discuss the questions.

1 Do you have any grandparents or older people in your life that you talk to a lot?

2 Have they taught you anything? What?

3 Have you ever taught anyone anything? What did you teach them? How did it go?

2 Read an article about old people and mentoring. Match paragraphs 1–5 with subheadings a–f. There is one extra subheading you don't need.

a Different kinds of mentoring

b The importance of similar experiences

c Ways to improve mentoring

d Lessons learnt by old people

e Sharing lessons

f Sharing is more important than learning

3 Read the Focus box. How do writers avoid repeating the names of people, places and ideas?

Recognising referents

Writers often introduce a person, place or idea in the first few lines of an article or paragraph. In order to avoid repeating the same word over and over again, writers will use different words or phrases to refer to the same thing. These words or phrases are often called referents. Writers use different types of referent:

• alternative names: *Professor Green, John Green, Johnny*

• general nouns: *the professor, the academic, the teacher and researcher,* etc.

• pronouns and possessive adjectives: *he, him, his*

Using different referents makes the writing more interesting, but it can be confusing if the writer uses vocabulary you don't know. You might find it helpful to:

• identify the key names or ideas mentioned in the first lines of a text or paragraph.

• notice general nouns which may represent these people, places, etc.

• focus on words like *it, that, their,* etc. and make a connection in the text with what they refer to.

taking on a new role. There are a number of programmes that bring **ex-criminals** or addicts together with young people who have been arrested, in the hope that they will persuade the kids to take a different path.
35 Your doctor may even find you a **mentor** to support you if you want to lose weight, get fit or stop smoking.

4 _____

Obviously, mentors have something in common with teachers, but the most important difference is that they have been through the same experience as
40 the person they're working with. The idea is that people learn better from those who are close to them in age or background and from having **a role model** to follow. They may be encouraged that someone like them can achieve their goals.

5 _____

45 Does it work, though? Although it's normal to find that everyone involved in mentoring schemes feels positive about the experience, a number of recent studies have found it often has little impact on learning or behaviour. Perhaps we shouldn't be surprised. You can imagine that if the Cornell research was repeated in 60 years' time, people who are young today will
50 have made the same mistakes as **Pillemer's pensioners**. In fact, right now they may be in their offices working overtime and worrying about whether they'll get a pay rise next year! However, I'm not sure that it matters. Perhaps the learning is not the important thing about
55 mentoring; what's more important is the communication and the sharing. The Legacy Project and mentoring both reassure people that they are not alone and
60 everyone's experiences in life are valuable. And that's certainly no cause for regret.

4 Do the nouns relate to pensioners or mentors? Put them into the correct category.

- ex-criminals
- Pillemer's pensioners
- those interviewed
- retired people
- older students
- adult volunteers
- the old people
- experienced staff
- a role model

5 Read the article again. Find at least three different referents for *research at Cornell University*.

6 Work in pairs. Read the extracts from the article. What do the underlined words refer to?

1 _it_ had often stopped _them_ getting on (line 6)
2 _they_ now realise losing money _in such a way_ isn't so bad (line 14)
3 _Many_ felt they should've spent less time working (line 16)
4 share _their_ wise words (line 24)
5 _they_ will persuade _the kids_ to take a different path (line 34)
6 _They_ may be encouraged that _someone like them_ can achieve their goals. (line 42)
7 Does _it_ work, though? (line 45)
8 right now _they_ may be in _their_ offices working overtime (line 50)

7 Work in pairs and discuss the questions.

Do you agree that …
1 the Legacy Project findings are surprising?
2 the Legacy Project and mentoring schemes are similar?
3 it doesn't matter if the project and/or mentoring fail to change people's behaviour?

8 a Complete the phrasal verbs with the correct form of the verbs in the box.

get   go (x2)   pair   pass   set   take (x2)

1 I try not to have regrets and just _____ on with my life.
2 Last year, our school _____ up a group of mentors to support kids with their homework.
3 I've tried and failed in business twice. Both companies _____ bankrupt.
4 I'd like to _____ on the skills I have to my kids, but they are not interested in becoming farmers.
5 In my first year at university, I was _____ up with a second-year student, who I could ask for advice.
6 The company I work for has _____ on several young people. I think it's good to have a mix of ages amongst the staff.
7 I went straight to work when I finished school, but I wish I had _____ a different path – gone to university or done some training. I feel stuck in my job.
8 He's _____ through a lot, but I think the experience has made him a stronger person.

b Choose four of the phrasal verbs from Exercise 8a and make sentences that are true for you. Then work in pairs and compare your sentences.

9 a Think of two lessons you would like to pass on to a younger person:
- connected to the area you work in or study.
- about life in general.

b Work in pairs and compare your ideas.

c Summarise your discussion for the rest of the class. Were there any common themes? Were any of your lessons the same as in the article?

> **Goal:** write an essay

> **Focus:** answering the essay question

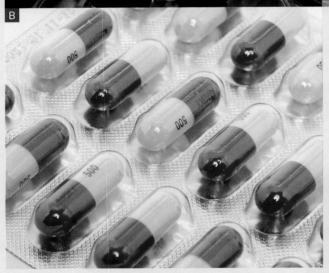

1 Look at the photos and discuss the questions.

1 What can you see in the photos?

2 Which things do you think have had the biggest impact on the world?

3 Think of three more things that have changed the world in different ways.

2 Work in pairs and read the essay questions. Which one would you choose to answer? Why?

1 Choose one invention that changed the course of history, but is no longer common today. Describe two ways it changed history and explain why it is no longer widely used.

2 Write a very brief history of the development of ready meals and describe how the market has grown. Explain two issues that might cause sales to fall and how they could be avoided.

3 Choose one object that is widely used today. Explain what impact it has had on two of these areas: the economy, society, history, the environment. Explain if these are positive or negative effects.

4 Choose one of the objects in the photos that you think has had a very negative impact on life today. Give examples of these negative effects and explain how we might overcome two of them.

3 Read the Focus box. Work in pairs and use the advice to analyse the essay questions in Exercise 2.

Answering the essay question

Before you start writing an essay, read the instructions carefully and ask yourself these questions to make sure you write what you need to:

- What is the main topic of the essay?
- Is there a maximum number of things I should write about?
- Do I need to include any of the following?
  - the background or history of something
  - the reasons why something happened/is happening
  - the effects of an event, product or process
  - the solutions to a problem
- Should I give my opinion about whether something is positive or negative?
- Is there a word limit?

In your answer, you need to make clear you are following the instructions by:

- explaining in your introduction how you are going to answer and in what order.
- organising the essay into paragraphs.
- using a sentence (usually at the start of a paragraph) to explain how that paragraph relates to the essay question.

4 Read the essay plan. Which question from Exercise 2 is it answering?

Intro: steam engine replaced something less efficient – efficiency of production/quick transport

1st para: started Industrial Revolution

2nd para: steam trains and shipping – much faster

3rd para: no longer used – relies on coal (dirty), large and heavy – been replaced

5 Work in pairs. Discuss what to put in a plan for one of the other essays.

6 Read the essay and answer the questions.

1 Which question is answered?
2 Which two areas has the writer chosen to focus on?
3 Which part of the question does each paragraph answer?

Ready meals are a very common feature of modern-day life. According to *Euromonitor International*, almost a third of people round the world buy a ready-made meal at least once a week. In this essay, I will explain the impact they have had on society and the environment.

¹_____ .

²_____ . Before they were widely available, women were mainly responsible for cooking and it took many hours of preparation each day. By reducing cooking to a few minutes, women have become free to do other more interesting and productive things.

³_____ .

⁴_____ . Ready meals have more fat and sugar compared with meals cooked from basic ingredients, which is one reason why we are becoming less healthy as a society. Also, because it is easy for anyone to put a ready meal in the microwave, families don't eat together as much and children are more likely to eat alone.

⁵_____ . They use more packaging and require fridges in transport and shops. As a result, they create far more greenhouse gases and rubbish than when you cook for yourself.

In summary, ready meals have had a positive effect on society by bringing women more freedom. However, the negative impact has been on people's health and relationships and increased greenhouse gases.

7 Complete the essay with sentences a–e.

a Furthermore, ready meals are bad for the environment
b Ready meals have been good for women
c However, ready meals have also had a negative impact on society, especially families
d If we had not had ready meals, it's likely that far fewer women would have received higher education and been able to work in professional jobs
e I will suggest these effects have been both positive and negative

8 Work in pairs and discuss the questions.

1 What do you think of the ideas in the essay?
2 Do you agree with them? Why?/Why not?

9 a Read sentences a–c and answer the questions about the underlined words/phrases.

a <u>As well as</u> recording our daily lives cameras have allowed us to share news stories from around the world.
b Photos and TV <u>not only</u> help us know about other parts of the world <u>but also</u> often lead to people sending help to others, for example those who are dying of hunger.
c <u>Furthermore</u> cameras allow us to protect ourselves and our property because thieves are more likely to be caught.

1 Which phrase(s):
a links two ideas in the same sentence?
b shows we are adding an idea connected to the previous sentence or paragraph?
c is followed by an -*ing* form?
2 Where should a comma be added to each sentence?

b Replace three of the underlined words/phrases in Exercise 9a with the words in the box.

do not just   moreover   apart from

10 Read the sentences and connect the ideas with the words in brackets. Make any other changes you need to.

1 There are millions of cameras spying on us on the streets. There are cameras in most shops and at every cash machine. (not only ... but also)
2 People are constantly taking photos and selfies on their phones. These photos get shared all over the internet. They get stored on strangers' computers. (and / furthermore)
3 Having so many cameras and photos reduces our privacy. It makes us obsessed with our image. (apart from)
4 People select photos. People use editing software to improve their image. There is some evidence that this negatively affects our self-image. (do not just / also / moreover)

Prepare

11 Work in pairs. You're going to answer essay question 3 in Exercise 2. Choose an object and discuss:
- which areas you are going to focus on.
- whether the effects are positive or negative.
- how you will organise your essay into paragraphs.

Write

12 Work alone and write your essay.

Grammar bank

1A Noun phrases 1

You often have to clarify and define the thing, person or place you are talking about by adding information after the noun or pronoun. You can use:

- a prepositional phrase to show, for example, where the thing is or what it has.

*I love that pizza place **in the centre of town.***
*There's a Greek restaurant **with a lovely terrace.***

- an infinitive with *to* to show the general function of the thing it defines.

*I need a room **to rent**. (= a room which I am renting or which I want to rent)*
*We're looking for somewhere **to eat**. (= a place where we can eat)*

- a relative clause to add (necessary) information about the noun.

*How about the place **we went to for my birthday**?*
*Do you know the woman **who has the dog?***

Relative clauses can always start with a relative pronoun:
*That's the person **that/who** I spoke to before.*
*I can give you the thing **that/which** I had.*
*The last time **that** I saw you was Wednesday.*
*The place **that** I went to was lovely. The place **where** we went last year was very expensive.*

You don't have to use a relative pronoun if the thing you are defining is the object of the verb in the relative clause. You do have to use a relative pronoun if it is the subject of the relative clause:
*Jo is **the friend** who has **the hotel** (that) I was staying in.*
*= **My friend** has the hotel. (who/my friend is the subject of the relative clause)*
*= I was staying in **the hotel**. (that/the hotel is the object of the relative clause)*

You can define the noun in more than one way.
*There's a great place **on Church Street which does excellent Lebanese food**.*

1B Modifying comparisons

To make comparatives, add *-er* to one-syllable adjectives and adjectives ending in *-y*. For most two-syllable and longer adjectives use *more* + adjective. You can modify comparatives to show how big the difference is.

- To show a big difference you can use:

a lot, far, much, miles + *more/less/-er* comparatives and *too*.
*It's **much too far** from work.*
*This flat is **miles better** than my last place.*
*Living in the city is just **much more convenient** than living in the country.*

nearly with *not as* comparatives and *not ... enough*.
*It wasn't **nearly as** cheap **as** I expected.*
*The house wasn't **nearly** close **enough** to where I work.*

- To show a small difference you can use:

a bit, slightly, a little + *more/less/-er* comparatives and *too*.
*It's **a bit too** big. I don't need two bedrooms.*
*The kitchen was **slightly bigger** than this room.*
*I need somewhere that's **a little less** expensive.*

quite with *not as* comparatives and *not ... enough*.
*It's **not quite as** easy to get to work (compared to where I lived before).*
*It's **not quite** big **enough** for me and my family.*

You can use *even* or *actually* to show the comparison is surprising.
*It's **even more noisy** since they opened the bar across the road.*
*It's **actually not as expensive as** you might think.*

You can also use a measurement to modify a comparative.
He's six years older than me.

You can also compare nouns in similar ways.
*There are **far/a lot more parks** now than before.*
*I don't have **nearly as** much space **as** I did before.*
*It costs **slightly/a bit more money** than my old place did, but I'm happy here.*
*It has **two more bedrooms** than I have now.*

1C Non-defining relative clauses

Use non-defining relative clauses to add extra information to sentences that are already clear and complete. These clauses always need a relative pronoun, and are more common in written English. They come after a comma, and if they come in the middle of a sentence, they are separated by commas at each end. In speech, these clauses are separated from the rest of the sentence by a short pause. You can add extra information about:

- places *We went on to this late-night place, **where we got talking to some locals.***
- how you felt *I met lots of my old friends, **which was great.***
- reasons and results *My friend knew the people organising it, **which meant** we got in free!/, **which is why** we got in free!*

- dates and time *We didn't get there until about eleven, **when** most people were starting to leave.*
- possession or connection *My friend Alex, **whose partner's a chef,** recommended this amazing seafood place in town.*
- part of a group of people *We went out with a big group of Mo's friends, **none of whom** I really knew!*
- people *My brother, **who** I haven't seen for ages, is visiting.*

In formal, written English you sometimes use *whom* instead of *who* when it is the object of a relative clause.
Mr Walsh, whom you met yesterday, is the manager. (very formal)
Mr Walsh, who you met yesterday, is the manager. (less formal)

PRACTICE

1A

1 Complete the text with one word in each space.

Last week, I went out for dinner with some friends [1]_____ university. We went to a place [2]_____ to the beach [3]_____ does discounts for students. Unfortunately, you can't book and by the time [4]_____ got there, there was a big queue. Luckily, we knew some of the people [5]_____ were queuing and so we were all chatting and the time passed quickly. When we finally sat down, we still had to wait for someone [6]_____ take our order. I was really hungry! I ordered a pizza [7]_____ ham as I thought it would be quick, but the rest of the people [8]_____ I was with took ages to decide. Honestly, I think the whole restaurant could hear the noise [9]_____ was coming from my stomach. The people [10]_____ the next table actually laughed at me – 'Oh, you're very hungry!' Then finally the waiter came with our food, but he didn't have the pizza [11]_____ I had ordered! I almost cried!

2 Complete the dialogues using the prompts to define the nouns.

1 A: What's the name of the friend _____? I've forgotten. (introduce / me / earlier)
   B: Heidi.
   What's the name of the friend (who/that) you introduced me to earlier?

2 A: Remind me again. What's the name of the guy _____? (read / news / Channel 1)
   B: Zach Gawlinska. How could you forget?

3 A: What was that place _____? (you / go / last summer)
   B: Pula?
   A: That's it! I was telling a friend from work you enjoyed it.

4 A: Why have I heard of Aliva before?
   B: Isn't that the place _____? (Julia / from)
   A: No that's Alcoy. How annoying! I'm sure I know it.

5 A: Who's Jimmy Wales?
   B: Isn't he the guy _____? Why? (start / Wikipedia)
   A: They're talking about him on the radio.

6 A: Where's the best place _____? (eat / round here)
   B: I'd say the place _____ , personally. (end / road)

1B

1 Complete the sentences with comparative forms using the pairs of words in the box.

quite/healthy   far/big   much/close   a lot/time
miles/good   slightly/central   nearly/sure

1 I don't really like being so far out in the suburbs. I'd prefer to be somewhere _____.

2 My parents are _____ as they used to be, so I'm thinking of moving _____ to where they live so I can spend _____ with them.

3 We want to start a family, so we're looking for somewhere _____ with at least one more bedroom and preferably two.

4 My partner says the school near there is _____ , which is why we're moving, but I'm _____ about the whole thing.

2 Complete the second sentence so that it means the same as the first. Use the words in brackets.

1 The film was nowhere near as good as the book.
   The book was _____ the film. (much)

2 The restaurant isn't quite as full on a Thursday.
   It's _____ on a Thursday. (less)

3 It's going to get a bit warmer later in the week.
   It won't be _____ later in the week. (cold)

4 There's not nearly enough money spent on education.
   The government should _____ money on education. (far)

5 There are far more tourists coming here than there were 20 years ago.
   Twenty years ago, there _____ much tourism as there is now. (nearly)

1C

1 Match main clauses 1–5 with two non-defining relative clauses from a–j.

1 I didn't get home until about 6 a.m.,
2 We went to that lovely Brazilian place on the main square,
3 We finished the last of our exams on Friday,
4 I got stuck in the kitchen with Sergei's friends,
5 I didn't have a late night. I just went out with my friend Ken,

a who doesn't usually stay out after ten!
b none of whom speak much English!
c which is why we all decided to go out.
d which meant two hours of listening to them talk about golf!
e whose dad runs that place I was telling you about.
f where we had to queue for about an hour to get in!
g when my flatmate was getting up!
h where we met some people I knew.
i when we threw a big party to celebrate!
j which meant I had to take the day off work!

Want more practice? Go to your Workbook or app.

2A Present simple and present continuous

Use the present simple to talk about:

• habits and routines.

Note that you usually add a frequency adverb or expression to show how often.

She goes swimming three or four times a week.
I don't usually work on Saturdays.
How often do you do that?

• things you see as facts, as always true.

I live quite near the park.
I don't have enough time to exercise.
Which gym do you belong to?

Use the present continuous to talk about:

• things started, but not yet finished at the time of speaking.

It's raining really heavily.
I'm not feeling very well.   Where are you going?

• things happening around now, but not at the moment of speaking.

I'm studying Spanish at university.
They're not talking to each other at the moment.
What are you training for?

Note that we often use the present continuous to talk about trends.

More people are choosing to work for themselves.
The number of young house-buyers is falling.

Some verbs aren't usually used in the continuous form. These are verbs that describe states and feelings, not actions. The most common state verbs are:

agree   believe   belong   know   mean   own   prefer   understand

2B Present habits

You can use lots of different expressions to say how often you do things – or how often things happen.

• Use *tend to* + infinitive to talk about things that you usually do or that are generally true. Note there are two possible negative forms.

I tend to start about nine most days.
I don't tend to/tend not to work weekends, if I can help it.
(= I don't usually work)

• Use *As a rule/On the whole* to show something is generally true. Use the present simple with both phrases, which usually go at the start of a sentence or clause.

As a rule, I don't read emails outside of work hours.
On the whole, it's quite a relaxed, informal kind of place to work.

• Use *regularly/frequently/often* before a main verb to show something happens often.

We regularly discuss goals for the coming months.
We often have short meetings via Skype.

• Use *from time to time* to talk about things that sometimes happen. It's used with the present simple and usually goes at the end of a sentence or clause. You can also use *every now and then* and *every now and again* in the same way.

We meet for dinner from time to time, but not often.
We have face-to-face meetings every now and again.

• You can use *has/have a habit of* + *-ing* and the present continuous with *always/constantly* to show that you find annoying something that happens a lot.

The coffee machine has a habit of breaking down when we most need it!
The coffee machine is always/constantly breaking down at the worst possible time!

Note that you can also use the present continuous + *always* to talk about positive things that happen a lot.

She's always smiling.
He's always helping me carry things up and down the stairs, which is kind of him.

2C *Used to, would* and past simple

Used to + infinitive, *would* + infinitive and the past simple can all be used to talk about things that happened in the past, but don't happen anymore.

• Use *used to* + infinitive, *would* + infinitive and the past simple to talk about repeated past actions.

When I was a kid, we always went away in the summer.
When I was a kid, we always used to go away in the summer.
When I was a kid, we'd always go away in the summer.

• To talk about past states (being, having or liking) you can use *used to* + infinitive or the past simple – but NOT *would*.

We used to have a dog called Spot when I was young.
We had a dog called Spot when I was young.

• To talk about single events in the past, you can only use the past simple – NOT *used to* + infinitive or *would* + infinitive.

I once got lost in the woods near my house.

Look at the ways to make negative sentences and questions with *used to.*

I didn't use to like it, but I do now.
I never used to like it, but I do now.
Did you use to live in Thailand?

2A

1 Complete the questions. Use the present simple or present continuous form of the verbs in brackets.

1. A: Where _____ you usually _____ tennis? (play)
   B: There are courts in the park near where I live, so we go there.
2. A: Why _____ you _____ ? (laugh)
   B: Oh, sorry. It's nothing. I just remembered something funny.
3. A: Why _____ you _____ to Ireland every year? (go)
   B: We love it there. It's a great place to surf.
4. A: What _____ you _____ at the moment? (read)
   B: I'm about halfway through *War and Peace*!
5. A: Where _____ your sister _____ these days? (work)
   B: She's just started at a new place, actually.
6. A: How often _____ they _____ ? (meet)
   B: Twice a week – Tuesdays and Thursdays.

2 Find the five sentences with a mistake and correct them.

1. Your hair is getting really long!
2. I'm afraid she works at the moment. Can I take a message?
3. How are you two knowing each other?
4. He doesn't live here anymore, I'm afraid.
5. I'm often going running before work.
6. How often are you playing football?
7. Greater numbers of people are taking up exercise every year.
8. I know he says he doesn't exercise much, but I'm not believing him.

2B

1 Complete the sentences with one word from the Grammar reference.

1. _____ a rule, we try to avoid having meetings unless they're really important.
2. We tend _____ to use first names in the office.
3. She's _____ coming in to my office and asking annoying questions!
4. I wear casual clothes _____ time to time, but I prefer to look smart at work.
5. We _____ eat lunch at our desks. It's pretty normal, to be honest.
6. He has a nasty _____ of saying one thing, but meaning another!
7. I think that on the _____ things are going quite well at the moment.

2 Find the five sentences with a mistake and correct them.

1. My boss is always asking us to work late. It's not fair!
2. We don't tend receive many letters. It's almost all emails these days.
3. As a rule, I get to work before eight.
4. He has a really annoying habit of interrupt when I'm talking!
5. She tends to be really good at making sure everyone knows how well they're doing.
6. You should take from time to time a few days off.
7. They're updating constantly our computer system!
8. On the whole, most of the big decisions are being made in our New York office.

2C

1 Cross out the alternatives that are not possible.

1. My dad *never used to/didn't* cook much when I was young.
2. I *didn't like/wouldn't like* vegetables when I was a kid – but now I'm a vegetarian!
3. Did you *use to go/go* swimming in the river when you were younger?
4. I *never used to/wouldn't usually* worry about anything when I was young.
5. My little brother and I *would often go/often went* on long walks in the countryside.
6. I somehow *lost/used to lose* the first phone I *had/would have*.
7. Our old house *was/would be* in the centre of town. It *was/used to be* great being so central.
8. My grandparents *used to have/would have* a house by the sea and *we stayed/we'd stay* there most summers.

2 Tick the correct sentences.

1. a We never used to going abroad on holiday when I was a kid.
   b We never went abroad on holiday when I was a kid.
2. a I used to live in Fez before I came to Amsterdam to study.
   b I'd live in Fez before I came to Amsterdam to study.
3. a I spend hours and hours writing letters to friends when I was younger.
   b I used to spend hours and hours writing letters to friends when I was younger.
4. a I play a lot of sport, but these days I don't have time.
   b I used to play a lot of sport, but these days I don't have time.
5. a I used to break my arm falling off a horse when I was nine.
   b I'd break my arm falling off a horse when I was nine.
6. a I didn't use to be interested in science, but then I had an amazing chemistry teacher.
   b I was never interested in science, but then I had an amazing chemistry teacher.
7. a I had really long hair when I was a teenager.
   b I would have really long hair when I was a teenager.

Want more practice? Go to your Workbook or app.

3A Present perfect simple questions and answers

Use the present perfect simple to talk about experiences. When you answer present perfect questions like *Have you (ever) been to…?* you can use a range of structures. For example:

- present perfect simple

to talk about experiences and desires from the past until now (no specific time reference).
Yeah, I've been there a couple of times.
No, but I've always wanted to.

- past simple

to give details of an experience you had (often with a specific time reference).
Yeah, I walked round there yesterday.
Yeah, but we didn't stay there long.

- present simple

to give your current opinions (based on your experience).
Yeah. It's amazing. There's so much to do there.

- *be supposed to*

to show opinions based on what you have read or heard.
No. It's supposed to get very crowded.

- *would like/love to*

to show your hopes for the future.
No, but I'd love to – it sounds really interesting.

- *be thinking of/might*

to show a possible plan.
No, but I'm thinking of going there tomorrow.
No, but I might go in the summer.

- *be going to*

to show a firm plan about the future.
No, but I'm actually going to visit next year.

You can also respond to a *Have you ever been to…?* question by asking questions of your own.
Yeah, I have. What did you think of it?
No. Have you?   No. What's it like?

3B Present perfect simple and continuous

Use the present perfect to talk about actions or events that started before now and have a present connection or result.

- Use the present perfect simple to focus on the completed action and the present result of that action. It often explains *how much* or *how many* (including none).

Apparently, they've found a new cure for hair loss, so there's still hope for you. (completed action)
The population rate has risen by 10 million over the last 30 years. (how much)
Doctors have done over 20 tests to find the cause of his illness, but without any luck. (how many)

- Use the present perfect continuous to focus on an action that lasts for a period of time and/or that is unfinished now. It is also used to focus on an action that is repeated over a period of time. It often explains *how long*. It is wrong to use the present continuous for this meaning.

I've been doing research into hair loss. (unfinished action)

The population has been growing steadily over the last fifty years. (how long)
I've been going to the cinema every Saturday since I was a child. (repeated)
They have been working on the project for several years. NOT *They ~~are working~~ …*

Don't use the present perfect continuous with passive verbs or state verbs (e.g. *know, belong*).
So far, all the research has been paid for by the government. (passive)
I've known him for ages.

In many cases, the present perfect simple can be used instead of the continuous form with no difference in meaning for the listener. This is true of verbs like *live, work, study* and *teach*, whose meaning suggests continuation.
I've lived here for the last ten years.
I've been living here for the last ten years.

3C Obligation and permission

- Use (semi-) modal verbs such as *needn't, must, should* and *can* to show obligation or permission. They are followed by an infinitive.

At busy stations, you should walk on the left.
You needn't walk on the left when it isn't busy.
You can drink soft drinks on public transport.

- You can also use some common passive verbs or *It's* + adjective. They are all followed by an infinitive with *to*.

be required to means people have to or must do something (absolute obligation).
You're required to register with the police.
be not required to means you don't have to or needn't do it if you don't want to.
You're not required to get a ticket …

be allowed to means you have permission to do something. *You're allowed to eat on the tube.*
be not allowed to means you mustn't or can't do something.
We're not allowed to give advice on visa issues.
be not supposed to/meant to means people shouldn't or ought not to do something (weak obligation).
On the tube, people sometimes put their feet on the seats, but you're not supposed to/but you're not meant to.
It's illegal to or *it's against the law to* show you mustn't do something.
It's (im)polite or *it's best (not) to* show weak obligation/advice.
It's polite to wear headphones when playing music or video on your device.
It's best to go to one of the walk-in centres.

3A

1 Read the responses to the question *Have ever you been to Japan?* Complete them with an appropriate verb form and any preposition you need.

1 No, but I'd love _____ Mount Fuji one day.

2 Yeah, I _____ a month there as part of my university degree.

3 No, but it's supposed _____ amazing.

4 No, but to be honest, I _____ . It's so far and I hate flying.

5 Yes. Several times. I _____ it there. I'm thinking _____ again in the summer.

6 No, but my parents _____ a friend there, so I might _____ her sometime.

2 Make questions and answers using the prompts.

1 A: you / fly business class?
   B: No / you?

2 A: you / go rafting?
   B: No / always want / love that kind of thing

3 A: any of you / visit here before?
   B: A few of us / come last year

4 A: you / look round the museum?
   B: No, / we / go later / but I'm not sure we'll have time

5 A: you / watch whales / or do anything like that?
   B: No / love / I bet it would be amazing

6 A: you / see / the new *Star Wars* film?
   B: No / pretty bad

3B

1 Complete the sentences with one verb in the present perfect simple and one in the present perfect continuous.

1 We _____ (not / work) on this project for very long so we _____ (not / make) any major discoveries yet.

2 A: We _____ (conduct) an online survey to investigate people's attitudes.
   B: How many people _____ (complete) it so far?
   A: Almost six thousand.

3 I _____ (not / see) him much recently, but we _____ by phone quite a lot. (talk)

4 She _____ (be) here for almost a year, but she _____ only _____ (stay) with us since November.

2 Find the five sentences with a mistake and correct them.

1 Only a very small part of the oceans has been exploring.

2 It's quite worrying that the ten hottest years on record have all occurred since 1998.

3 I'm running the same test over and over again with the same results each time.

4 What have you found out from all the research you've been doing?

5 You're sitting there for almost an hour now. Have you decided what to do?

6 The amount of pollution in the city has been falling by 20 percent since they banned cars.

7 I have worked for the same drug company for about ten years now.

8 For the past week, several people have been being connected to a device to see how their heart rate changes during the day and night.

3C

1 Write rules and customs about the UK using the prompts.

1 you / suppose / wait for people to get off the train first

2 against the law / own some kinds of dog

3 polite / give your seat to an elderly person on the tube

4 require / buy a licence to watch TV

5 you / not allow / smoke inside any place of work

6 you / not suppose / eat the fish you catch when you go fishing

2 Complete the text with one word in each space.

Different countries have different systems to allow people born outside the country to become a citizen. In Austria, you're [1]_____ to live continuously for at least ten years in the country before you're [2]_____ to apply for a passport, while in FYR Macedonia some people [3]_____ become citizens within a year and you [4]_____n't even live in the country! All they [5]_____ do is put €400,000 or more of their own money into a new business that employs local people. In South Korea, you [6]_____ to prove you can sing four verses of the national anthem, while the Dutch test has questions about normal behaviour such as 'If neighbours you don't know well are getting married, is [7]_____ polite to: send a postcard, give a present or give flowers?' The UK has a test on rules, facts and customs, which all British people are [8]_____ to know, although a recent survey found most would fail!

Want more practice? Go to your Workbook or app.

4A Past simple and past continuous

- Use the past simple to talk about single completed actions.

My daughter broke her arm over the summer.
I didn't see anything.
Where did you stay?

- Use the past continuous to suggest an action was in progress around a time in the past – or around the time another action happened. Note that it is usually used with the past simple.

We were both living in China when we met.
I wasn't feeling very well, so I just stayed at home.
What were you doing when this happened?

When you use the past simple and past continuous in the same sentence, you often introduce the past simple clause with *when*. You can also introduce past continuous clauses with *when* or *while*.

I was coming downstairs when I slipped and fell.
When/While I was cooking, I cut my finger.

You sometimes use the past continuous in both clauses of a sentence, when two actions were in progress around the same time.

While you were enjoying yourself with your friends, I was repairing the washing machine!

You can also use both the past simple and continuous to talk about the duration of an action or state. The past continuous emphasises the repetition of an action that continued for some time without stopping. When we use the past continuous like this, we usually add a time adverb (*for hours*, etc.).

I spent two weeks in hospital.
It was raining all morning so I couldn't put the washing out.

4B Past perfect simple

Use the past perfect simple to make it clear that one action happened before another in the past. You often use time expressions like *before, after, by the time* and *already* to show the order of actions.

I'd never seen anything like that before I went to China.
After I'd been there a couple of months, I started to feel a bit more comfortable.
He'd already made his first million by the time he was 21.
They'd already left by the time we got there.

The past perfect is often used after 'thinking' verbs such as *realise, remember* and *notice* and after clauses with *when*.

I was on my way to the airport when I suddenly realised I'd forgotten my passport.
I was just leaving the house when I suddenly noticed I'd left a window open.
When they arrived, everyone had left.

Note that where the order of actions is clear, we often use the past simple instead of the past perfect simple.

I rang the police after I saw/had seen the attack.
He was only freed/He'd only been freed from prison the week before it happened.

4C Reported speech

When we report speech, we often – but not always – move the tense back one step into the past. Look at the direct and reported speech below.

- to report statements about a situation or action at the time it was said/thought:

They said, 'You need to show us the receipt.'
They said I needed to show them the receipt.

- to report statements about an action in progress at the time it was said:

He said, 'I'm going to complain.'
He said he was going to complain.

- to report statements about an action further back in time before it was said:

She said, 'I've sorted it out.'
She said she'd sorted it out.

- to report statements about a plan or prediction for the future at the time it was said:

I asked and they said, 'We'll try.'
I asked and they said they would try.

When the statement you are reporting is still true, you can use present and other tenses as they apply to now.

He told me he's never had any problems with the one he owns.
They said they'll send a refund sometime this week.

When you report *Wh*-questions, use the normal word order of statements.

I said, 'What's the problem?'
I asked what the problem was.

When you report *yes/no* questions, use *if/whether*.

She said, 'Do you need any help?'
She asked if/whether I needed any help.

Remember that when you report speech, you often change the pronouns and time expressions.

She said, 'I saw you yesterday.'
*She told me **she**'d seen **me the previous day**.*
He said, 'I'll do it tomorrow.'
*He said (that) **he**'d do it **the next/following day**.*

Note that *say* can't take a direct object.

He said he'd do it. NOT *He said me he'd do it.*

4A

1 Complete the sentences with one word. Contractions count as one word.

1 A: I dropped a knife on my foot while I _____ cooking.
  B: Oh no! _____ it hurt?

2 I _____ three years in Huddersfield but to be honest, I _____ really like living there.

3 He borrowed my car without asking me first. I _____ very happy about it!

4 A: I saw him this morning at around nine. We had coffee together.
  B: How was he then? _____ he feeling OK?

5 You were young when it happened. But at that time, _____ you know what you _____ doing?

6 I was shocked by how bad the car looked afterwards. I mean, they _____ driving very fast when it happened.

7 She _____ travelling abroad all week, so she couldn't see her daughter in the school play.

2 Complete the sentences with the correct form of the verbs in brackets.

1 I _____ (open) my front door when I _____ (hit) myself in the face with it.

2 I _____ (slip) while I _____ (get out) of the bath.

3 I _____ (do) the ironing while Dave _____ (have) fun at his office party!

4 My brother _____ (get into) the car when I _____ (shut) the door on his hand! Luckily, he _____ (not break) anything!

5 I _____ (jog) in the park when I _____ (trip) on a stone and _____ (fall over).

6 I _____ (fall off) the ladder while I _____ (clean) the windows and I _____ (break) my ankle.

7 I _____ (ride) my bike in the countryside when a car _____ (come) round the corner and almost _____ (hit) me.

4B

1 Choose the correct alternatives.

1 I *worked/had worked* part-time in that store when I was at university.

2 I suddenly remembered where I *saw/had seen* him before.

3 He *was/had been* arrested at the airport late last night.

4 She lost her job after her boss learnt she *lied/had lied* to him about why she needed time off.

5 The gang broke into the house and *had demanded/demanded* money.

6 My wife *rang/had rung* the emergency services while I was helping the victims.

7 By the time I realised what *happened/had happened*, it was too late.

8 I noticed that my neighbour *was leaving/had left* his front door open.

2 Complete the story with the correct form of the verbs in brackets. Use the past simple, past continuous or past perfect simple. Where both the past simple and past perfect are possible, use the past simple.

Police last night [1]_____ (arrest) a man who [2]_____ (fall) down a chimney while he [3]_____ (try) to escape from a house that he [4]_____ just _____ (break into). The owners [5]_____ (call) the police and emergency services after they [6]_____ (hear) the man's calls for help! Earlier, the man [7]_____ (climb) out through a window with all the money and jewellery that he [8]_____ (take) from the house and was on the roof when the accident [9]_____ (happen). By the time the police arrived, the emergency services [10]_____ already _____ (rescue) the man.

4C

1 Complete the reporting sentences with three words.

1 'I'll email you later today.'
  You promised me you _____ later that day, but I never received anything.

2 'I want to speak to the manager.'
  He said he _____ to the manager – and I told him he was speaking to her.

3 'I'm afraid we're still waiting for a delivery.'
  They said they _____ for a delivery, so I decided to look elsewhere.

4 'I saw him in his office earlier.'
  I spoke to her yesterday and she said she _____ in his office earlier.

5 'This is the first time I've ever done anything like this.'
  You said that was the first time you _____ anything like that – but you lied!

6 'How do you know?' He asked me _____ – so I told him.

7 'When was it sent?' I asked them when it _____ , and they had no idea.

Want more practice? Go to your Workbook or app.

5A Future forms

There are lots of different ways of talking about the future in English. While one structure may be preferred for certain meanings, in many cases more than one structure can be used with little or no change of meaning.

• present continuous

Use this to talk about events in the future that have usually been decided and organised with other people. A time phrase which refers to the future is often used to avoid confusion with the present. You can also use *be going to* with no change in meaning.

We're having a party on Friday to celebrate our first year of business. (or *We're going to have*)

A: *Do you want to go to the cinema later?*

B: *Sorry, I'm meeting a friend.* (or *I'm going to meet*)

• be going to + infinitive

Use this to talk about plans and decisions about the future that you have already made (but not necessarily started to arrange).

I'm going to try and get a loan from the bank to help me expand the business.

A: *What are you going to do after you graduate?*

B: *I'm just going to look for a job.*

• will + infinitive and **be going to** + infinitive

Use these forms to make predictions you feel sure about. *Will* is often introduced by *think* and *expect*.

A: *Do you think their new product will be a success?* (or *is going to be*)

B: *Yeah, it's going to do really well.* (or *it'll do*)

• might/may + infinitive

Use these to talk about things you think will possibly happen in the future. You can also use *will possibly* or *be possibly going to*.

We might have to get rid of some staff in the new year.

The economy will possibly improve next year, but I'm not very hopeful.

• future continuous (will be + -ing)

Use this to talk about actions that will be in progress at or around a certain point in the future. You can also use *be going to be + -ing*.

Don't disturb me between 3 and 4 as I'll be doing a presentation online. (or *I'm going to be doing*)

Look at how to make negatives and question forms.

I won't be working next week, so don't call me.

When will you be arriving? I'll come and collect you.

5B Adverbs used with the present perfect

Some adverbs are often used with the present perfect simple. Note that unless otherwise stated, these adverbs usually go between *have/has* (*not*) and the past participle.

• Use *still* and *yet* in negative sentences to emphasise that something is not completed, but we expect it to happen. *Still* goes before *have*. *Yet* goes at the end of the sentence.

I still haven't found a suitable place. I haven't found it yet.

• Use *just* to show something happened very recently.

I've just come back from Mexico.

• Use *already* to emphasise something is completed (often before it was expected).

I've already finished the whole book.

• Use *so far* at the start (or the end) of a sentence to mean until now.

So far, I haven't had much luck.

• Use *even* to show something is surprising.

I've been very busy. I haven't even had time to think.

• Use *only* to show that nothing else has been done.

I've only done the first year of my course.

• Use *lately* or *recently* at the end of a negative sentence or question to mean in the recent past.

I haven't been there lately/recently.

Have you seen any good films lately/recently?

5C Comment adverbs

Many adverbs describe verbs. They usually go just after the verb (and its object if there is one).

He was talking sadly about how things had ended.   I marked his work very carefully but I couldn't find any mistakes.

Adverbs can also modify an adjective. They usually go just before the adjective.

She did amazingly well in her exams.   It was quite hot in the classroom.   The present was beautifully wrapped.

Comment adverbs show your attitude about a whole sentence or clause. They are usually used at the start of the clause or sentence they describe, and are followed by a comma. Here are some of the most useful comment adverbs:

actually	(this is the real fact)	luckily	(this is good or lucky)
amazingly	(this is very surprising – in a good way)	personally	(this is my opinion)
apparently	(this is what I read/heard, it may not be true)	obviously	(this is clear because it's obvious or logical)
basically	(this is the most important thing)	sadly	(this is something bad or wrong)
clearly	(this is true – and most people can see this)	surprisingly	(this is not what I expected)
generally	(this is usually true, but not always)	unfortunately	(this is sad or unlucky)
hopefully	(this is what I hope)		

Basically, all we did was stay in and watch TV.   I haven't got my results yet, but hopefully I've passed.

5A

1 Replace the underlined form with *will* + infinitive where this is possible without changing the meaning.

A: Hey, I was just talking to Alexi. [1]We're going to get something to eat after the meeting. Do you want to come?

B: Erm, I [2]may just go home. I'm actually not feeling great.

A: Really? Why don't you go home now?

B: Well, [3]I'm doing a presentation in the meeting – I can't miss that. I also need to finish preparing some samples for Tomas. [4]He's going to be really annoyed if I haven't done them by tomorrow. I promised I would.

A: Can't he wait a day longer?

B: No, [5]he's travelling to Singapore tomorrow.

A: Really? [6]What's he doing there?

B: It's the annual sales conference, but [7]he's meeting some new clients while he's there too, so I think [8]he's going to need those samples.

A: I see. I guess [9]you're going to have to do the best you can.

2 Choose the correct alternatives.

1 I suppose they *are lowering/might lower* their prices, but I think they'll look at other options first.

2 Once the new store is open, we*'re focusing/'re going to focus* more on developing our brand.

3 A: When *is/may* the new store *open/opening*?

   B: A week on Friday.

4 My father's retiring, so this time next year, he'll be on the beach and I*'ll be running/'ll run* the whole company.

5 A: Do you think they*'ll continue/'ll be continuing* to expand the company like they have been doing?

   B: Why not? They're doing really well.

5B

1 Complete the dialogues with an adverb.

1 A: How's school going?

   B: Not so well. I've _____ passed three of my eight exams this term.

2 A: How's the job-hunting going?

   B: Great. I've actually _____ been offered a job in a company near you, so we could meet up for lunch sometimes.

3 A: How's it going at university?

   B: _____ , it's been great. I've been really enjoying it, and I've _____ made lots of new friends. But I haven't sat any exams _____ so ask me again in a month's time!

4 A: How's the training for the marathon going?

   B: OK. I've _____ done a 25 km run, which I got through OK, so I think I'll be ready for the full marathon in April.

5 A: How's your new job going? Have you been on any work trips _____?

   B: You're joking, aren't you! I've hardly _____ been out of the office! I'm stuck behind my computer all day.

2 Complete the sentences with the adverbs in brackets.

1 I started building the house two years ago, but I haven't finished it. (still)

2 I'm trying to visit every football ground in the league. I've been to 16. (so far)

3 I've had three job interviews this month, but I haven't heard anything. (already, yet)

4 I've returned from Moldova. I'm trying to visit every country in Europe. There are two I haven't been to now! (just, only)

5 I want to buy a flat, but I've saved €15,000 so far. You can't buy anything for that amount of money. (only)

6 I often go fishing, but I haven't had much luck. I haven't caught a small one for ages now. (lately, even).

5C

1 Choose the best alternatives.

1 *Personally/Actually,* most studies show that students do better in mixed level groups.

2 *Surprisingly/Generally,* I managed to pass all my end-of-year exams. I really wasn't expecting to.

3 *Basically/Apparently,* I think students today have an easier time at school than in the past.

4 You might not think our education system is doing well, but *personally/sadly,* I think it is.

5 My son has struggled a bit at school, but *luckily/hopefully* he has a really good teacher this year and he's doing better.

6 I was quite a wild child and, *unfortunately/apparently*, I left school without any qualifications.

2 Complete the sentences with the adverbs in brackets. The adverbs are not in the correct order.

1 I felt proud when I got my degree. (incredibly)

2 My daughter got the top mark in the whole of her year. (amazingly)

3 The exam lasted six hours! I was exhausted afterwards. (absolutely)

4 You checked your answers before you handed them in. (carefully, hopefully)

5 It takes 10,000 hours of practice to become a good concert musician. (apparently, really)

6 I thought I had explained things, but if people said they still didn't understand what to do, I didn't do it that well. (obviously, very clearly, personally)

Want more practice? Go to your Workbook or app.

6A Passive

The passive is formed with a form of the verb *be* + past participle.

Use the passive when you want to focus on the person or thing that an action happens to.

In passive sentences, the main topic of the sentence is not the doer – the person or thing that does the action. If you include the doer in the sentence, use *by*. However, the doer is often not mentioned because it is unimportant, obvious or unknown.

• present simple
*It's **watched** by millions every week.*

• present continuous
*Parts of the new James Bond movie **are being filmed** in my city!*

• past simple
*Friends **was** first **shown** back in 1995.*

• past continuous
*The scene **was being filmed** at night.*

• present perfect simple
*More than thirty local versions of the programme **have been made** around the world.*

• past perfect simple
*I'**d been told** by friends that it was amazing, but I thought it was pretty average, to be honest.*

• modal + passive form
*I read somewhere that it **won't be released** until next summer.*

• be going to + passive form
*The new series **is going to be shown** on Netflix.*

• gerund + passive form
*He is excited about **being awarded** the Oscar.*

6B *Have/get something done*

Get/have + object + past participle is a passive structure. You often use it to talk about services that you pay someone else to do for you.

• Compare:
*Did you **make it** yourself?*
*No. I **had it made** for me (by an old friend of mine).*
*We had to **get our roof repaired** after that big storm the other week.*

• Use this structure when you want to emphasise both the thing that an action happens to and the person that the thing belongs to. The doer – the person that does the action – is unimportant, unknown or obvious. If you do include the person who does the action, use *by*.

• Use *have something done* in more formal situations.
Please have every student's exam checked by an external examiner.

• You can also use this structure to focus on things that happen to you, often bad, but which you don't organise or pay for. For this use, use *have something done*.
I hate having my photo taken.
He had all his money stolen while he was on holiday.

• Negatives
*We **didn't get it delivered**. We collected it ourselves.*
*We **haven't had it fixed** yet.*

• Questions
Have you had your hair cut?
Where did you get your nails done?

6C Probability

When you ask for opinions about future probability, you usually use *will*, but *be going to* + infinitive is also possible.
Who do you think will win?
What do you think they're going to do about it?

There are a number of different ways to express probability. If you use *will*, it is common to modify it with, e.g. an adverb or other phrase.

• to say you're almost certain:
I read that he'll definitely miss the final.
It's bound to get better sooner or later.
Things will change, I'm sure of it.

• to say something is probable:
There's a good chance an agreement will be reached.
It'll probably sell for over fifty million.
I think she's fairly likely to become the next leader.

• to say maybe – or maybe not:
It might happen. It might not. It's hard to know.
There's a chance it won't happen.
There's a chance he could end up in prison.

• to say something probably won't happen:
The president is unlikely to support the idea.
There's only a small chance that the company will survive.
The company probably won't be here next year.

• to say something is almost certain not to happen:
I doubt he'll say much about it, to be honest.
He's not the first person to do that – and he definitely won't be the last!

Sometimes you can just give short replies to *yes/no* questions about the future:
Do you think you'll get the job?
I'm bound to. (= I'm 99% sure I will.)
I hope so. (= I want this to happen.)
I doubt it./I don't think so. (= I'm fairly sure I won't.)
I hope not, actually. (= I don't want this to happen.)
Note this pattern:
I think we'll win.
I don't think we'll win.
NOT *I think we won't win.*

6A

1 Put the words in the correct order to make passive sentences.

1 was / It / Tunisia / in / filmed
2 live / Saturday / shown / It's / next / being
3 been / off / I / believe / she's / can't / killed
4 millions / appear / being / He's / in / paid / to / the / film
5 offered / take / but / I / didn't / been / them / had / I / tickets
6 voted / soon / I'm / off / the / sure / will / sometime / she / programme / be
7 posted / million / since / been / times / viewed / It / two / over / it / was / has
8 films / stopped / from / the / They / making / any / should / in / more / series / be

2 Complete the article with the words in brackets. Put the verbs in the active or the passive form.

Decades such as the 1970s ¹_____ (often / call) the Golden Age of Film. Some people say that all the great stories ²_____ (already / tell) and that over the next few years, TV ³_____ (replace) film as our main source of visual entertainment. In the early 2000s, maybe these critics ⁴_____ (have) a point: new technology meant that films could ⁵_____ (make) by anyone with a mobile phone – but most of these films were terrible! Hollywood ⁶_____ (get) lazy and endless remakes of old movies ⁷_____ (release)! That was then, but now young film makers ⁸_____ (produce) incredible films. Cinema ⁹_____ (not / kill off) any time soon!

6B

1 Complete the sentences with the words in brackets and a *have/get* passive form.

1 You ought to _____ , you know. It might be broken. (your arm / look at)
2 I locked myself out of the house again! I really should _____ and leave it with a neighbour. (a spare key / make)
3 Sorry. We'll have to use the stairs. We're _____ at the moment. (the lift / repair)
4 I'm thinking of _____ sometime soon. Do you think I should? (my hair / cut)
5 I usually _____ every week, but my cleaner is away at the moment. (my apartment / clean)
6 I got compliments after I _____, so people do notice the difference when they're done professionally. (my nails / do)
7 I've been so busy with work recently, I haven't had time to cook. I _____ every night. It's sad! (a pizza / deliver)
8 Sorry I can't drive you there, but I still _____ yet. I just haven't had time to sort it out. (my car / not fix)

2 Find the four sentences with a mistake and correct them.

1 I need to get my suit to be cleaned. Do you know a good place nearby?
2 We're having a new kitchen fitted at the moment.
3 I had my car was broken into last night. Luckily, there wasn't much to steal!
4 They got built a swimming pool in their back garden last year.
5 He had his nose broken in a car crash.
6 I'm afraid you'll need to have the whole screen replaced.
7 You should get that looked at by a doctor. It looks nasty!
8 I'm going to have cut my hair this weekend.

6C

1 Complete the sentences with one word in each space. Contractions count as one word.

1 What do you think he's _____ to say about it?
2 If you think it's funny, then there's a good _____ other people will, too!
3 It's not been good recently and I _____ think things will improve next year, either. I think things _____ only get worse.
4 I'll _____ be there, I promise. I'm just not sure exactly what time I can get away from work.
5 They should try it. You never know. It _____ help.
6 There's only a _____ chance the plan will work, but it's worth trying anyway.
7 It's fairly _____ that robots will end up taking lots of our jobs. I mean, it's already started!
8 There are _____ to be problems to begin with. There always are with projects like that.
9 They said it probably _____ rain today, but take an umbrella just in case it does!

2 Choose the best short answer.

1 A: Do you think you'll ever have kids?
   B: *I hope so/I doubt it*. Just not yet.
2 A: Do you think we'll win the next World Cup?
   B: *We're bound to/I doubt it*, but you never know. It's not impossible.
3 A: Do you think you'll ever live abroad?
   B: *It's unlikely/I'm bound to*. My boss is always sending people overseas.
4 A: Do you think you'll stay in your current job?
   B: *I'm quite likely to/I hope not*. After all, I'm happy there.
5 A: Do you think they'll win the election?
   B: *I hope not/It's quite unlikely*. It'll be terrible if they do.

Want more practice? Go to your Workbook or app.

7A Verb patterns 1: verb + -*ing*/infinitive with *to*

When two verbs are used together, the second verb often takes either the -*ing* form or the infinitive with *to*. The choice of form depends on the first verb. There are no rules for this. You just have to learn which verbs are followed by which patterns.

- verbs followed by the -*ing* form
  avoid   consider   enjoy   finish   involve   keep   mind   miss   practise   recommend   suggest
- verbs followed by the infinitive with *to*
  agree   arrange   decide   expect   fail   hope   learn   need   offer   promise   refuse   want
- Some verbs can be followed by both the -*ing* form and the infinitive with *to* without any real change in meaning.
  begin   continue   hate   like   start

*When did you begin **to feel/feeling** like this?*
*I hate **to complain/complaining**, but sometimes it's necessary.*
*I don't like **to ask/asking** you, but I have to.*
*When did you start **to smoke/smoking**?*

- A small group of verbs can be followed by both the -*ing* form and the infinitive with *to*, but the different forms affect the meaning.

***Try drinking** lots of water and see if that helps.*
(= a suggestion)
*I **tried to stand** on it, but it was too painful.* (= some kind of effort or difficulty)
*I **stopped taking** the medicine because it wasn't helping.*
(= I used to take it, but I don't now.)
*I **stopped to have** a little rest. (= This is the reason I stopped doing what I was doing before.)*
*I must **remember to get** my medicine from the chemist's.*
(= It's important that I do this.)
*I **don't remember getting** the knock on my head.*
(= It happened, but I have no memory of it.)
***Don't forget to take** your medicine. (= Remember to do it because it's important.)*
*I'll **never forget seeing** him there. (= It happened and I still remember it.)*

7B Verb patterns 2: verbs followed by a clause

A lot of verbs are often followed by a clause – especially verbs connected to speech and thought.
agree   ask   bet   claim   forget   imagine   know   realise   remember   say   suppose   tell   think   wonder

You can link the verb and the clause with *that*, but it's more common to use no linking word, especially in spoken English.

I forgot (that) you speak Spanish.
I agree (that) it's not a great idea.
I know (that) you don't agree with me about this.
I told you (that) I can't remember.

You can also link some of these verbs to the clause that follows with *if* or a question word. Notice that when you do this, you don't change the word order, so what follows looks like a statement, not a question.

*I don't **know if** he's married or not to be honest.*
*I'm sorry, but I've **forgotten what** your name is.*
*I **wonder where** she's from.*

When you use *if* or a question word, it cannot be left out like *that* can.

Questions using these verbs are sometimes called indirect questions. In indirect questions, use the word order of a statement after these verbs.

*Do you **know why** he can't come to the meeting?*
*Can you **ask if** he remembered to send that parcel?*
*Do you **think (that)** she'll agree to the idea?*

7C Noun phrases 2: noun + noun/noun + *of* + noun

You can modify or add information to a noun in different ways. As well as the way described in Lesson 1A, you can also:

- use noun + noun.

*I drove almost fifty miles with an empty **petrol tank**.*
*I was wearing my new **five-hundred-pound suit**.*
*They have a **swimming pool**. Can you believe it?*

Here, the second noun is the main noun and can be singular or plural. The first noun is a classifier and acts like an adjective and doesn't become plural, even if it's a number.

These combinations of noun + noun are sometimes called compound nouns. They are often quite fixed – and some are written as two words, some as one word and some with hyphens.

A good learner's dictionary will tell you how each compound is usually written.

driving test, bus stop, windscreen, bathroom, great-grandparents

- use noun + *of* + noun

*I have a terrible **fear of flying**.*
*It's not **the end of the world**.*
*Six **cups of tea** and two **glasses of orange juice**.*

Here, the first noun is the main noun and can be singular or plural. The second noun defines the first noun or adds more detail or information.

Learn new combinations when you meet them. Sometimes both forms are possible, with no difference in meaning.

the hotel garden/ the garden of the hotel

You can also combine the two patterns:

the level of air pollution

7A

1 Choose the correct alternatives. In one sentence, both alternatives are possible.

1 I didn't learn *driving/to drive* until I was 35.
2 I'd recommend *talking/to talk* to someone about it if it doesn't get better soon.
3 When did you begin *feeling/to feel* it was becoming a problem?
4 I didn't expect *spending/to spend* Christmas in hospital, but it was actually lovely!
5 My job involves *dealing/to deal* with some very angry people sometimes.
6 It's hard to practise *speaking/to speak* a language if you don't know other speakers.
7 I promise *stopping/to stop* this year, but it's not easy.
8 I usually avoid *going/to go* to the dentist's unless I really have to.
9 I was lucky. The doctor agreed *seeing/to see* me first thing tomorrow.
10 I really tried *to eat/eating* less meat, but it was so hard. I kept *wanting/to want* burgers!

2 Complete the second sentence so that it means the same as the first. Use the verbs in brackets.

1 Start with a short walk of a kilometre or two. (suggest)
   I _____.
2 I just get really out of breath all the time. (keep)
   I _____.
3 It'd be best if you stayed in hospital overnight. (need)
   I'm afraid you'll _____.
4 I'll send her a card. Can you remind me later? (remember)
   I must _____.
5 They did lots of different tests, but in the end, they couldn't find anything wrong. (fail)
   After doing all sorts of tests, they _____ wrong.
6 You should think about becoming a doctor. (consider)
   Have you ever _____?
7 On my way to work, I went in to the doctor's surgery and made an appointment. (stop)
   I was walking past the doctor's surgery on my way to work and I _____ an appointment.
8 I wanted something for the pain, but the doctor wouldn't give me anything. (refuse)
   The doctor _____ for the pain.

7B

1 Complete the second sentence so that it means the same as the first.

1 How much did he borrow?
   Do you know _____?
2 Why have they decided to do that?
   I don't know _____.
3 You speak Greek! I didn't know.
   I didn't realise _____.
4 Where's the bank?
   Sorry, but could you tell me _____?
5 Why don't they complain about it?
   I wonder _____.
6 When's her birthday?
   Can you remember _____?
7 Could you lend me five pounds?
   Do you think _____?

2 Find the four sentences with a mistake and correct them.

1 I can't believe how much he does earn.
2 He admitted he'd stolen the watch.
3 I don't know she's coming to class today or not.
4 She asked me why do I work so much.
5 I could see that it wouldn't be easy.
6 I suddenly remembered I had a test the following day.
7 Can you tell me where can I find more information?
8 They're complaining that they haven't been treated fairly.

7C

1 Complete the sentences with the plural form of the compound nouns in the box.

> amount of money   driving test   road sign   traffic jam   car of the future
> train station   side of the road

1 Most _____ will have to be electric because oil is running out fast!
2 We got stuck in one of the worst _____ I've ever seen in my life!
3 He spends crazy _____ on that car of his!
4 Cars were parked on both _____ , which made it really hard to drive down.
5 In the last few months, I've taken three _____ and failed each one!
6 None of the _____ were in English, so I couldn't read any of them!
7 They've opened two new _____ in the city over the last few years.

Want more practice? Go to your Workbook or app.

8A First conditional

Use the first conditional to talk about possible situations in the present or future.

The sentences have two parts: a possible future 'condition' (an action or a situation clause) and the result of that action.

- The condition clause can be introduced with *if, unless, even if* or *in case*, and these conjunctions are followed by a verb in a present tense or *can* + infinitive.
- The result part of a first conditional sentence uses:
will/be going to + infinitive to show you're certain
may or *might* + infinitive to show it's only a possibility
should to show you think it's a good idea.
- *in case* means 'in order to be prepared for' something that may happen.

*They should start investing in better defences against the sea **in case** water levels rise.* (= They won't know if water levels are going to rise, but they should invest in better defences anyway.)

Compare:
*They should start investing in better defences against the sea **if** water levels rise.* (= They should invest in better defences only if they know water levels are going to rise.)

- *unless* means 'if not this situation.'

***Unless** we **act** now, things are going to get worse.*

Compare:
***If** we **don't act** now, things are going to get worse.*

- *even if* means that something will still be true if another thing happens, but this other thing is not likely to happen.

Even if we all start consuming less, we will still face serious problems in the coming years. (= We are not likely to start consuming less.)

Either the condition part of the sentence or the result can come first. It depends on what you want to focus on. When the condition part comes first, separate it from the result using a comma.

If we don't act soon, things will get worse.

Things will get worse if we don't act soon.

8B *Whatever, whoever, whenever, however, etc.*

Use *whatever, whoever, whenever, however* and *wherever* when:

- it doesn't matter what, where, when, etc.
- you don't have to be specific about the thing, place, time, etc.
- you don't know the thing, place, time, etc.

*I give up! **Whatever** I do, you never seem happy about it!* (= it doesn't matter what I do)

*You can park **wherever** you want. It's all free parking on Sundays.* (= you can park anywhere)

*Ask **whoever** you want. They'll all say the same thing.* (= ask anybody)

***Whenever** I go and visit her, she always cooks me a huge meal!* (= every time I visit her)

*She was always kind to me, **however** badly I'd behaved!* (= it didn't matter how badly I'd behaved)

*She can eat **whatever** she wants and never seems to put on any weight!* (= she can eat anything and everything)

*He always phones us every day **wherever** he is in the world.* (= it doesn't matter where he is)

8C Time conjunctions

Time conjunctions link two parts of a sentence – an event or action with another event or action – and show the order they happen in.

- *Until, after* and *before* can be used as prepositions and are followed by a noun.

*Happy birthday! Ten more years **until retirement**!*

*I found things really hard **after the birth of my first child**.*

*Please arrive at least fifteen minutes **before the start of the ceremony**.*

They can also be used as conjunctions and are followed by a clause.

*Most people in my country live at home with their parents **until they marry**.* (= First they live at home, then they marry.)

***After I retire**, I want to travel more.*

*Personally, I think it's better not to live together **before you get married**.*

- *As soon as, when* and *once* are conjunctions only and are followed by a clause only.

***As soon as I graduated**, I moved to London.* (= I graduated and immediately after that I moved to London.)

*I cried and cried and cried **when my son was born**.* (= My son was born and then I cried.)

***Once we got married**, we moved into our own home.* (= We got married and then we moved into our own home.)

- When you talk about future events and actions, you use a present simple or present perfect form in the clause that follows the time conjunction.

***Once I start** working, I'll start saving to buy a flat.* (= I will start working and then I will start saving.)

The present perfect emphasises one action will happen before the other.

*Things will get easier **once we have had paid off the mortgage**.* (= We will pay off the mortgage and then things will get easier.)

***After I've paid off** my mortgage, I'm going to buy myself a new car!*

8A

1 Choose the correct alternatives.

1 We're going to change to solar power in case they *might increase / increase* the price of gas.

2 If you *will want / want* to lose weight, you'll need to eat less sugar, for a start!

3 People might recycle more *if / unless* they're paid to do so.

4 Even if we *meet / will meet* our country's targets, 25 percent of the earth may still be drier.

5 If they *want / will want* us to move from oil and gas, they should invest more in other kinds of energy.

6 We're going to run out of air that we can breathe unless carbon *is / is not* cut.

7 Some people *will / should* always break the rules even if they introduce fines for doing so.

8 They're going to build a big wall along the river in case another flood *happens / will happen*.

2 Find the five sentences with mistakes and correct them.

1 Many cities will become terrible places to live if we do something about all the pollution.

2 Unless we stop building on green spaces, we soon don't have many rare animals left.

3 If we all make little changes to the way we do things, it'll have a big effect.

4 You should get insurance before you go in case you're going to have an accident.

5 Even you stop eating meat, people are still going to kill animals.

6 You really should start applying now if you want to go to university next year.

7 Unless we don't act soon, we'll see more and more natural disasters starting to happen.

8 If you're not at home during the day, you should turn all the lights off.

8B

1 Complete the sentences with the words in the box.

> whatever   whoever   wherever   however
> whenever

1 We get on OK _____ we meet, but I wouldn't say we're good friends.

2 Some people are just good at enjoying themselves _____ they are in the world.

3 Feel free to visit _____ you're in the area.

4 _____ he told you, it's not true.

5 She's from Manningtree, _____ that is.

6 What an amazing photo! _____ took that is really talented!

7 She has enough money to buy _____ she wants.

8 It's a big problem _____ you look at it.

2 Complete the second sentence so that it means the same as the first. Use three words.

1 I don't know who said that, but they're wrong!
_____ is wrong!

2 It doesn't matter where she goes. She always manages to make friends.
She makes friends _____.

3 It doesn't matter what people say about him. I still like him.
People can _____ want about him. I still like him.

4 Even if you're really talented, you still have to practise.
You still have to practise, _____ are.

5 Every time I hear this song, I think of you.
I think of you _____ this song.

8C

1 Rewrite the pairs of sentences as one sentence.

1 My dad is going to retire next month. He might go and spend some time with my sister in Spain.
After my dad _____ .

2 Let me speak to my wife first. After that, I'll call you back, OK?
I _____ once I _____ .

3 I'm going to see her later today. I'll tell her then.
I'll _____ when _____ .

4 We're getting married next month. We still have lots of things to sort out.
We _____ before we _____ .

5 I'm moving house next month. Things are going to be a bit crazy until then.
Things _____ until _____ .

2 Match sentence halves 1–6 with a–f and link them with a conjunction.

1 I used to really love rugby

2 I'll email you about it

3 Please don't play music in your room

4 My grandfather died one month

5 I'll be worrying about you, so call me

6 Could you wait here with me

a you've landed in London, OK?

b my bus comes?

c my daughter was born, so they never met.

d I was younger.

e I leave the office tonight.

f everyone else has gone to bed.

Want more practice? Go to your Workbook or app.

9A Patterns after *wish*

Use *wish* to say what you would like in situations that are impossible to change. *Wish* is followed by:

• past simple

Use *wish* + past simple to say how you'd like a present situation to be different.

I wish I wasn't here. I'd rather be at the beach!

You sometimes see *were* used instead of *was*, but this is becoming old-fashioned.

I wish it were true.

• could

Use *wish* + *could* to say what you'd like to be able to do in the present situation.

I wish I could drive. It would be easier to find a job.
I sometimes wish I could move abroad, but I can't.

• would

Use *wish* + *would* to say what you want someone/ something else to do now or in the future - even though you're sure they won't do it.

I wish the council would do something about all the rubbish in the streets.

Note that you do not use *wish* to talk about future desires that you think are possible. Use *hope*.

I hope I'll be OK tomorrow. NOT *I wish I'd be OK.*

Short responses

In conversations, you often use *I wish I was, I wish I did, I wish I didn't, I wish I could, I wish he would* etc. as short responses.

A: *Why don't you come for dinner tomorrow?*
B: *I wish **I could**, but I'm busy. Another time maybe.*
(= I wish I could come for dinner.)
A: *Do you have time for a coffee?*
B: *I wish **I did**, but I really have to go.* (= I wish I had time for a coffee.)
A: *Do you need a car?*
B: *Yeah. I wish **I didn't**, but I use it a lot for my job.*
(= I wish I didn't need a car.)

9B Second conditional

Use the second conditional to talk about imaginary situations now or in the future. The sentences have two parts, a condition clause and a result clause.

• In the condition clause, you often use *if* + the past simple/continuous.

1 If they lowered the voting age ... (They are not planning to lower the voting age.)
2 If I was living alone ... (I'm not living alone.)

• In the result clause, use *would* + infinitive to talk about certain results.

1 ... it would increase the number of people voting.

Use *might/may* + infinitive to talk about less certain results.

1 ... it might encourage young people to get more involved in politics.

Use *could* + infinitive to talk about less certain results involving ability.

2 ... I could invite friends round more easily. (= I would be able to)

The condition clause can come before or after the result clause - or can be left out if you feel the condition is clear from the context.

A: *I could invite friends round more easily if I was living alone.*
B: *Yeah, but **you'd also have to do all your own housework**!* (... if you were living alone.)

Note that you will sometimes see *were* used instead of *was*, but this is becoming less common:

If he were a good leader, he'd do something about the problem. But he isn't, and he won't!

When you think a situation is more likely to happen you use a first conditional. However, often this is just a point of view, so either a first or second conditional is possible.

*If the government **increase** taxes, **it will damage** the economy.* (= There is a plan to increase taxes.)
*If the government **increased** taxes, **it would damage** the economy.* (= There is no plan to increase taxes.)

9C Past modals of deduction

To make deductions and guesses about the past, use *must, might* and *can't* + *have* + a past participle.

• Use *must have* (*must've* in spoken English) when you are almost certain something was true (based on the evidence). *Something **must have scared** him.*

• Use *might have* (*might've*) when you think it's possible that something was true.
*He **might have had** an injury of some kind, I guess.*

• Use *can't have* when you are almost certain something wasn't true (based on the evidence).
*The Queen Mother **can't have been** very pleased!*

• Commenting

You often use these modals to comment on a story that someone is telling you or to comment on something that someone is reporting. The other person can respond to your comments as if they were questions:

A: *My son came last in the race.*
B: *Oh dear. He must've been disappointed.* (= Was he disappointed?)
A: *A bit, but he was also happy he'd got to the final.*

You also use *must, might* and *can't* with a simple infinitive to comment on present situations.

A: *I train three times a week.*
B: *That **must be** hard. You **can't have** much time for anything else.*
A: *It does take a lot of time, but I like it.*
B: *Be careful! You **might overdo** it.*

9A

1 Complete the sentences with one word. Contractions count as one word.

1 A: Why don't you look for another job?
  B: I wish I _____ , but I just don't have time!

2 A: She gets such good grades, she should apply to study medicine.
  B: I know. I wish she _____ , but she doesn't seem interested.

3 A: I've got my interview tomorrow for the marketing job.
  B: Oh yes. I _____ it goes well.

4 A: You look quite fit.
  B: Yeah? I wish I _____ , but I hardly do any exercise.

5 A: Do you really have to go tomorrow?
  B: I wish I _____ , but I need to get back as I've got work to do.

6 A: You seem to get a lot of support at work.
  B: Do you think so? I wish we _____ . They don't actually help that much at all.

2 Complete the second sentence so that it means the same as the first.

1 I'm tired and my husband doesn't help enough with the housework.
  I wish _____ more with the housework.

2 There's too much corruption in the government.
  I wish our politicians _____ honest.

3 The traffic is terrible round here.
  I wish they _____ something about the terrible traffic.

4 I would like to move to a better area, but I don't have enough money.
  I wish I _____ to move to a better area.

5 I'd love to spend more time with my family, but I have to work long hours.
  I really wish I _____ with my family.

6 My dad should really retire because he's not that well.
  I wish _____ before his illness gets worse.

7 My garden is dying because of the lack of rain.
  I wish _____ . My garden really needs it.

9B

1 Complete the dialogue with the correct form of the verbs in the box. Use a past form or *would* or *could* + infinitive.

| be   damage   do (x2)   expect   get   have to |
| increase   live   spend |

A: We should invest money in better healthcare.
B: I guess, but if we ¹_____ more on health, people ²_____ longer.
A: And what's wrong with that?
B: Well, they ³_____ retired for longer and the government ⁴_____ spend more money on pensions.
A: Well, what if they ⁵_____ the retirement age?
B: But that wouldn't be very fair! Imagine if you ⁶_____ to retire at 65 and then they suddenly increased the age to 70.
A: I know, but they ⁷_____ it more gradually and people wouldn't suffer. I think you just don't want your taxes put up.
B: Well, exactly! If they ⁸_____ that, it ⁹_____ the economy, which means the government ¹⁰_____ less money and they would have to cut spending – on health, for example.

2 Find the five sentences with a mistake and correct them.

1 If I am president, I would give everyone an extra week of holiday.

2 If we would pay everyone a basic income, there would be less poverty.

3 If the government isn't investing in support for young people, crime might go up.

4 People might trust politicians more if they didn't promise so much.

5 If we had better education, we might can end racism.

6 Companies improved their service if consumers complained more.

7 If the government had more money, they would probably just waste it.

9C

1 Complete the text about King Tutankhamun of Egypt with the correct form of the pairs of verbs in the box.

| may/murder   can't/be   may/like   could/fall   must/die   must/be   can't/find   might/cause |

Tutankhamun is today one of the most famous Egyptian kings because of the treasure discovered in his tomb. However, we know that because his tomb was so much smaller than other kings', he ¹_____ very important. Recent research has shown he ²_____ before he was 20, but there is uncertainty about the cause of his death. The first idea is that someone ³_____ him to gain power, because X-rays of the king's body showed damage to his head. However, more recent research suggests that a fall ⁴_____ the injury. It seems that Tutankhamun ⁵_____ sport – particularly racing horses and hunting. However, X-rays also show he had a problem with his foot and chest, which ⁶_____ very painful. These physical problems also mean he ⁷_____ it easy to stand up when racing and so he ⁸_____ during a race or when he was hunting.

Want more practice? Go to your Workbook or app.

10A Third conditional

Use the third conditional to talk about imaginary past situations and actions.

The sentences have two parts: an imagined past 'condition' (a situation or an action) and the imagined result of that situation or action.

result:
*His achievements **wouldn't have been** possible*
imagined situation/action:
*if the French army **hadn't entered** Spain in 1808.*
imagined situation/action:
*If Rosa Parks **had done** as she was told,*
result:
*modern American history **might have been** different.*

- In the condition clause, use *if* + past perfect simple or continuous.

1 If she hadn't encouraged me …
2 If I hadn't been staying in that hotel …

- In the result clause, use *would* (*not*) + *have* + past participle to talk about definite results.

2 … we would never have met.

Use *might/may* + *have* + past participle for less definite results.

1 … things might've been very different.
2 … I may not have ever got married!

Use *could* + *have* + past participle to talk about possibility and ability.

1 … I don't think I could have done it.

Once the situation has been established you often don't repeat the condition clause – you just talk about the imagined results.

*A: If I'd known it was going to be this boring, I **would've stayed** at home.*
*B: I know. We **could've watched** the football. Roma are playing.*
*A: I was actually thinking I **could've done** some work. I have a lot to do.*

10B *Should have*

Use *should(n't)* + *have* + past participle to talk about past events. It often expresses regrets about – or criticism of – actions.

I should've been more careful to begin with.
I shouldn't have been in such a rush.
They should've done more to help.

Use this structure to imagine better alternatives to what actually happened. It is often linked to a third conditional sentence – or an imagined result (*would've/might've/could've*).

I shouldn't have denied making the mistake. (If I'd apologised and corrected the mistake immediately, I wouldn't have got into an argument.)

When you use adverbs like *really* and *probably*, you commonly put them between *should(n't)* and *have*.

I shouldn't really have done that!
You should at least have asked me what I wanted!

However, if you want to add a particular emphasis, you can also put adverbs before *should(n't)*.

He definitely should've tried harder.

10C Adjective word order

You sometimes use two or more adjectives together. As a general rule, opinion adjectives (adjectives which tell us what the speaker thinks of something) come before fact adjectives (adjectives that describe age, size, colour, etc).

If you use two or more fact adjectives, you usually put them in this order:

size – age – colour – origin – 'material' – **noun**
I bought a lovely new Thai silk shirt.
She's got a beautiful big old blue French car.
Look at that ancient blue Chinese bowl.

However, note that you don't often use more than three adjectives together.

When you describe something with two colours, link them together with *and*.

He was wearing a stripy red and white top.
I love your orange and yellow silk bag.
My daughter's school has got a new grey and purple uniform.

Also, remember that you often make compound nouns by adding two nouns together.

football boots, shower curtain, coffee table, kitchen clock

The two nouns always stay together when you add descriptive adjectives because the first noun classifies the second noun.

*new red and white **football boots***
*an old plastic **shower curtain***
*a new wooden **coffee table***
*a second-hand French **kitchen clock***

10A

1 Match sentence halves 1–8 with a–h to make third conditional sentences.

1 The 1960s might have been very different in the US

2 France probably wouldn't have won the 1998 World Cup so easily

3 If we'd taken a taxi instead of the bus,

4 It's my own fault. I would almost certainly have passed

5 I would never have gone to university

6 If I hadn't broken my leg when I was 17,

a we wouldn't have missed our flight!

b I could've ended up playing for Barcelona!

c if I'd studied a bit harder.

d if John F Kennedy had lived.

e if I hadn't had such an amazing geography teacher.

f if Ronaldo had played for Brazil that day.

2 Complete the second sentence so that it means the same as the first.

1 Napoleon invaded Russia in 1812. His French army then suffered a terrible defeat.

If Napoleon _____ in 1812, his army _____ a terrible defeat.

2 Einstein almost didn't become a scientist. He thought about becoming a watchmaker.

If he _____ a scientist, Einstein _____ a watchmaker.

3 I was late for my interview. That's probably why I didn't get the job.

I _____ the job if I _____ for my interview.

4 I wanted to stay in Krakow. I only left because my wife got a job in Warsaw.

I _____ in Krakow if my wife _____ a job in Warsaw.

5 You didn't tell me about it! That's why I can't remember.

I'm sure I _____ if you _____ it.

10B

1 Complete the sentences with *should've* or *shouldn't have* + the verbs in the box.

agree   delay   force   get   know   rush

1 I didn't do as well as I was hoping to. I _____ better marks in my exams.

2 Looking back, I can see I _____ the changes onto my staff. It was a mistake.

3 After what happened last time, I _____ better. I just hoped things would be different!

4 We introduced the new plan too quickly. We _____ the introduction and talked to our staff more first.

5 I _____ to take the job. I honestly didn't realise how much work it'd involve.

6 I blame myself. I _____ the work. I didn't realise how much time I'd need.

2 Read the information in the first sentence. Then complete the second sentence with *should've* or *shouldn't have* + verb.

1 I forgot to tell them about all my experience of working in schools. Maybe that's why I didn't get the job.

I _____ about my school experience. I might've got the job if I had.

2 I missed the train because I got the time wrong and I arrived at the station too late.

I _____ the train time on the ticket more carefully. I wouldn't have missed the train then.

3 They caused the problem and then they blamed me!

They _____ me for causing the problem. It was their fault!

4 I regret not wearing a suit now, but I thought it was going to be quite informal.

I _____ a suit. Everyone else was wearing one!

5 It was silly to drive to my interview as I was almost late.

I _____ to my interview.

10C

1 Choose the correct option a–c to complete the sentences 1–6.

1 Can you pass me that _____ cup?
   a plastic red big   b red big plastic   c big red plastic

2 We went to see this _____ movie.
   a Russian new wonderful   b wonderful new Russian   c new wonderful Russian

3 He was wearing a _____ jacket.
   a dirty old leather   b old leather dirty   c leather old dirty

4 We stayed in a _____ town.
   a beautiful Spanish old   b Spanish old beautiful   c beautiful old Spanish

5 We got married in a _____ castle.
   a fantastic 18th-century Scottish   b Scottish fantastic 18th-century   c Scottish 18th-century fantastic

Want more practice? Go to your Workbook or app.

Vocabulary bank

1B Describing homes and areas

1 a Work in pairs and describe the photos. Use the descriptions 1–10 to help you. Which place would you prefer to live in?

1 It's very lively.
2 It's very rural.
3 It's very central.
4 It's very green.
5 It's convenient for the shops.
6 It's a bit rough.
7 It's tiny.
8 It's nice and bright.
9 It's huge.
10 It's quite noisy.

b Which of the descriptions in Exercise 1a are of homes and which are of areas?

2 Match comments a–j with the descriptions in Exercise 1a.

a It's miles away from the nearest town.
b It must have at least ten bedrooms.
c You can walk to the main square in a couple of minutes.
d You can do all your shopping near where you live.
e I don't feel safe on the streets after dark.
f The kids love the park and all the trees.
g You get a lot of natural light in there.
h There are lots of bars and restaurants there and it's always very busy.
i I sometimes get woken up by the music from downstairs.
j It's basically just one room and a toilet.

3 Work in groups. Use the descriptions in Exercise 1a to talk about places you know.

1C Phrasal verbs

1 Match the phrasal verbs in bold in sentences 1–10 with meanings a–j.

verb + *on*

1 Thanks for all your help. I knew I could **rely on** you.
2 I'm lucky because I **get on** with everyone I work with.
3 Can you **pass** the message **on** to Jan when you see her?
4 **Hang on**. I'll be with you in a minute.
5 Things can't **go on** like this. I can't stand it.

verb + *up*

6 I'll **pick** you **up** from your hotel at 7.15. Wait in the lobby.
7 We had a party in the house last night so I need to **tidy** the whole place **up**.
8 I **stayed up** until 3 last night chatting to some friends online.
9 **Hurry up** or we'll be late. The film starts in half an hour!
10 I know it's hard, but don't **give up**. You have to keep trying.

a do things more quickly
b trust or depend on
c didn't go to bed
d continue
e make somewhere look better by putting things in their correct place
f have a friendly relationship
g meet someone and take them somewhere in a car
h give someone something, especially information that someone else has given you
i wait
j stop doing something, especially something you do regularly

2 a Complete questions 1–5 with the correct form of the phrasal verbs from Exercise 1.

1 Who do you _____ most? Why? How do they help you?
2 When did you last have to _____ your flat/house? Why was it in a mess?
3 When was the last time you _____ really late? What were you doing?
4 Who do you _____ with best in your family? Why?
5 Have you ever tried to _____ something _____, but failed? Why couldn't you stop?

b Work in pairs. Take turns asking and answering the questions in Exercise 2a.

2A *Make* and *do*

1 Work in pairs. Complete the table by adding the words in the box to the correct columns.

> an exam   good money   the laundry
> a lot of damage   a mess   a speech
> a suggestion   the washing-up

make	do

2 a Choose the correct alternatives.

1 It doesn't matter if you succeed or fail. The important thing is to *make/do* your best.
2 You must *make/do* arrangements for the future.
3 People who've *made/done* a fortune are generally happier than others.
4 It's not a problem if you *make/do* mistakes. It's part of the learning process.
5 I'm not very good at *making/doing* decisions.
6 I'm going to *make/do* another English course once this one is finished.
7 I'm *making/doing* good progress with my English.
8 I'd like to *make/do* some research into something I'm interested in.
9 If you *make/do* an effort, you often succeed in life.
10 I'm not as fit as I'd like to be. I need to *make/do* a bit more exercise.

b Work in groups and discuss the statements in Exercise 2a. Do you agree with them?

2B Compound nouns

1 a Match 1–4 with a–d to make four compound nouns.

1 a department	a rise
2 a union	b drill
3 a pay	c member
4 a practice	d store

b Match 5–8 with e–h to make four more compound nouns.

5 work	e insurance
6 job	f experience
7 sales	g targets
8 health	h security

c Match 9–12 with i–l to make four more compound nouns.

9 a pension	i industry
10 the fashion	j market
11 the job	k car
12 a company	l scheme

2 Complete the sentences with the compound nouns from Exercises 1a, b and c.

1 I travel a lot for work, so they gave me a lovely new _____ to drive.
2 I won a prize because I met my annual _____ in the first six months of the year.
3 I'll be OK when I retire because we have a really good _____ at work.
4 I had to take a month off work after an accident, but luckily I had _____.
5 I've always loved clothes, so I'd like to work as a designer in the _____.
6 I work in Selfridges. It's a big _____ in the city centre.
7 Don't worry! It's not a real fire. We have a _____ once every couple of weeks.
8 This is my first job. The money's not very good, but at least I'm getting some _____.
9 There's no _____ where I work. Anyone can lose their job at any time.
10 Every year, over 250,000 young people enter the _____ for the first time.
11 If you have problems at work, you'll get more help if you're a _____.
12 I'm earning the same now as I was when I started. It's time I got a _____ !

3 Work in pairs. Take turns saying five true things about your life. Use compound nouns from Exercises 1a, b and c

It's hard for me, because I can't get the job I want without work experience – and I can't get any work experience because no one will give me a job!

3B Verbs with dependent prepositions

1 Read the verbs in the box and find:

1 four verbs followed by *in*.
2 four verbs followed by *on*.
3 three verbs followed by *to*.
4 two verbs followed by *of*.
5 two verbs followed by *for*.
6 one verb followed by *from*.

> apologise   approve   believe   care   comment
> concentrate   congratulate   consist   contribute
> depend   invest   participate   refer   respond
> succeed   suffer

2 Complete the sentences with verbs from Exercise 1. The prepositions are given.

1 It's important to teach young kids how to _____ for their pets.
2 The president refused to _____ on the stories about him in the media. He didn't mention them.
3 Our school is going to _____ in the new project.
4 It's so noisy in here! I can't _____ on my work.
5 I didn't feel I had anything to _____ to the discussion. I don't know much about the topic.
6 I'm not sure how to _____ to that question.
7 I'm calling to _____ for what I said yesterday. I'm sorry.
8 I _____ from a bad back and can't do much exercise.
9 The government should _____ more money in health and education.

3 a Complete the questions with the correct prepositions.

1 What's the best thing you've succeeded _____ doing over the last few months?
2 When was the last time you had to apologise _____ something?
3 When was the last time you congratulated someone _____ something? What was it?
4 Do any of your friends ever do things that you don't approve _____ ?
5 What do you think is the best thing to invest _____ ?

b Work in pairs. Take turns asking and answering the questions in Exercise 3a.

3C Social norms and customs

1 Match verbs 1–8 with phrases a–h.

1 try   a your nose in public
2 ask   b for everyone to be served before eating
3 hold   c a present in front of the person who gave it to you
4 open   d to bring the price down when you're shopping
5 split   e hands in public
6 wait   f how much people earn
7 shake   g hands when you meet friends
8 blow   h the bill at the end of a meal

2 a Complete the second sentence with three words so that it means the same as the first.

1 It's best not to hold hands in public here.
It's not acceptable _____ in public here.
2 When I meet friends, I usually kiss them on each cheek.
Here, it's normal _____ on the cheek when you meet them.
3 In my country, I always try to bring the price down when I'm shopping.
In my country, it's usual _____ bring the price down when shopping.
4 We generally don't ask how much people earn.
It's not the done thing _____ much someone earns.

b Work in pairs. Which of the customs in Exercise 2a are/aren't normal in your country? Use the sentence starters in the second sentences to help you. Can you think of any other social norms and customs?

4A Verbs and nouns with the same form

1 a Complete the questions with the words in the box.

export	flood	object	present	promise
protest	research	trust		

1 Have you ever attended a public _____ ? What against?
2 What kinds of things does your country _____ ?
3 Have you ever done any _____ ? What on?
4 Who do you _____ most in the world? Why?
5 Has there ever been a bad _____ in your town/city? When? What happened?
6 What's your favourite _____ that you own? Why is it so important to you?
7 Have you ever made a _____ and then broken it? When and why?
8 What's the best _____ you have ever been given?

b Complete the questions with the words in the box.

challenge	control	increase	refund	struggle
update				

9 What do you most _____ with when learning English?
10 How often do you _____ your status on social media?
11 Can you think of anything there has been an _____ in recently? Why has this happened?
12 Do you ever find it hard to _____ your feelings? When?
13 What's the biggest _____ that you've ever had in your life?
14 When was the last time you had to get a _____ ? Why? What was the problem?

c Look at Exercises 1a and b. In which sentences did you add verbs? In which did you add nouns?

d Work in pairs. Take turns saying the fourteen words as verbs and as nouns. Which have the same stress in both forms? Which have different stress? How is it different?

2 Work in groups. Ask and answer the questions in Exercises 1a and b.

4C Prefixes: *over-* and *under-*

1 Add *over-* or *under-* to the correct form of the words in the box to complete the sentences.

achieve	charge	cook	develop	estimate
ground	pay	use		

1 I need to change my job. I'm overworked and _____ .
2 I can't eat this steak. Look at all this blood. It's very _____ !
3 If you ask me, footballers are _____ . No one should earn that much money!
4 My country is still _____ . We need better technology, better education and better jobs.
5 I think 'nice' must be the most _____ adjective in the English language!
6 He's talented, but he doesn't try hard enough. I'd say that so far he's _____ in his career.
7 They made a mistake in the shop and _____ me by £5, but I'm honest so I told them.
8 We completely _____ the cost of the project. It cost a lot more than we expected.
9 Cheap airline companies could bring new business to many _____ airports.
10 I never expected to do this well by the age of 30. I sometimes feel like I've _____ for my age.

2 Work in groups. Choose two of the topics to talk about. Compare your ideas.
- workers that you think are underpaid (or overpaid)
- someone who has underachieved in their career
- an area that's now overdeveloped (or that's still underdeveloped)
- something – or someone – you underestimated
- a time you were overcharged (or undercharged)
- a word/phrase that you think is overused

5A Word building: verbs to nouns

1 a Complete the pairs of sentences with the correct verb or noun form of the words in the box.

| create   act   persuade   compete   authorise |

1 a They need to take _____ to deal with the situation.

   b If we don't _____ soon, the problem is just going to get worse.

2 a Sorry, but I can't _____ payments over £1000. You'll need to talk to my boss.

   b I'm afraid you can't enter this area without official _____ .

3 a We can't _____ with them on price, so we need to be sure our products are better quality.

   b There's a lot of _____ between the different companies in this field.

4 a I've been with the company since its _____ in 2002.

   b We're hoping that we can _____ around 50 new jobs this year.

5 a I just couldn't _____ her to change her mind.

   b I think with a little _____ we can get them to reduce the price.

b Work in pairs. How many other nouns ending in *-ion* do you know? Work in groups and compare your lists. Who had the most words?

2 Work in groups. Choose two of the topics to talk about. Compare your ideas.

* something silly you were persuaded to do
* action that needs to be taken
* something you're (not) authorised to do at work
* an area where there's not enough competition
* something you've created

5C Confusing words

1 Choose the correct alternatives.

1 a I've been *studying/learning* German for two years now, but I haven't *studied/learnt* much.

   b I have to stay in tonight and *study/learn* for my test tomorrow.

2 a Sorry I'm late. I *lost/missed* my bus.

   b Sorry I'm late. I *lost/missed* my house keys and couldn't go out without them.

3 a My mum's doing a Spanish *career/course* because she's going to Mexico in the summer.

   b I started my *career/course* as a lawyer, but about ten years ago, I decided I needed a change.

4 a I trust her not to do anything silly. She's very *sensible/sensitive* for her age.

   b Be careful what you say to him. He's very *sensitive/sensible* and gets upset very easily.

5 a My uncle *advised/recommended* me to do my Master's degree in the US.

   b A friend of mine *advised/recommended* this school. That's why I'm here.

6 a He spent a year in England, but it didn't have much *affect/effect* on his accent.

   b I didn't sleep well last night. I hope it doesn't *affect/effect* how I do in the test today.

2 a Complete the questions with words in italics from Exercise 1.

1 What would you most like to _____ how to do? Why?

2 If you could do any _____ on any subject, what would you choose? Why?

3 Have you ever _____ anything important? What happened? Did you find it again?

4 Have you ever _____ a flight? If yes, what happened?

5 What was the last book/film/song/place you _____ ? Who to? Why?

6 What did your parents _____ you to do – or not to do? Did you follow their advice?

b Work in pairs. Take turns asking and answering the questions in Exercise 2a.

6A Adjectives to describe films and TV programmes

1 a Complete descriptions 1–10 with the adjectives in the box.

complex	confusing	dreadful	enjoyable
ordinary	predictable	ridiculous	romantic
shocking	violent		

1 I liked it. It wasn't amazing or anything, but it was very _____ .

2 It was very _____ to be honest. It really wasn't anything special.

3 The whole story was completely _____ . I just didn't believe any of it could ever happen.

4 I thought it was absolutely _____ . I watched half an hour of it and then turned over.

5 You knew how it was going to end after the first ten minutes. It was very _____ .

6 It's a really _____ film! It made me angry and upset and surprised all at the same time.

7 I'm surprised they let kids watch it. It's very _____ – lots of blood and fighting.

8 It's a love story about a couple from very different backgrounds. It's very _____ .

9 She's not a simple character. She's very _____ and hard to understand.

10 I couldn't work out what was going on or who anyone was. It was very _____ .

b Choose five sentences from Exercise 1a to describe films/TV programmes you have watched. Work in groups and explain your choices.

6B Prepositional phrases

1 a Complete the questions with *on*, *in* or *by*.

1 What's the best thing you've ever found _____ **chance**?

2 Do you know any poems or any songs _____ **heart**?

3 _____ **average**, how many emails/messages do you send every day?

4 Have you ever deleted an important document _____ **accident**?

5 How often do you find that you're _____ **a real hurry**? Why?

6 Do you know anyone who's ever been _____ **debt**? Why? What happened?

7 Do you prefer travelling with friends or _____ **your own**? Why?

8 Do you know anyone who lives _____ **the coast**? Would you like to?

9 How important is it for you to get to places _____ **time**?

10 Do you ever go out in the evening _____ **yourself**?

11 When you were younger, did you ever get _____ **trouble** at school?

12 Have you ever been _____ **tears** at the end of a film? Why? What was the film?

b Work in pairs. Take turns asking and answering the questions in Exercise 1a.

6C Newspaper headlines

1 Match the words in bold with definitions a–h.

1 PRESIDENT TO **QUIT**

2 £150 MILLION **BID** FOR BRAZILIAN STAR

3 HOUSE PRICES **DROP** 5%

4 GOVERNMENT PROMISES TAX **CUTS**

5 COAST **HIT** BY STORMS

6 ARMY **SEIZE** CONTROL IN CAPITAL

7 BUS DRIVERS IN NEW PAY **ROW**

8 BIG **RISE** IN VIOLENT CRIMES

a an increase

b take something, using official power and force

c an offer to pay a particular price for something or someone

d a serious disagreement with another person or group

e leave your job – forever

f go down to a lower value

g damaged or affected in a bad way

h a reduction in the number or amount of something

2 Work in groups. Use four of the words in bold in Exercise 1 to talk about news stories you know.

Doctors have been involved in a pay row. They want more money.

7A Phrases with *have*

1 Use *have* + the nouns in the box to describe the photos.

> an appointment   a headache
> an infection   an injection
> insurance   an operation
> a rest   stitches   a temperature
> treatment   a virus   an X-ray

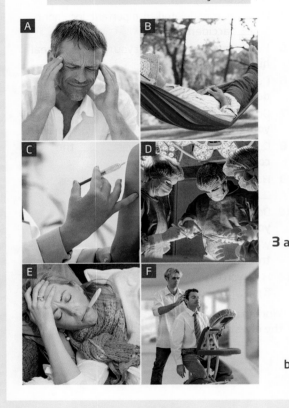

2 Complete the sentences with the nouns in the box in Exercise 1.

1 I'm afraid I don't have an _____ , but I really need to see a doctor.
2 I have a terrible _____ . It's really painful! I can't concentrate on my work at all.
3 We don't want you feeling any pain, so you'll need to have a little _____ .
4 I had some kind of _____ and spent most of the week in bed. It was horrible.
5 He had a problem with his heart and had to have an _____ to make it better.
6 I had an _____ in one of my teeth, so I had to take time off and go to the dentist.
7 It was a really nasty cut. I had to go to hospital and have ten _____ .
8 She had a _____ of 39 degrees, so we decided to call the doctor.
9 I broke my arm while I was in Boston. Luckily, I had health _____ , which covered the costs.
10 The doctor said I'm probably just exhausted. I need to go home and have a good long _____ .
11 We need to find out if it's broken or not, so you'll have to have an _____ .
12 He injured himself playing tennis last year and is still having _____ on his back.

3 a Complete the questions with nouns from Exercise 1. Only write questions that you would be happy to answer.

1 When was the last time you had (a/an) _____ ?
2 Have you ever had (a/an) _____ ?
3 Have you ever had to have (a/an) _____ ?
4 Do you know anyone who's ever had (a/an) _____ ?
5 Is it true that you've never had (a/an) _____ ?

b Work in pairs. Swap questions and take turns asking and answering.

7B Money and banks

1 Match verbs 1–8 with phrases a–h.

1 withdraw
2 transfer
3 check
4 invest
5 open
6 take out
7 charge
8 be

a money from one account to another
b in property
c a joint account
d money from your account
e a loan
f 20 percent interest
g in debt
h your balance

2 a Complete the sentences with the verbs from Exercise 1.

1 You should _____ your bank balance at least twice a day.
2 No companies should ever _____ more than ten percent interest. It's just wrong.
3 It's not safe to _____ money online.
4 The best thing to _____ in is your own education.
5 It should be easier to _____ a bank account.
6 It should be harder for people to _____ loans.
7 You should pay to _____ money from your account while you're abroad.
8 It's better to _____ in a lot of debt than a bit!

b Work in groups and discuss the statements in Exercise 2a. Do you agree with them?

8A Phrasal verbs with *out*

1 Complete the sentences with the correct form of the phrasal verbs in the box.

check out	die out	fall out	hang out
miss out	sort out	speak out	work out

1 If you _____ , you spend a lot of time at a particular place or with a particular person.

2 If something _____ , it becomes less and less common and eventually disappears.

3 If you _____ , you lose an opportunity to have something or do something fun/useful.

4 If you _____ a person, a place or a thing, you look to see if you like them/it.

5 If you _____ , you say publicly what you think about something, especially as a protest.

6 If you _____ a solution to a problem, you solve it by thinking/talking abut it.

7 If you _____ the details of something, you make arrangements/decide what will happen.

8 If two people _____ , they have a big argument and stop talking to each other.

2 Match sentence halves 1–8 with a–h.

1 It took me quite a while to
2 Most weekends, I just
3 Our Spanish teacher suggested
4 When should we
5 I'm not happy about what's happening, but I'm too scared to
6 My brother and I
7 We'd better get tickets early if we don't want to
8 In the late 1600s, dodos

a checking out that new Peruvian restaurant.
b sort out where we're going to stay?
c work out what was causing the problem.
d speak out.
e died out.
f hang out at the shopping mall with my friends.
g fell out about money last year. We haven't spoken since.
h miss out.

3 Work in pairs. Take turns asking and answering the questions.

1 Have you ever failed to work out the solution to a problem? When? What happened?
2 Where did you hang out when you were growing up? Who with?
3 Have you ever missed out on a really great opportunity? Why?
4 Have you ever spoken out about something you thought was wrong? When? Why?
5 Have you ever fallen out with anyone? Why? Are you friends again now?

8B Relationships

1 a Replace the underlined phrases with the phrases in the box.

come from similar backgrounds	very close	don't see eye to eye	lost touch
get on very well	go back a long way	have a lot in common	went their separate ways

1 We understand each other because we <u>grew up in similar conditions and went to similar schools</u>.
2 We <u>have known each other for years</u>. We went to school together.
3 They were in quite a serious relationship for a long time, but they <u>broke up</u> last year.
4 I don't <u>have a very good relationship</u> with my brother. We're very different and we argue a lot.
5 We used to be really good friends, but we moved to different places and <u>stopped communicating</u>.
6 I find her very easy to talk to. We <u>are quite similar and share a lot of interests</u>.
7 We're <u>really good friends</u>. We see each other a lot and tell each other everything.
8 We <u>have very different opinions</u> about politics. It makes life difficult sometimes.

b Choose four sentences from Exercise 1a that describe people you know. Work in groups. Tell your group as much as you can about your choices.

9A Word building

1 Complete the table with the adjective forms of the nouns.

adjective		noun
		ability
		anxiety
		charity
		community
		equality
		creativity
		generosity
		nationality
		normality
		probability

2 a Complete the sentences with adjectives and nouns from the table in Exercise 1.

1 Every year the people in my area raise thousands of pounds for _____ .
2 It isn't just home to people of one _____ . You get people from all over the world living here.
3 I live in the countryside and we're not always _____ to get a fast internet connection.
4 Since the trouble last year, a degree of _____ has returned to the area.
5 The area has a strong sense of _____ . Everyone knows everyone else and we all help each other.
6 Some people who've lived there a long time are _____ about the way the area is changing.
7 They need to do more to fight poverty and increase social _____ in the area.
8 It's quite _____ that they're going to build some cheap new housing in the area soon.
9 The area is starting to attract lots of _____ young people like designers, artists and musicians.
10 There are lots of homeless people, but everyone is very _____ and gives food and money.

b Which of the places in Exercise 2a do you think offer a good quality of life? Why? Work in groups and discuss your answers.

9B Society

1 Complete the sentences with the pairs of words in the box.

access/higher education   beg/homeless
healthcare/life expectancy   rights/wages
divorced/middle class   poverty/benefits
pollution/vandalism   social care/elderly

1 We need to invest in _____ to make sure that the _____ are looked after properly.
2 You're more likely to get _____ if you're _____ than if you're working class.
3 Having excellent _____ is one important reason why _____ is so high.
4 There's too much graffiti and _____ here - and there's a lot of noise _____ , too.
5 Everyone should have full _____ to education and _____ should be free for everyone, too.
6 If the government cuts _____ , we'll see more children growing up in _____ .
7 _____ aren't going up fast enough and we need to do more to protect workers' _____ .
8 People _____ for money for many reasons and they become _____ for many reasons.

2 a Complete the sentences with the phrases in the box.

all walks of life   a fact of life   later in life
life's too short   quality of life   see life
that's life   the time of your life

1 Before getting married and having kids it's important to get out into the world and _____ .
2 Bad things happen to everyone from time to time, but _____ .
3 It's important to meet and talk to people from _____ .
4 If you're not happy at work, change your job. _____ to do things you hate.
5 Don't worry if you're not sure what job you want. Lots of people don't know until _____ .
6 Everybody loves Disneyland. If you go there, you're sure to have _____ .
7 There's not much you can do about crime. Sadly, it's just _____ .
8 It's more important to have a decent _____ than it is to be rich.

b Work in groups and discuss the statements in Exercise 2a. Do you agree with them?

10A History

1 a Match the verbs in the box with the pairs of nouns/phrases they go with.

abolish	discover	elect	form	introduce
invade	invent	launch	sign	transform

1 _____ a rocket into space/a new product
2 _____ a country/someone's privacy
3 _____ a female president/a new government
4 _____ a new law/a whole new system
5 _____ the way we communicate/the film industry
6 _____ the steam engine/a new kind of battery
7 _____ a group/a new political party
8 _____ a cure for a disease/a new planet
9 _____ a contract/a treaty
10 _____ the death penalty/a law

b Work in pairs. Add one more noun/phrase to 1–10 in Exercise 1a. Use a dictionary to help you if necessary.

2 a Complete the questions with the correct form of the verbs in Exercise 1a.

1 When _____ the first iPhone _____ onto the market?
2 Who _____ the 45th president of the United States in 2017?
3 Where _____ paper _____ ?
4 When _____ the death penalty _____ in France?
5 In which city _____ The Beatles _____ ?
6 When _____ Napoleon and his army _____ Russia?
7 In which century _____ chocolate first _____ in Europe?
8 Which football player _____ Paris Saint-Germain _____ for almost £200 million in 2017?
9 Who _____ gravity?
10 How _____ Johannes Gutenberg _____ Europe in the 1400s?

b Work in groups. Try to answer the questions in Exercise 2a.

10B Word building

1 Complete the sentences with the verb form of the nouns in brackets.

1 When did you _____ as a lawyer? (qualification)
2 Do you think you could have a look at my essay and _____ any mistakes you find? (correction)
3 Luckily, the bomb failed to _____ . (explosion)
4 If enough people _____ the plan, the government may decide not to go ahead with it. (opposition)
5 I was a bit shocked. I didn't expect her to _____ like that. (reaction)
6 It took him a long time to _____ he'd done anything wrong! (admission)

2 Work in pairs and discuss the questions.

1 Can you think of two things there has been opposition to recently?
2 Do you know anyone who's gained a qualification recently?
3 How much do you like to be corrected when you're speaking English?
4 Can you remember a time when you were shocked by someone's reaction?
5 Have you ever not admitted that you'd made a mistake? When? What happened?

10C Colour expressions

1 Complete the sentences with the phrases in the box.

black and blue	the green belt	in the red
a white-collar job	feeling a bit blue	

1 They've promised not to build any more houses on _____ around the city.
2 It's much easier to find work in a factory or on a building site than it is to find _____ .
3 The last time I played football, I woke up _____ the next day! It took me days to recover.
4 I need a better-paid job. I'm fed up with being _____ at the end of every month.
5 I'll be OK tomorrow. I'm just a bit tired and I'm _____ . That's all.

2 Choose the correct alternatives.

1 They talked about it for ages, and then decided to give the plan the *green/orange* light.
2 I fell and hit my face and woke up the next day with a *blue/black* eye.
3 It's a *golden/red* opportunity. You'd be stupid to miss it.
4 I was really surprised to hear from her again. It was completely out of the *white/blue*.
5 I checked my bank balance earlier. It's nice to actually be in the *red/black* for a change.
6 It's not as *black and white/white and black* as people often think. It's a complicated issue.

3 Work in groups and discuss the questions.

1 Have you ever missed a golden opportunity to do something special? What?
2 Have you ever heard from an old friend out of the blue?

Communication bank

1C Develop your listening

3d

Presenter: Back in 1667, Paris became the first city in the world to light its streets at night. It soon became popular to go out at night and suddenly when and how long you slept became a matter of choice. Rather than everyone getting up with the sun and going to bed soon after dark, we've now moved to a 24-hour culture, where we divide ourselves into being morning people or night owls, working day shifts or night shifts – but where we all sleep less.

Lesson 1B

9

Lesson 1D

7a

Lesson 4B

9a

Student B

It was nearly the perfect crime. The owner of an apartment in Montreal, Canada had hidden her jewellery and computers, and had smashed her own back window before ringing the police. The man who answered the call was Indian-born police officer Dipesh Kurian. When he arrived at the apartment, Kurian found a woman crying and screaming. The woman said a thief had broken in through the window and had taken everything! As the police officer was taking notes, the phone rang and the victim answered.

It was her French-speaking father and she explained – in French – that the whole thing was just a trick to try to claim money on her insurance. What she didn't realise was that Officer Kurian had understood every word as he speaks seven languages including French! 'By the end, I had about ten pages of notes,' he said.

Lesson 4B

9a
Student A

A Texan man who became trapped inside an ATM passed notes to customers through the front of the cash machine, while asking them to help him escape.

Tim Summer, the local chief of police, said the man had got stuck on Wednesday night, when he was changing the lock on a Bank of America door that leads to the ATM.

'Apparently, he'd left his phone and the card he needed to get back through the door in his truck,' Summer said.

The man then passed notes through the machine to customers taking out cash, asking them to call his boss. One read: 'Please help. I'm stuck in here.'

Eventually, someone called the police, who heard a voice coming from inside the ATM. An officer broke in and freed the man, whose name was not given.

Lesson 3B

12
Student B

Read the article and answer the questions.

1 What have they been doing research into? Why?
2 What have they discovered so far?
3 Are there any concerns about it?

Can we live forever?

How long people live has increased a lot over the last one hundred years. Worldwide, the average male today can expect to live to around 67, while the average female will reach 71. This is twice as long as people lived just one century ago. Some scientists have started to think that we could live much longer and that we can solve the problems connected with old age.

Google has invested a huge amount of money in the California Life Company, which is one of many companies developing anti-ageing drugs. Our knowledge of what causes us to age has grown dramatically over recent years. Research into genes, diet, etc. has taught us a lot about the kind of drugs that may help. Some scientists now believe that that many of us could live to at least 100 and maybe even 120. On top of that, we'll live healthier lives, with far fewer diseases, such as diabetes and cancer.

However, increasing the number of older people in the world could cause a number of problems. The population has already grown to a size where some of the world's resources are at risk of running out. If the population continues to grow, it might also make climate change worse or mean that we don't have enough food for everyone.

Lesson 4C

11

Student A

Conversation 1

You have just come back from holiday and are going to complain to the manager of the company that you booked your trip with.

The agent you spoke to before you left promised:
- free wifi in all the rooms.
- clean, comfortable rooms with excellent views.
- a range of restaurants providing top-quality international cuisine.
- a hotel near the beach.
- a car to take you to and from the airport.
- a full refund if you weren't satisfied.

1 Decide which of the things above you didn't get and what you got instead. What do you want the manager to do about this?
2 Complain to the manager. Try to make sure you get what you want from the situation.

Conversation 2

You work for a mobile phone company. Student B is going to complain about a bad experience with your company. Your main goals during the conversation are to:
- explain why the problems happened.
- keep the customer happy.

Lesson 5A

11b

Student A

Choose a business from a–c below. Then decide how you will answer the journalist's questions 1–4.

1 What do you do?
2 How long have you been doing that?
3 How's the company doing at the moment?
4 What are your plans for the future?

a Dance studio

You've only recently set up a company teaching modern dance. You have rented a large space. You're making a loss and don't have much money. What are you going to do to get more business? How will you survive? Where do you want the company to be in five years?

b T-shirt company

You and your partner have a small company designing T-shirts, which you then sell in local markets. This year, you think you will break even and maybe even make a small profit on top of the small amount you pay yourselves. Because you design the T-shirts yourself and sell them, you only have time to visit one market a day. How are you going to improve the business and expand? Do you borrow more money? Or do you do something else?

c Specialist electrical goods

You've been running a small company making electrical products for the last eight years. You have ten people working for you and your company has expanded quite a lot over recent years. However, you have recently lost one important customer and you had a problem with a new product you recently launched. Because of this, sales have dropped. What will you do about these problems?

Lesson 5B

12

Student B

1 You're going to ask your partner about their projects. Start with questions 1 and 2. Think of three other questions you could ask your partner.

1 Have you found a new job yet?
2 How's the house-building going?

2 Look at your two projects, 1 and 2. Decide which stage you are at (from lists a–e and a–f) and what you have/haven't done. Think of extra details and add your own ideas to your lists.

1 How are the wedding plans going?
   a decide when and how big
   b sort out the place for the ceremony/party
   c send invitations
   d choose dress/food/flowers, etc.
   e any other things not done yet?

2 Have you found a new place to live yet?
   a look at houses
   b make an offer
   c get a loan
   d pack your things
   e move in
   f any repairs you have done or need to do?

Lesson 5C

12

- Class sizes should be reduced.
- All university education should be free.
- Single-sex schools are better for kids' education.
- Home-schooling should be encouraged.
- There should be greater use of technology in the classroom.
- Students should always be separated into classes of the same ability.

Lesson 5B
12

Student A

1 Look at your two projects, 1 and 2. Decide which stage you are at (from lists a–e and a–g) and what you have/haven't done. Think of extra details and add your own ideas to your lists.

1 Have you found a new job yet?
   a apply for jobs
   b have interviews
   c get offers
   d start the job
   e be given tasks/projects to do

2 How's the house-building going?
   a find land
   b get an architect
   c approve the plan
   d start construction
   e finish roof
   f move in
   g anything left to do?

2 You're going to ask your partner about their projects. Start with questions 1 and 2. Think of three other questions you could ask your partner.
   1 How are the wedding plans going?
   2 Have you found a new place to live yet?

Lesson 6B
9b

Student B

1 You're going to recommend to Student A:
   • a hairdresser.
   • a gym or personal trainer.
   • a dry cleaner or place to get clothes repaired.

   Think of either people or companies you know and why you would recommend them. If you don't know anyone, either invent something or recommend someone you think could help.

2 You're going to ask Student A for recommendations for:
   • a garage or mechanic.
   • a dentist.
   • a builder or someone to do work on your house.

   Think about why you want the services and what exactly you want done.

Lesson 4C
11

Student B

Conversation 1

You are the manager of a holiday company. Student A is going to complain about a bad experience with your company. Your main goals during the conversation are to:
   • explain why the problems happened.
   • keep the customer happy.

Conversation 2

You are unhappy with the company that provides your mobile phone and are going to call the customer service helpline to complain.

The agent you spoke to in the shop promised:
   • a good signal anywhere in the country.
   • free texts.
   • the same charges abroad as at home.
   • help available online 24 hours a day.
   • a cheap deal for the first year.

1 Decide which of the things above you didn't get and what you got instead. What do you want the company representative to do about this?

2 Complain to the company representative. Try to make sure you get what you want from the situation.

Lesson 6B

9b

Student A

1 You're going to ask Student B for recommendations for:
- a hairdresser.
- a gym or personal trainer.
- a dry cleaner or place to get clothes repaired.

Think about why you want the services and what exactly you want done.

2 You're going to recommend to Student B:
- a garage or mechanic.
- a dentist.
- a builder or someone to do work on their house.

Think of either people or companies you know and why you would recommend them. If you don't know anyone, either invent something or recommend someone you think could help.

Lesson 5A

11b

Student B

Choose a business from a–c below. Then decide how you will answer the journalist's questions 1–4.

1 What do you do?

2 How long have you been doing that?

3 How's the company doing at the moment?

4 What are your plans for the future?

a **A newsagents and grocery store**

You run a newsagents and small grocery store. You started six years ago, and the first few years were very hard but now you're making a very healthy profit. You're thinking of opening a new shop, but one of your big competitors, who has a group of similar shops, wants to take you over and is offering a lot of money. What are you going to do – expand or sell?

b **A restaurant**

You run a small restaurant. You started it ten years ago now, and it's going OK. You employ five other people and you make enough money to pay everyone basic wages, but nothing more. You are a bit bored of what you are doing. What are you going to do? Try to expand? How? Or will you sell the restaurant? What would you do instead?

c **A gym**

You work at a gym, but you are leaving to set up your own business as a personal trainer and eventually want to open your own gym. You have a few clients you think will join you. How are you going to get more? How will you get the money you need for the gym? When? Where will it be? How are you going to launch your new business?

Lesson 7D

7a

Student A

1 Read situations 1–3. What might the rule or problem be? You're the customer. What would you say to a member of staff to try to get what you want?

1 You bought a jacket and after you wore it a couple of times, you realised it has a tear under the arm. It also has a small mark on it. You want a refund.

2 You're renting a car, but you want to return the car when the office is closed.

3 You're checking into a hotel, but have forgotten the PIN for your card.

Choose one of the situations to roleplay.

2 You're a member of staff. Student B is a customer who has a problem. Your main goals during the conversation are to:
- try to follow your company's rules.
- offer solutions.

6C Develop your writing

8 Use the results from two of questions 3-5.

Question 3

	18-25	25-35	35-55
0-20%	0	0	1
20-40%	1	1	1
40-60%	2	1	2
60-80%	7	6	9
80-100%	90	92	87

Question 4

	18-25	25-35	35-55
TV	61	49	47
radio	19	19	25
newspapers (print or online)	9	21	23
social media	9	8	1
blogs	1	1	2
other	1	2	2

Question 5

All ages	Too much	Enough	Too little
politics	36	55	9
business	18	74	8
sport	35	47	18
science	2	38	60
weather	20	61	19
celebrities	36	61	3
positive	3	18	79
negative	89	10	1

Lesson 7A

12

1 When you woke up this morning, you felt stiff all over. Your muscles ached and when you looked in the mirror, you realised you were very pale. You checked your temperature, and it was much higher than usual. You've heard there's a terrible virus going around and you're worried that you've got it.

2 You usually do a lot of exercise, but two weeks ago you fell off your bike and bruised your back and legs quite badly. You keep getting a pain behind your knee and you're worried that maybe you have injured it. Your back hurts too, and you think you've maybe strained a muscle there.

Lesson 7B

9c

1. Qatar
2. 38
3. 5,732; 300,000
4. 6
5. San Francisco, $80,000
6. Switzerland
7. half
8. Belgium
9. Japan
10. Saudi Arabia

Lesson 9A

11

Quality of life survey

1 Have you learnt or done something interesting in the last few days?
2 Is the government doing enough to protect the environment?
3 Are you happy or unhappy with your job? How could it be better?
4 Do you have faith in the media here? Why?/Why not?
5 How do you feel the leader of your country is doing?
6 Are there any countries nearby where you think life is better/worse?
7 How happy are you with the roads and the public transport where you live?
8 Is the city/town where you live getting better or worse as a place to live? Why?
9 How happy are you with healthcare in your country?
10 Do you feel you have enough holidays/free time?
11 Can people in your country improve their lives by working hard?

Lesson 10A

4a

Student A

Read the article about Rosa Parks, then answer the questions.

1 What problems were there in the southern states of America in the 1950s?
2 How were the lives of black and white Americans different?
3 What happened to Rosa Parks in Montgomery, Alabama?
4 What was the result of her arrest?

Rosa Parks

The mother of the Civil Rights movement

In the 1950s, the southern states of the US were not a happy place. It was almost a hundred years since the end of the Civil War between the slave-owning south and the north, which was against white people being able to own black slaves. However, black and white Americans still led very different lives – and had very different opportunities.

There were strict rules about where non-whites were allowed to walk, talk, drink, rest and eat. Black and white children were educated separately. All of this meant anger started to grow about the fact that so many non-whites had to endure such a terrible situation in their own country. Several organisations began to fight for justice and equal rights for African-Americans and soon something happened in Montgomery, Alabama that became big news across the country.

One day in December 1955, a white bus driver called James Blake asked an African-American woman on her way home from work to move to the back of his vehicle so that a white man could sit down. If Rosa Parks had done as she was told, modern American history might have been very different, but she refused, and was then arrested. This caused a lot of public anger and – eventually – changes to the law. Interestingly, Parks had had problems with Blake before and later said that if she'd been paying attention, she would never have got on that bus! History is made in these moments.

Lesson 10A

4a

Student B

Read the article about Simón Bolívar and answer the questions.

1 Where was Simón Bolívar from?
2 When was he alive?
3 What is he most famous for?
4 What were his main skills?

Simón Bolívar
The father of South American independence

Born in 1783 to a wealthy family, Simón Bolívar was a Venezuelan military and political leader, who helped several Latin American countries become independent. The country of Bolivia is named after him, the money used in Venezuela is called the Venezuelan *bolívar* and there are many statues of him, not only across Latin America, but also all over the world. He is widely remembered today as *El Libertador* – the Liberator!

Bolívar managed to help Venezuela, Colombia (including Panama), Ecuador, Bolivia and Peru break free from centuries of Spanish rule. In addition, his military skills helped him win many battles, including the important Battle of Carabobo in 1823.

However, he was also great at recognising the best time to act. None of his achievements would've been possible if the French army, led by Napoleon, hadn't entered Spain in 1808. After that, Spain had to spend more time on local rather than international problems. As a result, independence for much of Latin America soon became possible.

In his youth, Bolívar studied in Europe and was influenced by many of the great European philosophers, especially their ideas about equality, human rights and freedom of speech. He was also very keen on political and military issues, and it was his influence and skill in leading his army that led to the country of his birth finally becoming fully independent in 1830, the year Bolívar died, aged 47.

Lesson 10D

6a

Choose two of the situations and allocate roles.

Situation 1

Student A: You're part of a host family. Offer to:
- take B's coat.
- show B round the house.
- get some food/drink for B.
- help B with the wifi.
- explain the local area and facilities.

Student B: You're a foreign student arriving at the house to stay. Think about how to respond to the offers.

Situation 2

Student A: You work for an international company and a colleague from abroad is coming to your office for a meeting. (You're speaking on the phone.) Offer to:
- book a room for the meeting.
- organise transport to/from the airport.
- book flights.
- book a local restaurant.
- book a tour of the town.

Student B: You're the colleague from abroad. Think about how to respond to the offers.

Situation 3

Student A: You're a neighbour. You're talking to a friend next door, who is a single parent and has had an accident and broken their leg. Offer to:
- do some shopping for B.
- drive B to hospital.
- walk B's dog for them.
- cook for B.

Student B: You're the next-door neighbour. Think of how to respond to the offers.

Lesson 3B

12

Student A

Read the article and answer the questions.

1 What have they been doing research into? Why?
2 What have they discovered so far?
3 Are there any concerns about it?

Can we use the ocean's resources?

Some scientists say we should call our planet Water instead of Earth, as water covers over 70 percent of the world. Exploring the oceans is important to everyone as we may be able to discover new sources of medical drugs, food, energy and other products. We can also learn more about how to predict earthquakes and tsunamis and how we are both causing climate change and being affected by it.

The deepest point in the ocean is almost seven miles down, and very few people have ever managed to visit it, which is why we know more about the moon than we do about what's at the bottom of our oceans. However, we have been sending robots down there, and we have already discovered animals that are new to us. One of them, the giant crab, has helped scientists develop new ways of treating memory problems in old people.

Unfortunately, one negative discovery is that the oceans contain huge amounts of incredibly small pieces of plastic – microplastics. These microplastics have also been getting into the fish we eat and the water we drink and nobody knows how eating this plastic will affect us in the future.

Lesson 9C

7

Lesson 7D

7a

Student B

1 **You're a member of staff. Student A is a customer who has a problem. Your main goals during the conversation are to:**
   - try to follow your company's rules.
   - offer solutions.

2 **Read situations 1–3. What might the rule or problem be? You're the customer. What would you say to a member of staff to try to get what you want?**

   1 You bought an electronic item and it's stopped working properly after 12 months. You want a new one.
   2 You're trying to get into a club/disco but you don't have any ID with you.
   3 The receptionist can't see a record of your booking for a family room at the hotel.

   Choose one of the situations to roleplay.

Irregular verbs

Verb	Past simple	Past participle
be	was	been
become	became	become
begin	began	begun
bite	bit	bitten
blow	blew	blown
break	broke	broken
bring	brought	brought
build	built	built
buy	bought	bought
catch	caught	caught
choose	chose	chosen
come	came	come
cost	cost	cost
cut	cut	cut
do	did	done
draw	drew	drawn
drink	drank	drunk
drive	drove	driven
eat	ate	eaten
fall	fell	fallen
feel	felt	felt
find	found	found
fly	flew	flown
forget	forgot	forgotten
freeze	froze	frozen
get	got	got
give	gave	given
go	went	gone
grow	grew	grown
have	had	had
hear	heard	heard
hide	hid	hidden
hit	hit	hit
hold	held	held
hurt	hurt	hurt
keep	kept	kept
know	knew	known
learn	learned/learnt	learned/learnt
leave	left	left

Verb	Past simple	Past participle
lend	lent	lent
let	let	let
lie	lay	lain
lose	lost	lost
make	made	made
mean	meant	meant
meet	met	met
pay	paid	paid
put	put	put
read	read	read
ride	rode	ridden
ring	rang	rung
run	ran	run
say	said	said
see	saw	seen
sell	sold	sold
send	sent	sent
shine	shone	shone
show	showed	shown
shut	shut	shut
sing	sang	sung
sit	sat	sat
sleep	slept	slept
smell	smelled/smelt	smelled/smelt
speak	spoke	spoken
spend	spent	spent
spill	spilled/spilt	spilled/spilt
stand	stood	stood
swim	swam	swum
take	took	taken
teach	taught	taught
tell	told	told
think	thought	thought
throw	threw	thrown
understand	understood	understood
wake	woke	woken
wear	wore	worn
win	won	won
write	wrote	written